Pragmatism

Pragmatism

EDITED BY
CHERYL MISAK

© 1999 Canadian Journal of Philosophy

University of Calgary Press
Calgary, Alberta, Canada

ISSN 0229-7051   ISBN 0-919491-24-3

© 1999 The Canadian Journal of Philosophy
ISBN 0-919491-24-3
ISSN 0229-7051
CJP Supplementary Volume 24 (1998)

University of Calgary Press
2500 University Drive NW
Calgary, Alberta
Canada T2N 1N4

Canadian Cataloguing in Publication Data

Main entry under title:
    Pragmatism

    (Canadian Journal of Philosophy. Supplementary volume,
ISSN 0229-7051 ; 24)
    Includes bibliographical references and index.
    ISBN 0-919491-24-3

    1. Pragmatism. I. Misak, C.J. (Cheryl J.) II. Series
B832.P724 1999   144'.3   C98-911168-7

Printed and bound in Canada.
♾ This book is printed on acid-free paper.

Table of Contents

Introduction

CHERYL MISAK
University of Toronto

Pragmatism has had to travel a rather rocky road to philosophical respectability. With some notable exceptions, such as F.P. Ramsey and Hilary Putnam, analytic philosophers have largely thought they ought to steer well clear of it.

Despite this reputation, many of the themes developed by the early pragmatists have made their way deep into the Anglo-American philosophical consciousness. I hope to have collected in this volume a set of papers which encourage a fresh look at the position. Not all of the authors here are self-described pragmatists, and some are engaged in setting obstacles in pragmatism's way, but they all consider it to be a philosophical position which should be taken seriously.

Contributors were given free rein to write about what they thought important in pragmatism. Dewey gets considerable attention, but most of the papers cluster around the founder of pragmatism, C.S. Peirce, and his views about doubt, belief, truth, and inquiry. Indeed, a good many of the contributors think we should return for a more careful look to Peirce's "On The Fixation of Belief," a paper epistemologists have often considered to be rather superficial, overly psychological, and just not very good.

That paper is the *locus classicus* of Peirce's argument that a true belief is one which would never lead to disappointment, or would not be defeated, were inquiry pursued as far as it could fruitfully go. Inquiry begins with settled belief, then proceeds, when prompted by a surprising experience or argument, to the irritation of doubt, and then aims at attaining a new settled belief. A belief which was settled for good, a belief which was as good as it could be by way of accounting

1

for the evidence and argument, would be such that nothing further could be asked of it. It would be true.

The central thought of pragmatism is that philosophy must be connected to practice. There is much contemporary interest in what this thought implies for the notions of truth and objectivity. The founders of the position — Charles Peirce, William James, John Dewey — argued, in different ways, that the notion of truth must not be disconnected from the practices of belief, assertion, and inquiry. We have seen that on Peirce's view a true belief is one which would not be improved by inquiry. Truth, that is, is what would be assertible were we to have deliberated as far as we could on the matter.

Here is Peirce speaking against the idea that a belief (or a proposition or a sentence) might correspond to an unknowable "thing-in-itself":

> You only puzzle yourself by talking of this metaphysical 'truth' and metaphysical 'falsity' that you know nothing about. All you have any dealings with are your doubts and beliefs ... Your problems would be greatly simplified, if, instead of saying that you want to know the 'Truth', you were simply to say that you want to attain a state of belief unassailable by doubt. (*Collected Papers* 5.416)

This is an early statement of the now-popular view that we must deflate the notion of truth. The metaphysician has lost sight of the connection between truth and the less glamourous notions of belief, assertion, doubt, and experience. He has lost sight of the point that arguing that *p* is true is just arguing for *p* itself.

It is also the thought which lies behind the disquotational schema — "*p*" is true if and only if *p* — which has attracted so much attention in recent years. Disquotationalists take the schema to entirely capture the content of the predicate "is true."

There are pressures on the pragmatist to deflate the notion of truth all the way. Indeed, some contemporary pragmatists (following Richard Rorty, who takes himself to be following Dewey) think that the disquotational schema is all there is to truth, and go on to argue that we should happily jettison the notion of truth in favour of warranted assertion relative to one group of inquirers or another. Truth, right reason, rationality, validity, and the like are myths. Truth is merely what passes for good belief; it is not the sort of thing about which one should expect to have a philosophically interesting theory. Were we to hold on to the term "truth," against Rorty's advice, we would have to take it to mean that beliefs which are currently approved of are true. The notion of objectivity must be reinterpreted to mean intersubjectivity or "solidarity." It is what *we* have come to take as true.

But there are ways of interpreting the pragmatist insight, of connecting the notion of truth to practice, which are not so severe. We can start with the idea that to say that *p* is true is to assert *p*. But, as Crispin Wright argues in his contribution to this volume, the crucial thing now is to ask what it is to assert or endorse a proposition. When I affirm a proposition's truth, I recommend its acceptance and I commend it as meeting certain standards for belief. Then the question presses as to what warranted acceptability or meeting the standards of good belief amounts to. Wright argues that one thing to say here is that when someone commends *p*, she goes beyond whatever good reason there is here and now to believe *p*, for she means to suggest that reason will continue to support *p*.

That, I suggest, is very close to Peirce's own view. He argued that a belief aims at being true, at being a belief which would be indefeasible or not defeated by reasons or evidence, no matter how far we were to push our investigations. When I believe *p*, I assert *p* as being true, as being the kind of belief which would stand up to the rigours of further investigation and argument.

David Wiggins, on the way to offering us an answer to Hume's problem of induction, also looks to what a person is committed to in asserting or believing. We have to ask how we are to inquire, if we are to produce genuine belief; we have to ask what constitutes having such a belief. He gets the answers by rekindling some insights from "On The Fixation of Belief." On Wiggins' view, part of what Peirce is doing in this paper is arguing that the very notion of belief is bound up with the notions of fact, reality, and truth. In an invigorating reading, Wiggins has Peirce holding that if a person aims at fixing belief, "all sorts of other things gradually but inevitably unfold." When a person believes or asserts *p*, she is, for instance, committed to *p*'s being sensitive to reasons, evidence, and the requirements of logic.

This volume begins with the papers by Wiggins and Wright. Both think that we are ill-advised to try to give an analysis of truth — a specification of the necessary and sufficient conditions under which any sentence is true. Wiggins takes his cue from Peirce here and Wright from the requirements of his own way of setting the debate. Wright is a pluralist about truth: truth may be different things in different discourses. He thus thinks that the attempt at analysis is an attempt at a false generality. Wiggins, on the other hand, is after some general thoughts about truth.

Mark Migotti then joins Wiggins and Wright in tracing the internal connections between belief, truth, inquiry, and dispositions to act. He takes us through the arguments of both "On The Fixation of Belief" and the equally influential "How To Make Our Ideas Clear." So we get a helpful overview of Peirce's account of truth and of the Pragmatic Maxim. Migotti sets out how Peirce can think that truth is both independent of us and accessible to us. These two aspects of truth are not in tension, he suggests, because of the fact that experience forces itself upon us: in Peirce's words, "the essence of truth lies in its resistance to being ignored." He also goes a long way towards ironing out some of the difficulties for the position, most notably those surrounding "buried secrets," such as sentences about the remote past for which the evidence has dried up.

Isaac Levi and Christopher Hookway focus, in different ways, on Peirce's idea that our body of background beliefs and our habitual practices of inference and investigation play an essential role in inquiry and must be assigned epistemic authority.

On Levi's anti-foundationalist view, there is no need to justify current beliefs, but only changes in belief — either an expansion of our current state or a contraction of it. He follows Peirce, James, and Dewey in holding that real doubt, doubt which calls for inquiry, arises only if the inquirer has acquired good reason for ceasing to believe what he initially took for granted. Levi sketches an epistemology on which it makes sense for me to expand or contract my corpus of belief, given my assumption that my current beliefs are true.

In Hookway's terms, if we are to reason well we require confidence in our evaluative habits. He examines the role of desire and emotion in practical reasoning. This is done from the perspective of a pragmatist epistemologist, but it will resonate happily with many who approach philosophy from other angles. Hookway argues, for instance, that rationality and inquiry require a kind of self-trust in our responses to propositions and inferences. And our instinctive-seeming feelings of trust should be (and in fact are) granted a defeasible authority over some sorts of philosophical challenges — challenges which, as Peirce put it, give rise only to paper doubts. So we have here, amongst many other things, an account of the pragmatist response to sceptical arguments.

Joe Heath then offers us a twist on the standard construal of the pragmatist idea that belief converges on the truth. (David Bakhurst's paper also gives us some important advice on how to sidestep the mischief done by the ideas of "the end of inquiry" and "agreement in the long run.")

Heath asks what sense can be made of the idea of convergence, once the pragmatist drops the notion of representation or correspondence from the theory of truth. And he asks how the pragmatist might explain, again without invoking the idea of representation, why we find more convergence in "factual" as opposed to evaluative and aesthetic discourse. Heath's suggestion is that the issue turns on the practical requirements of social interaction. What licences our expectations of convergence is the need to coordinate our actions. Heath utilizes some points arising from game theory to argue that, in contexts of social interaction, we all require the same set of beliefs about how all of us will act. Some discourses, such as that about physical or natural events, impose a strong normative convergence constraint on participants. In these discourses we expect resolution of disagreement. We think there is something wrong with someone who thinks there might be two equally good but conflicting answers; we think that one of two contradictory accounts must be wrong. In moral discourse we also expect a relatively high level of convergence, for a shared set of social norms is required for the stability of social interaction. We do not, however, need to have the same desires or the same beliefs about what outcomes are best. Here we can more easily agree to disagree.

The question about morals arises quickly and naturally from the pragmatist's thoughts about truth and inquiry. For if truth is that which our best inquiries would produce, there appears to be no *prima facie* obstacle in the way of moral statements aspiring to truth. Perhaps the pragmatist should abandon Peirce here and follow Dewey (at least in some moods: see Richardson's essay) in holding that the notions of inquiry, truth, and objectivity be extended to moral and political discourse.

Indeed, Wright thinks that a truth-predicate remarkably like the pragmatist truth-predicate holds *only* for discourses such as morality and aesthetics — discourses in which it is *a priori* that all truths are knowable. He argues that "superassertibility" is the relevant truth-predicate for these discourses: a statement is superassertible if and only if it is warranted and that warrant would survive close scrutiny of its pedigree and arbitrarily extensive increments to, or other forms of improvement of, our information. Other discourses have more robust truth-predicates.

But a number of other contributors encourage the thought that the pragmatist view of inquiry, truth, and objectivity can be viewed, in Wiggins's words, as "perfectly general and all-embracing." Bakhurst's "Pragmatism and Moral Knowlege" offers us an excellent outline of how we might extend the broadly Peircean view of truth to morals. He defends pragmatism as a kind of cognitivism, a defense which has the pragmatist joining forces with David Wiggins and John McDowell. Morality can be a human institution but can nonetheless be about objective values.

One of pragmatism's central claims is that our epistemological and moral theory should try to preserve our deeply held convictions and our ways of inquiring into various subject matters. For a theory of *x*, if it is to remain a theory of *x*, must try to preserve at least some of the features of *x*; it must try to preserve at least some of the phenomena that it is a theory *of*. One of the things Bakhurst does in his paper is to show how this thought can withstand scrutiny. He explores the prospects for a pragmatist account of moral knowledge. In his view Rorty is right that to call a belief true is to pay it a kind of compliment, but fails to see that some compliments are warranted and others are not. Bakhurst argues for the pragmatist idea that we are warranted in calling a belief true if we are warranted in thinking that good reasons support it and that those reasons would not be undermined, no matter how far we were to inquire into the matter. Of course, we might be wrong — our reasons might be defeated.

Henry Richardson also offers us a route to a pragmatist cognitivism — a kind of amalgam of the best of Dewey and the best of Peirce. Richardson asks how Dewey can take a critical stance towards existing desires, common actions, and political institutions without thinking that there can be a truth of the matter about final ends — things worth seeking for their own sakes, rather than as the means to some other end. He argues that the pragmatist who takes truth to be the end or aim of inquiry must not take truth to be a fixed or remote ultimate end. Rather, we can specify our end in inquiry though deliberation. Truth is the regulative end of inquiry, but we can reason or deliberate about how it is to be conceived. That leads us to the central question of a pragmatist epistemology: How can we conceive of truth such that it could function as the end of the practical activity of inquiry? Richardson's answer is that the pragmatist must be a cognitivist and a fallibilist all the way down. Truth is neither cast in stone nor erected as a fixed and remote end. We need a "working conception of truth," and Richardson's conception takes us in the direction of an account of democratic deliberation aimed at truth.

If we are to extend Peirce's view of truth and objectivity to morals, much has to be said about moral inquiry. How can we talk of convergence in the face of so much disagreement? What distinguishes moral inquiry from other kinds of inquiry? Some of the contributors here (Levi, for instance) question such an extension.

But were we to press ahead with the project of articulating a pragmatist account of moral inquiry, we might, as a first step, say that the products of a careful and extended deliberation would be the truth. Here our focus would be on the best that moral deliberation, in which the views of all were listened to and taken seriously, could do.

Judith Baker, while expressing some sympathy with this idea, presents us with some of the difficulties which face it. Listening to everyone, she argues, is not enough, as taking the views of everyone seriously might well involve unequal effort. Listening to those who have views similar to mine and those with whom I usually come to agree will involve relatively little effort. But it might take enormous effort and education and goodwill for me to be able to understand, let alone take seriously, the views of someone whose cultural and economic background is very different from my own. The energy required is increased when what I am trying to comprehend is the accusation of my own injustice. When a minority claims that those who enjoy the status of the majority have an unfair advantage, it is unsurprising if the majority fails to see any immediate plausibility in the claim. They might, at least at first, not be able to see the problem at all. The pragmatist who thinks that there are reasons — connected to truth — for giving additional weight to the views of marginalised groups must answer Baker's worries.

In coming to grips with such difficulties, the pragmatist takes a central place in contemporary debates about the objectivity of morals. For pragmatism is, if anything is, a view of truth and objectivity which might be fitting for moral and political philosophy, a view on which it might make sense to think that our moral and political debates aim at truth. The pragmatist idea has struck many as being especially valuable here, for a competing epistemology — we can call it realism — stacks the deck against objectivity in morals and politics. This kind of realist holds that a belief is true if it corresponds to something like facts in the believer-independent world. Since truth and objectivity in morals and politics cannot be anything like that, realism seems to lead directly to the conclusion that moral and political judgments cannot fall within our cognitive scope — within the scope of truth and knowledge. The would-be cognitivist must thus explore different theories of truth. That pragmatism presents itself as a plausible alternative is one of the reasons for the amount of interest recently expressed in it.

CANADIAN JOURNAL OF PHILOSOPHY
Supplementary Volume 24

C.S. Peirce: Belief, Truth, and Going from the Known to the Unknown

DAVID WIGGINS
New College, University of Oxford

The third philosophical stratagem for cutting off inquiry consists in maintaining that this, that, or the other element of science is basic, ultimate, independent of aught else and utterly inexplicable — not so much from any defect in our knowing as because there is nothing beneath it to know. The only type of reasoning by which such a conclusion could be reached is *retroduction*. Now nothing justifies a retroductive inference except its affording an explanation of the facts. It is, however, no explanation at all of a fact to pronounce it *inexplicable*. That, therefore, is a conclusion which no reasoning can ever justify or excuse. (Peirce, *Collected Papers* 1.139)

Abduction consists in studying facts and devising a theory to explain them. Its only justification is that, if we are ever to understand things at all, it must be in that way. (Peirce, *Collected Papers*, 5.145)

[Scientific procedure] will at times find a high probability established by a single confirmatory instance, while at others it will dismiss a thousand as almost worthless. (Frege, *Foundations of Arithmetic* (1884), p. 16)

In philosophy as we now have it, there is rarely any mention of Sufficient Reason. But the idea is not altogether lost. The rational residue of this metaphysical idea is a certain methodological outlook, an outlook that finds its most perfect expression in what C.S. Peirce calls abduction. But neither the idea of abduction nor its pretensions to help us find the truth — pretensions I shall defend even to the point of claiming that Peirce answers the Humean challenge over induction — can be properly understood otherwise than in the context of Peirce's theory of inquiry, reality, and truth. So it is here, and with Peirce's theory of inquiry in particular, that we begin. It will take a considerable time to reach Hume.

In "The Fixation of Belief" (1877) Peirce says that with respect to any question that concerns us, belief or opinion is the state we seek to attain and doubt is the state of irritation and dissatisfaction we seek to end. Belief in a certain proposition is a calm and satisfactory state, he says, the state which "we do not wish to avoid, or to change to a belief in anything else. On the contrary, we cling tenaciously, not merely to believing, but to believing just what we do believe."[1] It is not altogether obvious whether this is true, or if it is true, whether we should simply acquiesce in this tendency of ours. But in due course it will become clearer that all this is put forward subject to two Peircean explications, explications that Peirce did not pause to enter when he first advanced the claim. The explications are:

(1)   Belief is not as such a complacent or self-satisfied state, according to Peirce. It is exigent and persists *only on certain conditions*. (See the account in "Fixation" of the defects of the *a priori* method, discussed below.)

(2)   "Doubt [which irritates, Peirce says] is not the same as ignorance nor as the consciousness of being ignorant"; for "if one does not care to know, one cannot be said to be in doubt." The doubt that is described as irritation or dissatisfaction is not the same as "calm ignorance."[2]

Peirce's story can then continue as follows. Belief being the state we seek to attain, and doubt being the state of irritation we seek to end, one turns to inquiry in order to better one's state of mind. Since the fixation of belief is the whole object of inquiry, the chief question is *how* one is to conduct one's inquiry in order to achieve this fixation. But once we know that, we know everything we need — indeed, everything (or so I shall claim) that even Hume could justifiably demand.

---

1   *Writings of Charles S. Peirce*, C. Kloesel, ed., Bloomington: Indiana University Press, p. 247. Cited hereafter as W[vol. Number: page number].

2   MS 8828 p. 1 and MS 334, page marked "C," quoted in Misak, *Truth and the End of Inquiry* (Oxford: Clarendon Press, 1991), 49.

The question of how to proceed is a practical one. But the Peircean answer, for reasons that become more and more apparent as methods of fixing belief are passed in review, is part and parcel with his account of the science of logic. What, then, according to Peirce, is logic? In Peirce's broad nineteenth-century understanding of the term, logic is the art of reasoning and subsumes the art of making inferences from the known to the unknown. Logic embraces not only deduction, and not only induction, which is the testing of hypotheses, but also abduction, which is the framing of explanatory hypotheses. "Reasoning is good if it be such as to give a true conclusion from true premises and not otherwise [good]," Peirce wrote. (He later amended this sentence to say "Reasoning is good if it be dominated by such a habit as generally to give a true conclusion from true premises.")[3]

Peirce published the celebrated essay "On the Fixation of Belief," from which I have just quoted, as a popular essay. But it was one to which he must have attributed not only the literary felicity that we ourselves find in it, but also high philosophical importance and effectiveness. For he constantly returned to it in the ensuing decades as a vehicle for clarification of his thoughts, either in order to enter corrections and amplifications or to adapt it to new philosophical initiatives. Some of the amendments were designed to adapt the essay to the projects of "The Grand Logic" and "The Search for a Method."

The essay reviews four different and progressive methods of fixing belief: the method of dogmatism or tenacity, the method of authority, the *a priori* method, and the method that Peirce approves and commends to his reader. This last method embraces logic in the sense already explained and is intended to integrate all the virtues of all virtuous modes of investigation. "The distinction between good and bad investigation ... is the subject of the study of logic .... logic is the doctrine of truth, its nature and the manner in which it is to be discovered" (*Collected Papers* 7.320–21).

Before we go any further, we need to consider in a little more detail Peirce's explicit claim, already quoted and promised some qualifica-

---

3 *Collected Papers of Charles Sanders Peirce* (Cambridge, Mass: Belknap Press), 2.1: "Logic is the theory of the conditions which determine reasonings to be secure."

tion, that the sole object of inquiry is the fixation of belief. What Peirce wrote was this:

> With the doubt ... the struggle begins, and with the cessation of doubt it ends. Hence, the sole object of inquiry is the settlement of opinion. We may fancy that this is not enough for us, and that we seek, not merely an opinion, but a true opinion. But put this fancy to the test, and it proves groundless; for as soon as a firm belief is reached we are entirely satisfied, whether the belief be true or false. And it is clear that nothing out of the sphere of our knowledge can be our object, for nothing which does not affect the mind can be the motive for a mental effort. The most that can be maintained is, that we seek for a belief that we shall *think* to be true ... and, indeed, it is a mere tautology to say so. ("Fixation," W3:248)

Peirce derives from this conclusion three attractive corollaries concerning the impossibility cum pointlessness, in the absence of real and living doubt, of questioning either everything or anything. I like that. But I have to acknowledge that one ought not to permit the claim that the sole object of inquiry is the fixation of belief to escape criticism just because it delivers conclusions that we have other reasons to find attractive. So the claim needs more extended comment.

The directive "seek a true belief," Peirce seems to argue, has no more practical content than "seek a belief you think true." And then he continues, "We think each one of our beliefs is true. It is a mere tautology to say so." If doubt irritates us, Peirce seems to say, we may as well be advised "seek for a belief" as "seek for a true belief." But the defect of Peirce's way of arguing becomes evident so soon as we recall that similar claims used to be made to the effect that there is no practical difference between the directives "do your duty" and "do what you think is your duty." Makers of such claims paid too little attention to the fact that it is not without consequence which of these directives you second. One who fails to think hard what his duty is but does what he *takes* to be his duty obeys the directive to do what he thinks is his duty, but he does not necessarily do his duty.

This is a grave oversight in Peirce's exposition. But there are two ways in which it misses the point to insist too much upon it.

In the first place, it becomes clear later in Peirce's essay that he is deeply impressed by a particular and special point about belief that is conceptual and constitutive of belief. It is this: the belief that p is a state that needs, on pain of extinction, to see itself as a state *not* "determined by circumstances extraneous to the facts [concerning whether or not *p*]." Belief is a touchy, uncomplacent condition which will not stay around on just any old terms. Once we absorb this point, we can see Peirce's insistence that the sole object of inquiry is the settlement of opinion as tantamount to his saying this: "Believe what you will — end the irritation of doubt as you will — provided only that the belief with which you conquer doubt will *stick*, provided it really will conquer doubt." What this advice will imply, as we make the transition through all the defects of the earlier methods, is that, given the exigence that Peirce finds latent in the state of belief, the injunction to get oneself a belief in order to end the irritation of doubt *cannot* be satisfied by possessing oneself of just any belief. It cannot be satisfied, in fact, by any belief that one takes oneself to have acquired in a manner extraneous to the circumstances that the belief is concerned with. One cannot be satisfied by any belief that one takes oneself to have acquired in a manner that is not proper to its content. The injunction to seek a belief can only be satisfied if we manage the irritation of doubt and conduct our efforts at inquiry in such a way that the beliefs we acquire are acquired in a manner that is *not* so extraneous.

An analogy may be helpful. Augustine wrote "*Dilige [deum] et quod vis fac.*" The exhortation "Love God and do what thou wilt" may seem to be utterly permissive. It seems so until you reflect that such an injunction requires you to desire nothing God would not wish you to desire (or nothing you think he would not wish you to desire). It does not entail that you should do whatever you will.[4]

There is a second reason to think it misses the point to insist too much on the criticism urged. We have evidence from Peirce himself about how he intended the reader to take the claim that the fixation of belief was the sole aim of inquiry. It seems the point he really wanted to make is not best stated in the manner of the paragraph quoted. The declaration that the aim of inquiry was the simple fixation of belief was part of an argument to show that, *once you follow through* upon the

---

4 There is no doubt how Augustine's double direction is to be understood. It is a question whether "imperative logic" would need general modification lest "conjunction elimination" destroy the sense of such double commands.

simple object of fixing belief, you will be forced to see yourself as finally committed to the ideas of fact, reality, and truth. The evidence I have in mind is that, in 1906, Peirce wrote:

> My paper of 1877, setting out from the proposition that the agitation of a question ceases when satisfaction is attained with the settlement of belief ... goes on to consider *how the conception of truth gradually develops* from that principle under the action of experience. (*Collected Papers* 5.564)

Whether this is a natural reading of the essay in its 1877 condition is much less important than the fact that it shows how it was Peirce's considered view (reflecting the reading with which he revised "Fixation" over and over again) that, from the fixation of belief's being *taken as the aim of inquiry*, all sorts of other things gradually but inevitably unfold, not least the aim to have one's beliefs determined by circumstances not extraneous to the facts, the ideas of truth and fact, and, in the longer run, the commitment to permit the social art of logic, including the canons of abduction and induction, to play its role in effecting the fixation of opinion.

I conclude that, given the difficulties that his doctrine has in practice occasioned in both his critics and his admirers, it would have been far better if Peirce had said that the fixation of belief was *the whole inclusive aim of inquiry* rather than *the sole aim of inquiry*. He should not have issued the denials I have quoted. The thing that is perfectly certain, however, is that he was aware that, with the transition from the *a priori* method to his method, there arrives on the scene a distinctively refined motivation, a motivation that supersedes the simpler construals that are put on the fixation of belief by the three unsatisfactory methods.[5] And the need for this transition incorporates a real elucidatory

---

5 Indeed, in something he wrote before "On the Fixation of Belief," he had already noted that there is an important difference between the settlement of opinion which results from investigation and every other such settlement. It is that investigation "will not fix one answer to a question as well as another, but on the contrary it tends to unsettle opinions at first, to change them and to confirm a certain opinion which depends only on the nature of investigation itself." (*Collected Papers* 7.317)

insight about truth as a property forced upon us by reflection upon the state of belief.

There is one more false expectation that has been aroused by Peirce's exposition. I have said that, in so far as Peirce signals that the fixation of belief is (as I have put it) the whole inclusive aim of inquiry, truth is never abandoned — far from it, just the reverse — but simply waits for its moment to show itself. But how does Peirce himself conceive of this thing that is waiting for that moment? Does he conceive of truth simply as any old property in a belief that will make the state of belief be a satisfactory and non-irritable state? Some popular accounts of Peirce, which would assimilate him to a popular pragmatist or a job-bing anti-realist, suggest that that is *all* that is expected of truth in his construction. Worse, a footnote to the passage most recently quoted, continuing it into an after-thought dated 1903, may seem to confirm that expectation:

> Truth is neither more nor less than that character of a proposition which con-sists in this, that belief in the proposition would, with sufficient experience and reflection, lead us to such conduct as would tend to satisfy the desires we should then have. To say that truth means more than this is to say that it has no mean-ing at all.

This sounds awful. But perhaps we misunderstand Peirce if we take him, either here or in comparable passages, to be offering an "analytic definition" of truth. For, being a pragmaticist, Peirce would have little interest in such definitions. By "mean" he ought to mean something pragmaticist.[6] We misunderstand Peirce yet more unfairly if we take the characterization in this passage to be a definition of truth that is further intended to bring out what is so good about truth. We attribute to Peirce a cynical instrumentalism that is utterly alien to his actions,

---

6 One does not have to be a pragmaticist to want to be careful here. If I say that the character of being red is nothing more nor less than the character of being the colour thought by blind people to be well grasped by a comparison with the sound of a trumpet, do I have to be interpreted as offering a definition? For the importance in these connexions of Peirce's pragmaticist theory of meaning, see Misak, *Truth and the End of Inquiry*, chapter 1.

his character and his expressed views of science and life itself — *and* alien to the later sections of "On the Fixation of Belief."[7]

What, then, *is* going on in the 1903 addition? This, I suggest: Peirce is equating truth which waits in the wings, and is latent in the project of fixing belief, with a certain character that he relies upon the reader to know of already. There are all sorts of alternative ways of thinking of that character. We may think of it as (1) the character that beliefs aspire to; (2) the character beliefs have if and only if they correspond to a fact; (3) the character beliefs will have if actually they prompt correct anticipations of experience and never collide with it, the character in a belief that actually secures us from unpleasant surprises and will protect us (or so we may confidently trust) from the frustration of our desires; or (4) as the character enjoyed by beliefs that will actually survive, we hope, however long or far inquiry is pursued or prolonged. *De facto*, I suggest these alternatives all give a fix on the same character (if on any) — or so a serious inquirer had better suppose. But, in different connections, some of these ways of thinking of the thing we view as truth are more illuminating than others.

In Peirce's view, characterization (2) is useless for all relevant purposes. Its dependence on the idea of correspondence makes it useless in metaphysics.[8] It is useless in the actual *conduct* of inquiry too, because what inquiry has to be concerned to do is to *identify* the facts. But even in the *theory* of the conduct of inquiry, (2) will be equally useless. For (2) does not prompt that theory to engage with the efforts of *inquirers*. Nor, then, can it cast any light on the idea of truth that is strong enough to illuminate it.

Characterization (1) is more benign. But it must be said that it will scarcely help the inquirer who asks, "What shall I do to rid myself of the discomfort and irritation of doubt?" If we do get ourselves a belief, we shall think it a true belief. ("It is a mere tautology to say so," etc.) But the question will remain of what beliefs *to* adopt and how to acquire them, and what beliefs to hold onto.

---

7 See here my *Needs, Values, Truth* (Blackwell: Aristotelian Society, 1987) and Misak, ibid., 35–45.

8 See Misak, ibid., 37–45.

Now concede to Peirce that the first question for the theory of inquiry must be how an inquirer is to see his enterprise if his beliefs are to be determined by circumstances not extraneous to their content (not extraneous to the facts that the belief records). Then the thing I suggest the inquirer is going to need *within his inquiry* is some way to see truth that connects truth with his experience *in the conduct of inquiry.* But here precisely is the virtue of characterization (3), and (consequentially upon that) the virtue of characterization (4). *Neither of these fixes upon truth,* I have said, *is a definition.* The inquirer needs the thought that he wants his beliefs to be true in an ordinary pre-philosophical sense, yes. But lacking any viewpoint external to his inquiry, he will *also* need another, more operational, fix upon the character of truth. He needs a fix that connects that character with his experience as an investigator. But that can be provided by passages like the footnote of 1903, provided that they are read in the light of passages like that quoted from *Collected Papers* 5.564.[9]

Where are we? The settlement of opinion being the whole inclusive aim of inquiry, and truth, which waits in the wings, being the character you always thought it was but something that will only show itself again, as if face to face, when we understand better what inquiry is, the chief question must be *how* to inquire in a way that will be productive of genuine belief. The progression through the four methods of fixing belief begins in the primitive need to scratch one's doubt whenever it itches, in the hope of stopping that itch. But it will end in the perfected mentality of cheerful open-minded confidence that is the proudest attribute of enterprising and humbly experiential inquirers, the race apart of dedicated scientists or "laboratory men." Let us review the stages by which their outlook comes into being.

Peirce reviews first the method of tenacity or dogmatism. He says that the social impulse, which comprises the inner compulsion to pay anxious heed wherever others think differently from oneself, practically guarantees the total ineffectiveness of this method to determine opinion.

---

9 The meaning that Peirce says it lacks to say that truth means "more than this" is presumably pragmatic meaning.

Next Peirce cites the method of authority, consisting of dogmatism supported by the repression of social impulses that unsettle opinion.

> Let [men's] passions be enlisted, so that they may regard private and unusual opinions with hatred and horror. Then, let all men who reject the established belief be terrified into silence. (W3:250)

But, even if it seems to promise the end of doubt, Peirce declares (in passages which seem in the light of the past decade's events in Eastern Europe little less than prophetic) that this will not work either:

> No institution can undertake to regulate opinions upon every subject. Only the most important ones can be attended to, and on the rest men's minds must be left to the action of natural causes. (W3:251)

Under these conditions, people are bound to see in the end that their having the approved beliefs in which they are schooled is "the mere accident of having been taught as [they] have." For this reason,

> a new method of settling opinions, must be adopted, which shall not only produce an impulse to believe, but shall also decide what proposition it is which is to be believed. Let the action of natural preferences be unimpeded, then, and under their influence let men, conversing together and regarding matters in different lights, gradually develop beliefs in harmony with natural causes. (W3:252)

This method, which Peirce calls the *a priori* method,

> ought to be followed, as long as no better methods can be applied. But its failure has been the most manifest. It makes of inquiry something similar to the development of taste; but taste, unfortunately, is always more or less a matter of fashion ... [And] I cannot help seeing that ... sentiments in their development will be very greatly determined by accidental causes. Now, there are some people, among whom I must suppose that my reader is to be found, who, *when they see that any belief of theirs is determined by any circumstance extraneous to the facts, will from that moment not merely admit in words that that belief is doubtful, but will experience a real doubt of it, so that it ceases to be a belief.* (W3:253, my italics)

This last sentence, which I have already had occasion to quote in discussion of Peirce's conception of belief, is of course the point of transition to Peirce's celebrated fourth method, by which our beliefs may be caused by nothing human, but by some external permanency — by something upon which our thinking has no effect. It must be something which affects, or might affect, every man. And, though these affections are necessarily as various as are individual conditions, yet the method must be such that the ultimate conclusion of every man shall be the same. Such is the method of science. Its fundamental hypothesis, restated in more familiar language, is this: There are real things, whose characters are entirely independent of our opinions about them; those realities affect our senses according to regular laws, and, though our sensations are as different as are our relations to the objects, yet, by taking advantage of the laws of perception, we can ascertain by reasoning how things really and truly are, and any man, if he have sufficient experience and reason enough about it, will be led to the one true conclusion. The new conception here involved is that of reality. (W3:243-4)

Did Peirce mean to describe this last method in such a way that it was restricted to the procedures that impressed and inspired him in the laboratory and observatory? It may seem these are the terms in which it is most rational to picture the "Reals" which Peirce describes in terms of an "external permanency." But might not Peirce have intended it to be a perfectly general and all-embracing method, one applicable to ordinary life outside the laboratory? In that case, it will be a method whose most conspicuous and illuminating instance or paradigm is the procedure of practising scientists or "laboratory men." But their procedures, for all their purity and force, will not be the only possible exemplification of the method. In this case, when the rhetoric and excitement of Peirce's exposition are allowed for and then discounted, Peirce's Reals are place-holders for the propositional or other objects of *any* mode of thinking that is in good enough order to fix genuine beliefs. They will be place-holders for objects of any mode of thinking that is well enough managed (or well enough manageable) for the following to hold: if you engage in the form of thinking, then "secondness jabs you perpetually in the ribs" (*Collected Papers* 6.95). Having reached by patient labour a complex and many-layered state of readiness, you arrive, when jabbed, at a belief *malgré vous*, as Leibniz would have said. Your will is engaged first by curiosity or irritability. Patiently, you manage your inquiry as best you can to quell that irritation, and then at some crucial point something that is not up to you, but is of the right sort, brings it about that you are convinced, fallibly but fully.

Let us take stock. If we are influenced by Peirce's gloss of 1906 upon his essay of 1877, then we interpret him to say that anyone who begins with the idea that the whole aim of inquiry is the fixation of belief will realize that this apparently simple aim comprehends within it nothing less than this: that any belief of ours to the effect that *p* should be determined by circumstances that are not extraneous to the fact that *p*. But reflecting on this constitutive aim, the philosopher of inquiry will see that this last is all that is needed for the idea of Reality. It is all that is needed, then, for the idea of the Reals to which the belief that *p* is answerable. Inquirers scarcely lie under any obligation to reflect in this way. But, if, even as we experience, we do reflect about our procedures and their rationale, then that which is discovered to us are the ideas of truth, of fact, and of Reals. This is the rich outcome of the apparently meagre resources we began with. And along with the ideas of truth, fact, and Real, we find the fundamental hypothesis, which speaks of our ascertaining "by reasoning how things really and truly are." It is in this quiet way that retroduction or abduction enter into the picture, and with them the old idea of Sufficient Reason. The fundamental hypothesis also forces upon us the task of arriving at a proper conception of experience — or of that by which we can expose our mind to and make our beliefs answerable to Reals. In this last connexion we should take note of a manuscript of 1893–95 helpfully adduced by Cheryl Misak:

> As for the experience under the influence of which beliefs are formed, what is it? It is nothing by the forceful element in the course of life. Whatever it is ... in our history that wears out our attempts to resist it, that is experience ... The maxim that we ought to be 'guided' by experience means that we had better submit at once to that to which we must submit at last. 'Guided' is not the word; 'governed' should be said.[10]

The idea of Reality is one thing. A Real is another. "It may be asked," Peirce notes, "how I know that there are any Reals." To this question Peirce gives four replies, of which the most striking, interesting, and conclusive is this one:

---

10 Misak, *Truth and the End of Inquiry*, 83.

> The feeling which gives rise to any method of fixing belief is a dissatisfaction at two repugnant propositions. But there already is a vague concession that there is some one thing, which a proposition should represent. Nobody, therefore, can really doubt that there are Reals, for, if he did, doubt would not be a source of dissatisfaction. The hypothesis, therefore, is one which every mind admits. So that the social impulse does not cause men to doubt it.

At this point, the idea can arise in the reader's mind that Reals must be something in an altogether different category from facts, truths, and the like. For it may be supposed that Reals are items with a distinctive causal role. That would certainly have the effect of restricting the ambit of the doctrine drastically, and it would commit Peirce to a strange new ontology. But is it necessary to read Peirce so?

The idea of inquiry is an entirely general one. It is as general as the ideas of truth, knowledge, fact, and the rest. Sometimes Peirce strained consciously to confer an equal generality upon the ideas of experience and its secondness. Seeking that sort of generality and avoiding at the same time any ontological commitment at all, one might try saying that what is minimally required is that any belief to the effect that p shall be determined by circumstances not extraneous to the circumstance that p.

As it stands, such a formula covers the future as well as the past and the abstract as well as the concrete. If we want to preserve this generality, then it seems we must resist any complete take-over by the idea of causality. And we must think that the letter "p" is not here a variable. It functions by holding a place for a sentence. Thus the minimal claim about the formation of the belief that p is seen as a notionally simultaneous assertion of all instances of a schema, with different fillings for the letter "p." In putting the claim forward, we *gesture* at something entirely general. In this way, we understand the secondness requirement and other requirements by applying schemata over and over again to different examples. The same might even be proposed for Peirce's way of understanding his own talk of Reals. In logical terms, what he says can be interpreted or elucidated by a schema. Philosophically, that means that it can be filled out for different kinds of case according to the subject matter and in the light of that which Peirce's logic will add to his characterization of the fourth method.

In the fundamental hypothesis itself, recently quoted, where I do not deny that causality or causal explanation is uppermost in his mind,

Peirce speaks of "Reals affect[ing] our senses according to regular laws" and of anyone who has sufficient experience and willingness to reason "taking advantage of the laws of perception" to "ascertain by reasoning how things really and truly are." The thing we must ask next is what kind of reasoning this is, and how Peirce envisages its workings. Its working is abductive or retroductive, but in a special way. Unluckily, Peirce offers no systematic account of this special case. But from the lectures he gave in 1903 in Cambridge we get some indications of the link he saw between this kind of reasoning and states like memory and perception:

> I once landed at a seaport in a Turkish province; and as I was walking up to the house which I was to visit, I met a man upon horseback, surrounded by four horsemen holding a canopy over his head. As the governor of the province was the only personage I could think of who would be so greatly honoured, I inferred that this was he. This was an hypothesis ...
>
> Fossils are found; say, remains like those of fishes, but far in the interior of the country. To explain the phenomenon, we suppose the sea once washed over this land. This is another hypothesis ...
>
> Numberless documents and monuments refer to a conqueror called Napoleon Bonaparte. Though we have not seen the man, yet we cannot explain what we have seen, namely, all these documents and monuments, without supposing that he really existed. Hypothesis again.
>
> As a general rule, hypothesis is a weak kind of argument. It often inclines our judgment so slightly toward its conclusion that we cannot say that we believe the latter to be true; we only surmise that it may be so. But there is no difference except one of degree between such an inference and *that by which we are led to believe that we remember the occurrences of yesterday from our feeling as if we did so.* (*Collected Papers* 2.625, my italics.)

This is the case of memory. For the case of perception, we have the following:

> ... abductive inference shades into perceptual judgment without any sharp line of demarcation between them; or, in other words, our first premisses, the perceptual judgments, are to be regarded as an extreme case of abductive inferences, from which they differ in being absolutely beyond criticism. The abductive suggestion comes to us like a flash. It is an act of insight, though of extremely fallible insight. (*Collected Papers* 5.181)

What did Peirce have in mind when he claimed that perception and memory were abductive? Any adequate answer would need to cohere with two other Peircean doctrines (the first familiar from our earlier mention of "secondness"):

> Direct consciousness of hitting and getting hit enters into all cognition and serves to make it mean something real. (*Collected Papers* 8.41)

and

> The chair I appear to see makes no professions of any kind, essentially embodies no intentions of any kind, does not stand for anything. It obtrudes itself upon my gaze; but not as a deputy for anything else nor "as" anything. (*Collected Papers* 7.619)

A full reconstruction of Peirce's doctrine would have to cohere not only with these clues, with his fallibilism (which suggests that what is "beyond criticism" must be not any perceptual belief but the perceptual state that can sustain a belief), but also with Peirce's numerous but sketchy hints about the distinct roles in perception of *percipuum, percept,* and *perceptual judgment.* The thing I shall offer here, however, is only an interim statement. It is intended to cohere with these constraints, but it is not given in Peircean language.

Suppose object and perceiver encounter one another in perception. Then independently of will or reason, the perceiver may be moved to report what she sees by saying "six windows obtrude, it seems, upon my gaze." No abduction yet. But for the perceiver to take what she is confronted with *for* six windows just *is* — whether she knows it or not — for her to take it that the best explanation of her perception is that there are six windows there. (Certainly she must not believe there is any other explanation, though of course there may be.) And similarly *mutatis mutandis* for the remembering case. From remembering (or its being as if one remembers) the messenger giving one a letter yesterday one concludes that the messenger did indeed give one a letter yesterday. Again, whether one knows this or not, this is abductive.

Can we generalize this? Well, it seems the relation of experience and belief must be this: that the experience creates the fallible presumption that what we are moved to report that we see or remember is that which accounts for our being so moved. One might say that the acceptability of retroduction is quietly and tacitly *institutionalized* in our experience or in the title we claim that that experience affords us to make empirical claims.

Here ends the interpretation and explication of "The Fixation of Belief." But we are not yet at the end of the fourth method, which is still in the condition of a program needing to be worked out. To enlarge upon the fourth method and establish the general role therein of abduction, we now have to draw upon writings Peirce devoted to logic and his theory of inference.

Peirce classifies inferences as deductive/analytic/explicative and as synthetic/ampliative. And the synthetic/ampliative he subdivides into (1) abduction, hypothesis, or retroduction and (2) induction. It will be useful to have some characterizations of each. Let us begin with induction:

> Induction is where we generalize from a number of cases of which something is true, and infer that the same thing is true of a whole class. Or, where we find a certain thing to be true of a certain proportion of cases and infer that it is true of the same proportion of the whole class. (*Collected Papers* 2.264)

Hypothesis, on the other hand,

> is where we find some very curious circumstances, which would be explained by the supposition that it was a case of a certain general rule, and thereupon adopt that supposition. Or, where we find that in certain respects two objects have a strong resemblance, and infer that they resemble one another strongly in other respects. (*Collected Papers* 2.624)

Or, as Peirce describes abductive thought elsewhere:

> The first starting of a hypothesis and the entertaining of it, whether as a simple interrogation or with any degree of confidence, is an inferential step which I propose to call abduction. This will include a preference for any one hypothesis over others which would equally explain the facts as long as this preference is not based upon any previous knowledge bearing upon the truth of the hypotheses, nor on any testing of any of the hypotheses, after having admitted them on probation. I call all such inference by the peculiar name, *abduction*." (*Collected Papers* 6.525)

Here the restrictions Peirce starts to draft may need very careful statement, for we may also need to preclude this form of inference from allowing into the place of a hypothesis — into the place marked by "A" in our next citation — suppositions that are contrary to things in the reasoner's evidential background or that are gratuitous relative to that background. The thought that we may need to do this becomes more evident when abduction is set out as starkly as it is in the following citation:

> The hypothesis cannot be admitted, even as an hypothesis, unless it be supposed that it would account for the facts or some of them. The form of inference, therefore, is this:
> The surprising fact, C, is observed;
> But if A were true, C would be matter of course;
> Hence, there is reason to suspect that A is true.
> Thus, A cannot be abductively ... conjectured until its entire content is already present in the premise, 'If A were true, C would be a matter of course'. (*Collected Papers* 5.189)

When the form of this reasoning is set out thus, the question that takes shape is whether any supposition at all that would make C a matter of course should be permitted (subject to the restrictions Peirce gives in 6.525, cited) to count as a hypothesis, as something ready to move to the next stage of being subjected to refutation or adoption. (Peirce sometimes talks like this: "Abduction commits us to nothing. It merely causes a hypothesis to be set down upon our docket of cases to be tried" [*Collected Papers* 5.602].) Or are there criteria for the selection of things that shall count as hypotheses?[11] And where do *they* spring from? Do they spring from the need to fix belief? I shall not answer these questions here.

According to Peirce's doctrine, retroduction or abduction (however we enlarge upon it) is a distinctive mode of thinking. It is reducible neither to deduction, whose role is the ancillary one of drawing out the consequences of hypotheses, nor to induction, to which Peirce assigns the special role of testing (refuting or supporting) the hypotheses that are submitted to it by abduction. Induction can *support* generalizations, but in or of itself it does not license us to go from positive instances of an arbitrary putative generalization to the assertion

---

11 See Misak, *Truth and the End of Inquiry*, 99.

of that generalization. For first the generalization has to enjoy the status of a hypothesis. It can only attain that status if it renders less surprising something that was surprising or that wanted explaining· It follows that no methodological paradoxes such as Hempel's (of the ravens, etc.) or Goodman's (of "grue," etc.) can gain any purchase on the Peircean account of inquiry. Nothing in it corresponds to Nicod's postulate.[12]

Thinking in this way, Peirce is distinctively anti-Bayesian. His is not the only anti-Bayesian theory. But nor yet is Peirce's theory quite the same as Popper's theory or Reichenbach's. Indeed, Peirce's account of these matters is not a notational variant of any of the theories that are normally pitted against one another in present-day discussions. Now I shall try to do for it what Peirce himself never did (so far as I know), namely, reconstruct the singular way in which it measures up to the challenge that David Hume issued to all forms of reasoning from the known to the unknown.

Hume points out that all reasonings concerning matters of fact are founded in the relations of cause and effect, and that the foundation of our understanding of these is experience. But how, he asks, does experience found the conclusion (e.g.) that bread will nourish us? How may I infer from past bread eatings having nourished me that similar eatings *will* nourish me? If there is such an inference it is not *intuitive* (knowable without demonstration), nor yet is it *demonstrative*. What is it then? It is experimental, Hume imagines you saying. But to this he replies that all experimental reasonings presuppose that the future will resemble the past. Therefore, they cannot *prove* that the future will resemble the past. So it is not reasoning which engages us to suppose the future will resemble the past. Hume concludes that it is habit.

---

12 On Nicod, see C. G. Hempel, 'Studies in the Logic of Confirmation', *Mind*, 54, 1945. If a white shoe really confirmed to some degree that "all non-black things are non-ravens" — that is the effect of Nicod's postulate — then it would have to confirm to the same degree its contrapositive equivalent "all ravens are black." And that is absurd. See the striking observation of Frege's that stands as the third motto. But in Peirce's conception of inquiry, Nicod's postulate is entirely dispensable.

Peirce would begin by agreeing that inference from the known to the unknown is indeed a matter of habit and not demonstrative. But habits, he would insist, can be good or bad. And good habits can exemplify a distinctive form of reasonableness. After all, we *need* to argue from the unknown to the known. If we need to, then it is reasonable for us to do so — provided that we do not do so in a manner that is unreasonable (e.g., by following a policy that will harm us) or question-begging.

It is easy to imagine that Hume would then press harder upon the question how Peirce can argue non-question-beggingly from past nourishings by bread to future nourishings by bread, if this presupposes the *general* claim that the future will resemble the past, which is something yet harder to establish than future nourishings by bread.

To this Peirce would surely reply (here anticipating Popper) that good arguments from the known to the unknown had better *not* presuppose that the future will resemble the past. For it is not even true that it will!

> Nature is not regular ... It is true that the special laws and regularities are innumerable; but nobody thinks of the irregularities, which are infinitely more frequent. (W2:264)

Moreover, when we argue from past nourishing by bread to future nourishings by bread, we are *not*, according to Peirce, simply extrapolating a past regularity. That is never, in his view, a valid procedure. If that was what Hume was attacking, Hume was right (but short of the conclusion he was aiming for). When we extrapolate a regularity, there has to be another reason to do so beside the fact that the regularity has held so far. Even in the special case of the *particular* methods so beloved of the inductive reliabilists such as Mellor and Papineau (if I understand them), it would be utterly invalid simply to argue from the past success of a method to its future success. There has to be something else that commends any method. That is the role of abductive thought.

How, then, according to Peirce, does experimental reasoning carry us (e.g.) from past nourishings by bread to future nourishings by bread? To this I think Peirce can reply in steps. First, if we are to do what we are naturally committed to do and we are to argue from the known (e.g., the past) to the unknown (e.g., the future), then we must begin by trying to understand the known — in this case, bread. This problem of understanding the known does not need to be one we can solve on its own, without reference to the state of our inquiries into other empirical questions. Nor yet do we need to be assured that we *can* succeed in this. If it is not possible to succeed, then what we are naturally committed to attempt (argument from known to unknown) will be impossible. Wherever that is so, there's an end on it. But even that would not show that it was *irrational* to attempt the investigation — if it was important to us to find the answer to a certain question. If our need is great enough, we have no alternative but to proceed as if progress is possible. (And it may indeed *be* possible, remember.) If we have no alternative but to proceed, then it is reasonable for us to apply at any moment the most promising investigative strategy that is then known to us. What, then, shall that be? Well, Peirce says, something suggested by the fundamental hypothesis. If we want fuller generality, is there something more general than the fundamental hypothesis? Only one answer presents itself, namely this: "Nothing holds or is so or obtains but that there is some reason why it is so." Readers of Leibniz will recognize the thought. *This* claim is as general as the claim that the future will resemble the past. But it is a far better candidate to be the regulative assumption of inquiry. At least it is not manifestly false. Even better, it scarcely needs to count as a general claim about reality. It is enough for it to determine an attitude towards reality that it would be unreasonable not to share in.

What then is the connection between Sufficient Reason and the twofold procedure that Peirce commends to us? Surely this: Suppose our attitude has to be that nothing holds unless there is a reason why it should. Then if some phenomenon C holds, something must be true which explains why C holds. But then it must be possible to argue backwards against the current of deductive sequence, and infer from C's obtaining whatever *best* explains why C obtains. But that is nothing other than abduction, which supplies materials to induction. For instance, if stuffs like this and that and the other nourish, there must be something or other about them in virtue of which they nourish. The only question is what this something or other is — a question that we attempt from the midst of a large background of collateral beliefs, suspicions, conjectures, questions, and the rest. The label "bread" is, if you like, a sort of place-holder for that something or other. (Just as even that comical old abstraction *virtus dormitiva* is a good enough place-holder for the something or other in opium that "explains its always putting people to sleep"; cp. *Collected Papers* 4.234.) Is not "bread" a good enough place-holder to provide us with a hypothesis that can be tested, qualified, reformulated, tested again, and so on? In practice and so far, some hypotheses have stood up. When they fail we will start repairing them. This is the only rational way for us to proceed.

None of this proves that bread will continue to nourish.[13] Such a proof was not what Hume took himself to be entitled to. What he asked was, what kind of reasonable inference it is that gives the conclusion that bread will nourish? The answer to his question is that, just as Hume says, the inference is not intuitive and it is not demonstrative. It is a fallible extrapolation which we should be practically irrational not to attempt from an abductive hypothesis that we should have been practically irrational not to try to formulate and test, an abductive hypothesis arrived at in accordance with the branch of thinking that the nineteenth century called logic. Except insofar as it subsumes the science of deduction, it is not the business of such logic, and it does not need to be its business, to furnish infallible directions by which to argue from the known to the unknown[14] — only directions that it would be very irrational not to employ.

---

13 Or that the world will not be stood on its head. If the world is swept away, then better answers may be swept away with everything else.

14 Or even to furnish procedures that "will, if persisted in long enough, assuredly correct any error concerning future experience into which [they] may temporarily lead us" (*Collected Papers* 2.769). Peirce does make such claims, but they are inessential to his contribution to the "problem of induction" (see Misak, *Truth and the End of Inquiry*, 111, 115).

CANADIAN JOURNAL OF PHILOSOPHY
Supplementary Volume 24

Truth: A Traditional Debate Reviewed*

CRISPIN WRIGHT
University of St. Andrews and Columbia University

I

Every student of English-speaking analytical metaphysics is taught that the early twentieth century philosophical debate about truth confronted the correspondence theory, supported by Russell, Moore, the early Wittgenstein and, later, J.L. Austin, with the coherence theory advocated by the British Idealists.[1] Sometimes the pragmatist conception of truth deriving from Dewey, William James, and C.S. Peirce is

---

* A version of this paper was originally written for delivery as a lecture in the series "Unsere Welt: gegeben oder gemacht? Wissensproduktion zwischen sozialer Konstruktion und Entdeckung" held at the Johann Wolfgang Goethe-Universität in Frankfurt in the spring of 1996. It is published in German in Matthias Vogel and Lutz Wingert (eds.), *Unsere Welt gegeben oder gemacht? Menschliches Erkennen zwischen Entdeckung und Konstruktion* (Frankfurt/M.: Suhrkamp, 1999). Thanks to the discussants on that occasion and also to participants at colloquia at University College, Dublin; the University of Kent at Canterbury; Columbia University; and the 1998 Austin J. Fagothey S.J. Philosophy Conference on Truth at Santa Clara University; and to Bob Hale, Fraser MacBride, Stewart Shapiro, and Charles Travis.

1 Two *loci classici* of coherentism are H.H. Joachim, *The Nature of Truth* (Oxford: Oxford University Press, 1906) and F.H Bradley, *Essays on Truth and Reality* (Oxford: Oxford University Press, 1914). Ralph Walker has argued that coherentism is implicit also in the forms of anti-realism canvassed by Michael Dummett and Hilary Putnam (at least, the Hilary Putnam of *Reason, Truth and History*). See Ralph Walker, *The Coherence Theory of Truth: Realism, Anti-Realism, Idealism* (London: Routledge, 1989). Myself, I doubt this — for further discussion, see my critical study of Walker's book in *Synthese* 103 (1995): 279–302.

regarded as a third player. And as befits a debate at the dawn of analytical philosophy, the matter in dispute is normally taken to have been
the proper analysis of the concept.

No doubt this conception nicely explains some of the characteristic
turns taken in the debate. Analysis, as traditionally conceived, has to
consist in the provision of illuminating conceptual equivalences; and
illumination will depend, according to the standard rules of play, on
the analysans' utilizing only concepts which, in the best case, are in
some way prior to and independent of the notion being analyzed —
or, if that's too much to ask, then concepts which at least permit of
some form of explication which does not in turn take one straight back
to that notion. Thus if it is proposed, in this spirit, that truth is correspondence to external fact, it will be possible for a critic both to grant
the *correctness* of the proposal and to reject it nevertheless — because,
it may be contended, it fails to comply with the conditions on an illuminating *analysis*. In particular, it will be an obligation on an analysis
of truth in terms of correspondence that it be possible to supply appropriate independent explications of the notions of "correspondence"
and "fact," and it is exactly here, of course, that many of the traditional difficulties for the correspondence proposal have been located.
Likewise, if we propose to analyze truth in terms of coherence, or on
broadly pragmatist lines, we must be prepared to allow that any and
every occurrence of "true" as applied to what the analysis recognizes
to be its primary bearers — sentences, or propositions, or whatever —
may be replaced, without change of meaning,[2] by an expression of the
preferred analysans. And, again, many of the knots into which critics
have tied proposals of these kinds depend upon exploitation of this
constraint. As recently as 1982, for instance, Alvin Plantinga observed
that if "true" just means *would be believed by cognitively ideal subjects
operating under cognitively ideal conditions*, then there seems to be no

---

2 How this constraint may be made to consist with the requirement that analysis
be illuminating is, of course, the heart of Moore's paradox of analysis. But the
sort of objection about to be noted need read no more into sameness of content
than sameness of truth-conditions.

prospect of recovering, without paradox, an account of the content of the thought: it is true that conditions are not cognitively ideal.[3]

When the debate is all about the analysis of the concept of truth, then at least two other kinds of position have to be possible — and, historically, they have indeed been occupied. One is the indefinabilist view adopted by Frege: that truth allows of *no* analysis, because it is too simple, or primitive, or because any notions involved in a formulation which is at least correct will rapidly bring one back to truth, so compromising illumination. Frege held this view for reasons whose cogency is a matter of dispute,[4] but the apparent paucity of successful analyses of *anything* in analytical philosophy, and the inchoate and uneasy state of the methodology of analysis itself, must encourage the thought that this negative stance will not easily be dismissed. Quite different — and rather more interesting — is the proposal that correspondence, coherentist, pragmatist, and even indefinabilist conceptions of truth all err in their common conviction that "true" presents a substantial concept at all. This is the deflationist tradition, which is usually thought to have originated in Ramsey, was defended in rather different ways by Ayer and Strawson, and which survives in contemporary writers such as Paul Horwich and Hartry Field.[5] According to

---

3 Alvin Plantinga, "How to be an Anti-Realist," *Proceedings and Addresses of the American Philosophical Association* 56 (1982): 47–70. Plantinga's point also engages certain formulations of the coherence theory. For instance to suppose that "true" means *would be believed by a subject who had arrived at a maximally coherent and comprehensive set of beliefs* is again implicitly to surrender the means to construe the truth of the thought: no-one holds a maximally coherent and comprehensive set of beliefs. The problem is a special case of the so-called conditional fallacy: any analysis in terms of subjunctive conditionals is potentially in trouble if its intended range comprises statements which are incompatible with the protases of the relevant conditionals.

4 For discussion, see Peter Carruthers, "Frege's Regress," *Proceedings of the Aristotelian Society* 82 (1981): 17–32. See also the useful account in Ralph C.S. Walker's survey article "Theories of Truth" in the Blackwell *Companion to the Philosophy of Language*, ed. Bob Hale and Crispin Wright (Oxford: Blackwell, 1997), esp. Section 6.

5 Paul Horwich's *Truth* (Oxford: Blackwell, 1990) provides a detailed defence of the deflationary tradition and a useful bibliography of its literature. While Field's

deflationism, there simply isn't anything which truth, in general, *is*. It's a misconstrual of the role of the adjective "true" to see it as expressing the concept of a substantial characteristic of which one of the traditional accounts might provide a correct analysis, or which might allow of no correct analysis. Those who think otherwise are missing the point that the role of a significant adjective doesn't have to be to ascribe a genuine property.

My first principal point is that, notwithstanding the fact that it rationalizes many of the moves made, and doubtless reflects therefore the intentions of many of the protagonists, the conception of the traditional debate about truth as centred upon reductive analysis of the concept is not best fitted to generate the most fruitful interpretation of that debate. To see this, suppose for the sake of argument that the indefinabilists are right: that "true," like, say, "red," admits of no illuminating conceptual breakdown. It is striking that philosophical discussion of colour has hardly been silenced by the corresponding point about the concept *red* or basic colour concepts generally. The contention that there is, as Locke thought, an interesting distinction between primary and secondary qualities of objects and that red is a secondary quality; the contention that whether an object is red is, in some way, a "response-dependent" matter, or more generally that there is some form of implicit relativity in the idea of an object's being red; the contention that red is, on the contrary, a non-relational property of objects or, more specifically, that red things form a natural kind; even the "error-theoretic" view that a complete inventory of characteristics found in the real world would contain no mention of colours — all these views, and an acknowledgement of the interest of the debates to which they contribute, are consistent with recognition of the indefinability of colour concepts. So, consistently with its indefinability — if it is indefinable — a similar range of issues can be expected to arise in connec-

---

"The Deflationary Conception of Truth" (in *Fact, Science and Morality*, ed. G. Macdonald and C. Wright [Oxford: Blackwell, 1986], 55–117) eventually suggests that there are purposes for which a correspondence conception is needed; his more recent "Deflationist Views of Meaning and Content" (*Mind* 103 [1994], 249–85) takes a more committed deflationary line.

tion with truth. "True" — even when taken, in the broad sense which interests us, as a predicate of content-bearing things — is predicated of a variety of items: beliefs, thoughts, propositions, token utterances of type sentences. But whatever such items we have in mind, we can ask whether one of them being true is in any way an *implicitly relational* matter — and if so, what are the terms of the relation; whether it is a *response-dependent* matter, or in any other way dependent on subjectivity or a point of view; whether there is indeed nothing generally in which the truth of such an item consists — whether an inventory of all the properties to be found in the world would include mention of *no such thing as truth.*

Indeed, such issues arise for any putative characteristic, Φ. Should we (ontologists) take Φ seriously at all, or is some sort of error-theoretic or deflationary view appropriate? If we do take it seriously, should we think of the situation of an item's being Φ as purely a matter of how it is intrinsically with that item, or are we rather dealing with some form of relation? Is an item's being Φ an objective matter (and what does it mean to say so)? These are analytic-philosophical issues *par excellence*, but their resolution need not await — and might not be settled by — the provision of a correct conceptual analysis.

II

Suppose we discard the analysis-centred conception of the traditional debate and look at it instead in the way suggested by the foregoing reflections. Clearly the deflationary option remains in play, holding that truth is not a genuine characteristic of anything — that it would find no place in an inventory of what is real. The other views all allow the reality of truth but differ about its *structure*, or in respects relevant to the broad question of objectivity. Correspondence theory holds that truth is a relational characteristic whose terms are respectively propositions — to pick one among the possibilities[6] — and *non-propositional*

---

6 Sentences, token utterances, statements, beliefs, and thoughts are some among the other content-bearing items which we ordinarily think of as apt for truth.

items — facts, or states of affairs — in an independent world.[7] The proposal thus bears both on structure and, so proposers of correspondence intend, on objectivity too. Coherence theory agrees about the relationality of truth, but disagrees about the terms of the relation: on this type of view, the truth of a proposition consists not in a relation to something non-propositional but in its participation in a system, meeting certain conditions, whose other participants are likewise propositions — so ultimately in relations to those other propositions. This is again, in the first instance, a view about the structure of truth, but it was intended by its original proponents to provide a vehicle for their idealism. And pragmatism — the view that truth is, broadly, a matter of operational success of some kind — while making no clear suggestion about structure (though there may be commitments in this direction once the relevant dimensions of success are clarified), stands in opposition to the correspondence theorists' thoughts about objectivity without — intentionally anyway — implying anything like such idealism.

Let's focus for the time being on the question of structure, and return later to some of the issues connected with pragmatism. We may chart the possibilities in a tree as follows:

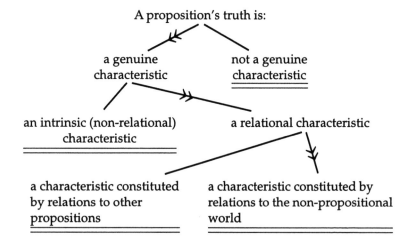

---

7 Excepting, of course, the case where a proposition is itself about propositions.

Essentially, then, just four structural proposals are possible: deflationism; intrinsicism; and the two forms of relationalism, coherentism, and correspondence. I think it's fair to say that this conception of correspondence, shorn of any further analytical or explanatory obligations, comes across as highly common-sensical. In general, we'd want to think both that there's a real distinction marked by the classification of some propositions as true and others as false, and that it is a distinction which cannot generally be understood without reference to things which are not themselves propositions, and so cannot be understood in intrinsicist or coherentist terms.

This piece of common sense is not to be confused with the idea that, understood one way, correspondence is nothing more than a platitude. The platitude is that predications of "true" may always harmlessly be glossed in terms of correspondence to fact, telling it like it is, etc. These paraphrases incorporate no substantial commitment about the structure of truth — any more than the paraphrasability of "she did it for John" by "she did it on John's behalf" involves a commitment to the view that altruistic action is really a three-term relation. By contrast, the ordinary, common-sensical conception of the kind of thing a proposition's truth is involves exactly the structural commitments associated with the feathered path on the above tree.

It will be a second main contention of this paper that there is no stable alternative to allowing at least some scope to this common-sensical conception.

III

In order to make good that contention, we need to see that each of the three alternatives gives rise to intractable problems.

Intrinsicism is the easiest case to deal with. Fix attention on the case of contingent truths. If its truth-value were an intrinsic — but contingent — property of a particular proposition, then no contingent change in any other object should entail change in the proposition in that particular respect. That's an instance of a quite general principle. The mass, for instance, of a given body is a contingent but intrinsic property of that body only if no contingent change in any other object would entail change in that object's mass. By contrast, a property — for instance, being a grandfather — is essentially relational, even if expressed by what looks like a semantically simple predicate, if change in other objects may entail that a particular object sheds, or acquires, that property. By this simple test truth is, manifestly, not an intrinsic property. For the truth-value of any contingent proposition must co-vary with hypothetical changes in the characteristics of things it concerns — so that a hypothetical change, for instance, in the location of my coffee cup may entail an alteration in the truth-value of the proposition that there is no coffee cup on my desk, even though that proposition and the particular coffee cup in question are quite distinct existences. To be sure, this line of thought creates no difficulty for the idea that the truth-value of a *necessary* proposition might be an intrinsic property. So, indeed, it may be. But clearly intrinsicism cannot handle the general run of contingent cases.[8]

It might be rejoined that the canvassed account of the contrast between intrinsic and relational properties is incorrect or circular. For a property F may be an intrinsic characteristic of an object and yet its loss, say, may still be entailed by change in another object provided that latter change is permitted to be in *non-intrinsic respects*. For instance, if G is a ("Cambridge") property possessed by any object just in case *a* has intrinsic characteristic F, then any other object's losing G will entail that *a* has lost F. This observation is, however, beside the point. All the objection to intrinsicism needs is that the account be correct, not that it be explanatory. If it is at least granted that F is an intrinsic property of *a* just in case no *intrinsic* change in any other object can entail change in *a* in that respect, it will follow as before that truth cannot be an intrinsic property of any proposition whose content is that another object has some particular intrinsic but contingent property.

IV

It is a rather more complicated business to elicit what is fundamentally unsatisfactory about the deflationary conception of truth. The difficul-

---

8 I do not know that anyone has ever seriously proposed an intrinsicist conception of truth quite generally.

ties here are owing partly to the point that deflationism is more of a "tendency" than a definite philosophical position, and different deflationists display differences of formulation and emphasis which make it hard to see what may be essential and what optional in their views. There are, however, a number of characteristic, inter-related claims: first,

(i)   that there is no property of truth which is an appropriate object of philosophical attention: something which we might try to analyze, or in whose structure we might be interested, or which might give rise to issues about objectivity. Contrary to the presupposition both of the traditional debate and of its revision canvassed above, there is *nothing* in which the truth of a proposition, e.g., consists. "True" expresses no real property.[9]

That negative contention is then characteristically augmented by a variety of considerations about the meaning or positive function of the word "true"; for instance:

(ii)   that, as applied to sentences, "true" is just the device of *disquotation* — a device for affirming at the metalinguistic level (by locutions of the form: "P" is true) exactly what can be affirmed at the object-language level by an assertoric use of "P";

(iii)   that the Disquotational Scheme
        "P" is true ↔ p,
        (or if the primary grammar of "true" is considered to be that of an operator on (or predicable of) propositions, the Equivalence Schema
        It is true that P/that P is true if and only if P)
        is (all but) a complete explanation of the meaning of "true";

(iv)   that "true" is just a device of endorsement — we only have any use for such a term because we sometimes choose to endorse

---

9   Horwich is more guarded on this than many writers in the deflationist tradition. But although he seems unwilling expressly to deny that truth is a property, it is not, he contends, a "complex property" — not "an ingredient of reality whose underlying essence will, it is hoped, one day be revealed by philosophical or scientific analysis" (*Truth*, 2). Thus there is, for Horwich, nothing to say about what truth really consists in, no real question for, e.g., correspondence and coherence accounts to address themselves to.

propositions indirectly, without specifying their content ("The sixth sentence of *Remarks on the Foundations of Mathematics* IV, §3 is true" or "Fermat's Last Theorem has turned out to be true") and sometimes want to endorse whole batches of propositions at once ("Almost everything Chancellor Kohl says is true"). In other kinds of case we can dispense with the word altogether.

Deflationism has been subjected to a variety of criticisms: for instance, that its characteristic lionization of the Disquotational Scheme is in tension with the manifest unacceptability of that principle when vagueness or other phenomena leading to failures of bivalence are operative;[10] that it is inconsistent with a truth-conditional conception of meaning or more generally with the semantic role of truth;[11] that it cannot accommodate the idea of scientific progress; most generally, that it violates our intuitions about correspondence, about truth as bestowed by fit with an external, objective world.[12] Here I shall rehearse an argument I have given elsewhere to the effect that deflationism is internally unstable.[13] Specifically, there is a contradiction between the kind of account of the function of "true" which deflationists broadly want to give and the contention that the concept of truth, properly understood, is not the concept of a genuine, substantial property.

Let us focus, for ease of exposition, on "true" as predicable of propositions, and on the positive deflationist contention that, in its most basic use, the word is essentially a device of endorsement which, except in cases where the content of the proposition endorsed is not explicitly given, or where quantification over propositions is involved, may be dispensed with altogether in favour of a simple assertion of the proposition characterized as "true."

---

10 This criticism is first lodged, I believe, in Michael Dummett's early paper "Truth," *Proceedings of the Aristotelian Society* 59(1959): 141–62.

11 This claim, too, is advanced in Dummett's "Truth."

12 All these directions of criticism are usefully referenced and reviewed in Horwich's *Truth.*

13 See Chapter 1 of my *Truth and Objectivity* (Cambridge, MA: Harvard University Press, 1992).

It is hardly deniable that "true" does have this kind of function and that its uses may often be paraphrased away without materially affecting the content of what is said. The issue is rather whether the point can carry the intended deflationary implications. And the crucial question for that issue is, what is it to *endorse* a proposition? Endorsement generally involves an element of recommendation, or approval of an item as meeting a certain standard. That's what I'm doing when, for example, in helping my child choose an ice cream I point at the pistachio and say "That's a nice one." What kind of commendation is involved in the case of "true"? Plausibly, that if I affirm a proposition's truth, I'm recommending its acceptance, commending it as meeting a certain doxastic standard, as it were. In this way, affirmations of truth — and likewise denials of truth — are normative claims. To endorse a proposition as true is to affirm that it is acceptable as a belief or statement; to deny that a proposition is true is to affirm that it's correspondingly unacceptable.

To be sure, nothing in that should impress as immediately uncomfortable for deflationism. No deflationist has wanted, or ought to have wanted, to deny that believing and statement-making are normatively constrained activities — activities governed by standards, noncompliance with which opens a thinker to criticism. However, once that is accepted, the question has to be confronted of what the relevant standards are. In particular, if "true" is essentially just a device of endorsement, then in using it I'm saying that a proposition is in good shape as far as certain relevant norms are concerned. What, for deflationism, are those norms? What does "good shape" here consist in?

Believing and stating are, naturally, subject to rather different norms. In very many contexts, justification for a belief is insufficient to confer justification for its public expression, partly because assertion is socially constrained — the public expression of a fully justified belief may give offence, or bore people, etc. — and partly because complex principles of conversational implication make it possible to encourage false beliefs in an audience by the judicious selection and assertion of fully justified ones.[14] However, if one wanted to criticize an assertion

---

14 The classic treatment of this phenomenon is, of course, H. P Grice's "Logic and Conversation," reprinted in his *Studies in the Way of Words* (Cambridge, MA: Harvard University Press, 1989).

on this type of broadly social or pragmatic ground, one wouldn't do so by denying its truth. So, as a first approximation, it seems the deflationist should say that the use of "true" in the basic kind of case is to endorse a proposition as *epistemically justified*, or to endorse an utterance as acceptable just insofar as the epistemic justification of the proposition it expresses is concerned.

In any case, what the deflationist clearly *cannot* allow is that "true," when used to endorse, has the function of commending a proposition for its satisfaction of *some distinctive norm* which contrasts with epistemic justification and which only "true" and equivalents serve to mark. For if there were a distinctive such norm, it could hardly fail to be reckoned a genuine property of a proposition that it did, or did not, comply with it. And if the norm in question were uniquely associated with "true" and its cognates, that would be as much as to allow that there was a special property of *truth* — at which point the deflationary game would have been given away. So for the deflationist, it appears, the basic use of "true" has to be to signal a proposition's compliance with norms whose proper characterization will not proceed in terms of equivalents of "true." If it is propositions, rather than utterances, that we are concerned with, epistemic justification would then seem to be the only plausible candidate.[15]

It would follow that the basic use of "not true" should be to signal a proposition's *non*-compliance with relevant norms of epistemic justification. But if that were so, there should in general be nothing to choose between the denial that a proposition is true and the denial that it is justified. And not only does that misrepresent the ordinary usage of the terms: it is inconsistent with principles to which deflationism itself is committed, and which are, indeed, at the heart of the deflationary account: the Disquotational Scheme and, its analogue for propositions, the Equivalence Schema.

I'll illustrate the relevant point as it flows from the latter. The schema provides that, for an arbitrary proposition *P*,

---

15 This would be less than a commitment to the idea that "true" *means* epistemically justified. There is a distinction between holding that a word expresses no property but is used to commend items for their possession of a certain property and holding that it expresses that very property.

It is true that $P \leftrightarrow P$.

If we substitute "not-P" for "P" at both occurrences, we have

It is true that not-$P \leftrightarrow$ not-P,

while if we negate both sides, we derive

It is not true that $P \leftrightarrow$ not-P.

And from the latter two principles, via transitivity of the biconditional, we have

It is not true that P if and only if it is true that not-P.

In brief: the Equivalence Schema entails, given only the most basic assumptions about its scope and about the logic of negation, that truth and negation commute as prefixes. Manifestly, this is not true in general of warrant and negation: there is, in general, no sound inference from

It is not the case that P is warranted

to

It is the case that not-P is warranted.

This pattern of inference cannot be sustained in any case where the correctness of its premise is owing to the *neutrality* of our state of information — to the fact that we have no evidence bearing either on p or its negation.

The Equivalence Schema itself, then, is a commitment to repudiating the idea that "... is not true" is a device for denying that a proposition complies with norms of warrant/justification — for if it were such a device, it ought not to commute with negation. But what other account can deflationism offer of what the denial of truth amounts to, given its express contention that "... is true" is merely a device of endorsement, so a device for affirming a proposition's compliance with some norm or other, and given that the only norms on the board — in a context in which the existence of any self-standing norm of truth has been rejected — are justificatory ones?[16]

---

16 There is scope for some skirmishing. Ian Rumfitt has responded (in "Truth Wronged," *Ratio* 8 [New Series] [1995]: 100–7) that the divergence in the

In fact, it's intuitively perfectly evident that the use of "true" *is* tied to a norm — to a way in which acceptance of a proposition may be in good, or bad, standing — quite separate from the question of its justification in the light of the acceptor's state of information. An acceptance that grass is green, that is, may be open to censure if there is no

---

behaviour of "true" and "assertible" just noted may straightforwardly be accommodated in a fashion entirely consonant with the purposes of deflationism, without admission of a distinctive norm of truth, provided the deflationist is prepared to allow primitive norms of *warranted denial* to operate alongside those of warranted assertion. Rather, that is, than restrict his distinctive deflationary claims to the word, "true," the deflationist should contend "that 'is true' and 'is not true' function purely as devices for endorsing *and rejecting* assertions, beliefs and so on ... and which therefore register no norms distinct from justified assertibility *and justified deniability*" ("Truth Wronged," 103; compare my *Truth and Objectivity*, 30). How would this help to explain the commutativity of truth and negation? Rumfitt is not entirely explicit, but the point may seem clear enough. Since denying a statement is asserting its negation, a primitive warrant — an *anti-warrant* is Rumfitt's term — for the denial of *P*, registered by a claim of the form, it is not true that *p*, will be *eo ipso* a warrant for asserting the negation of *P*, so — via the Disquotational Scheme — for asserting that it is true that not-*P*. So the problematical direction of commutativity is secured, while the invalidity of the corresponding principle for assertibility is vouchsafed, as before, by the possibility of states of information in which one has neither warrant nor anti-warrant for *P*.

However, the problem recurs. Consider again the problematical equivalence,

It is not true that *P* if and only if it is true that not-*P*.

and the result of negating both its sides:

It is not not true that *P* if and only if it is not true that not-*P*.

Supposing that the role of "(is) not true" were merely to register the presence of an anti-warrant, there seems no way of shirking the transition to

It is not anti-warranted that *p* if and only if it is anti-warranted that not-*p*.

But that, of course, is no less unacceptable when neutral states of information are possible than is

It is not warranted that *P* if and only if it is warranted that not-*P*.

In short, for any discourse in which neutral states of information are a possibility, the Equivalence Schema imposes a contrast both between "is true" and "is assertible"; *and* between "is not true" and "is anti-warranted." Rumfitt's proposal that the deflationist should recognize anti-warrant as primitive — whatever its independent interest — is thus of no assistance with her present difficulty.

warrant for accepting that grass is green; but it is in bad standing in quite another way if, warranted or not, it is actually not the case that grass is green. Correspondingly it is in good standing, in one way, just if accepted on the basis of sufficient justification, whether or not grass is green; but it is in good standing in another way if, irrespective of what justification may be possessed by the acceptor, grass is actually green. The concept of truth is a concept of a way a proposition may or may not be in good standing which precisely *contrasts* with its justificatory status at any particular time. That's the point which we've elicited from the Equivalence Schema. But it is independently evident, and any satisfactory philosophy of truth has to respect it.

There is no hope, then, for a deflationary account of truth which allows, or is anyway committed to the idea, that "true," in its most basic use, is a device for endorsing propositions as complying with other norms. A device of endorsement it may be, at least in the basic case. But the concept of the associated norm is of something *sui generis*.

Can the deflationist regroup? What the foregoing forces is an admission that, for each particular proposition, we have the concept of a norm which is distinct from warrant and is flagged by the word "true." And once it's allowed that the role of "true" is to mark a particular kind of achievement, or failing, on the part of a proposition, contrasting with its being warranted or not, there will have to be decent sense in the question, what does such an achievement, or failing, amount to? To be sure, that is a question which may turn out to admit of no very illuminating or non-trivial answer — but if so, that would tend to be a point in favour of Frege's indefinabilism, rather than deflationism. If a term registers a distinctive norm over a practice, the presumption ought to be that there will be something in which a move's compliance or non-compliance with that norm will consist. And whichever status it has, that will then be a real characteristic of the move. So what room does deflationism have for manoeuvre?

There are two possibilities. First, it might be contended that all, strictly, that has been noted — has been shown to follow from the Equivalence Schema — is that "true" is so used as to *call for* — express — a norm over the acceptance of propositions which is distinct from warrant. It's quite another matter whether there *really is* such a norm — whether there really is such a way for a proposition to be in, or out, of good standing. It's one thing for an expression to be used in the making of a certain distinctive kind of normative claim; quite another matter for there to be such a thing as a bearer's *really qualifying for* a judgment of that kind. An error-theorist about morals, for example like John Mackie,[17] would presumably readily grant that moral language is *used* normatively — is used to applaud, or censure, particular actions, for instance. What he would deny, nevertheless, is that there are any real characteristics which respond to this use — any real characteristics by possessing which an action may qualify for a deserved such appraisal.

It is easily seen that deflationism cannot avail itself of any counterpart of this first line of defence. For the deflationist must surely be quite content to allow that all manner of statements *really are true* — when the right circumstances obtain: that grass is green, for instance, really is true just when grass is green; that snow is white really is true just when snow is white; that the earth's orbit is an ellipse is true just in case the earth's orbit really is an ellipse; and so on. For deflationism, there has to be, for each proposition — or at least for those of an objective subject matter — *an objective condition*, viz., the very one specified by the appropriate instance of the Equivalence Schema, under which it qualifies as true. So there is no possibility of refuge in error theory in this context. The Equivalence Schema itself determines what the conditions of rightful application of "true" to a particular proposition, *p*, are; if as a matter of fact they obtain, then this, coupled with the distinctive normativity of the predicate, enforces the recognition that there really is such a thing as *p*'s complying, or failing to comply, with the distinctive norm of truth. It is not merely that our concept of truth calls for such a norm; the call is answered.[18]

---

17 J.L. Mackie, *Ethics: Inventing Right and Wrong* (Harmondsworth: Penguin, 1977).

18 This simple observation is a partial response to a recent tendency of Richard Rorty's, viz., to dismiss those features of our practice with "true" which are recalcitrant to "pragmatist" interpretation as mere reflections of the concept's absorption of a misguided representationalist metaphysic. See, for instance, his "Is Truth a Goal of Enquiry? Davidson *vs.* Wright," *Philosophical Quarterly* 45 (1995): 281–300. But it is to be expected, of course, that Rorty would refuse to hear any but a metaphysically inflated reading of "an objective subject matter."

We should conclude that two characteristic claims of deflationism are lost. It is not true, first, that "true" *only* functions as a device of (indirect, or compendious) endorsement; it also functions, for each proposition, to advert to the satisfaction of a distinctive norm, whose satisfaction is — at least for a proposition with an objective subject matter — a real matter of fact. Second, it is hard to hear a distinction between that last point and the admission that truth, for each such proposition, is a real property. But there is still a final line of defence — one last characteristic deflationary claim which a proponent might try to salvage. The question remains so far open whether the property in question should be regarded as *the same* in all cases. Perhaps the deflationist can dig a last ditch here. For if the property were not the same, we might yet have the resources to undercut the classical debates about the *general* constitution of truth; and that those debates were bad was one major point that deflationism wanted to make.

A line of thought with that tendency is nicely expressed by Simon Blackburn as follows:

> compare "is true" ... with a genuine target of philosophical analysis: "is conscious", or "has rights", for example. We investigate these by looking for the principles which determine whether something is conscious, or has rights. These principles are intended to govern any such judgement, so that we get a unified class: the class of conscious things, or things that have rights. Each item in such a class is there because it satisfies the same condition, which the analysis has uncovered. Or, if this is slightly idealised, we find only a "family" of related conditions or "criteria" for the application of the term. Still, there is then a family relationship between the members of the class. But now contrast "is true". We know *individually* what makes this predicate applicable to the judgements or sentences of an understood language. "Penguins waddle" is a sentence true, in English, if and only if penguins waddle. It is true that snow is white if and only if snow is white. The reason the first sentence deserves the predicate is that penguins waddle, and the reason why the judgement that snow is white deserves the predicate is that snow *is* white. But these reasons are entirely different. There is no single account, or even little family of accounts, in virtue of which each deserves the predicate, for deciding whether penguins waddle has nothing much in common with deciding whether snow is white. There are *as* many different things to do, to decide whether the predicate applies, as there are judgements to make. So how *can* there be a unified, common account of the "property" which these quite different decision procedures supposedly determine? We might say: give us any sentence about whose truth you are interested, and simply by "disquoting" and removing the reference to truth, we can tell you what you have to judge in order to determine its truth. Since we can do

> this without any analysis or understanding of a common property of truth, the idea that there is such a thing is an illusion.[19]

Blackburn here captures with characteristic felicity a thought which has unquestionably influenced many deflationists (though he does not himself explicitly endorse it). However, it surely provides no very good reason for the intended conclusion — that truth is no single property. For the pattern it calls attention to is a commonplace, exemplified by a host of properties which we should not scruple to regard as unitary, or as potentially open to philosophical account. *Many* properties, that is, are such that their satisfaction conditions vary as a function of the character of a potential bearer. Consider the property of having fulfilled one's educational potential. What it takes to instantiate this will depend naturally on other characteristics of the individual concerned; but that ought to be quite consistent with the substantiality and commonality of the property in question, since there is a clear sense in which anyone who has fulfilled his educational potential has done the same thing as anyone else who has done so, and what they have both done may be expected straightforwardly to allow of a uniform account. In general, how *x* has to be in order to be *F* can depend in part on how things stand in other respects with *x*, and vary accordingly, without any motive thereby being provided for regarding it as an error to suppose, or to try to characterize, a general condition which being *F* involves satisfying. Otherwise, you might just as well say that there is no single thing in which being twice as old as one's oldest child consists (being a *doubletenarian*), since for me it would involve being twice as old as Geoffrey, for Prince Charles being twice as old as William, and for Blackburn being twice as old as Gwen.

The general pattern, it should be evident, is that of properties whose satisfaction consists in an individual's meeting a condition implicitly involving existential quantification over the right field of a relation. To fulfil one's educational potential is for there to be certain levels of academic attainment such that under certain normal educational conditions it is possible for one to meet them, and such that one has met them.

---

19 Blackburn, *Spreading the Word* (Oxford: Oxford University Press, 1984), 230–31.

To be twice as old as one's oldest child is for there to be some individual of whom one is a father or mother and whose actual age is half one's own. In general, to be the bearer of such a property will be to stand in a relation of a certain kind to an appropriate instance or instances of this implicit quantifier, and the identity of that instance or instances may vary depending on the identity and character in other respects of the bearer in question. It is in the *nature* of properties of this general character to admit such variation, and it compromises their unity not at all.

There is accordingly no comfort for a deflationist in the platitude that how things have to be in order for particular propositions to be true varies. Propositions vary in *how they claim matters to stand* — as parents vary in how old their children are, or people vary in what their educational potential is — and propositions' truth-values will naturally be a function of the specific such claims they make. To impose the rubric explicitly: for any proposition *p*, it is true that *p* just in case *there is a way things could be* such that anyone who believed, doubted, etc., that *p* would believe, doubt, etc., that things were that way, and things are that way.[20] This paraphrase is doubtless wholly unilluminating — it offers little more than a long-hand version of the Correspondence Platitude. Its merit is to serve as a reminder how truth is naturally conceived to share a conceptual shape with, e.g., double-tenarianship, or fulfilment of educational potential, and thus to bring out why no conclusions follow about its integrity from the line of thought outlined in Blackburn's remarks.

A sympathizer with deflationism may essay a final throw. It may be contended that the position at which we have arrived, although inconsistent with the traditional formulations of deflationism, is still nothing terribly at odds with its spirit. Maybe it has to be recognized that truth is a property after all, contrasting with justification, and normative over assertion and belief. But the conviction of the traditional debate is that it is a *metaphysically deep* property, whose essence is

---

20 For truth as a property of sentences, the rubric might naturally be applied to issue in something along the lines: for any sentence *s*, an utterance of *s* in a particular context is true just in case there is a proposition, that *p*, which such an utterance would express, and which is true.

unobvious and controversial. By contrast, the characterization of it now offered by way of rebuttal of the tendency of Blackburn's remarks is nothing if not obvious and *trivial*; and this triviality surely just as effectively cuts the ground from under the traditional debate as would the findings that truth is no unified property, or no property at all. The victory over deflationism is therefore Pyrrhic: the skirmishing has led us to say what truth in general is in such a way as to drain all metaphysical interest from the question.[21]

Someone inclined to resist this would not be prudent to stake all on the possibility of a less trivial account of truth. Where the rejoinder goes astray is in its oversight, rather, of the contrast, drawn at the start, between the project of analysis of the concept of truth and the debate about the structure and objectivity of the property of truth. One meritorious claim in the deflationist portfolio — though not its exclusive possession — may well be that the success of any purported analysis of the concept must pay a price in terms of triviality. But the above account of truth for propositions, trivial as it may be, simply does not engage the structural alternatives charted earlier nor the debate they delimit. Anyone who has mastered the concept of truth and does not scruple to quantify over "ways things could be" can accept it as necessary and sufficient for the truth of a proposition that there be a way things could be which anyone who believes that proposition will suppose realized, and which is indeed realized. To accept that much enjoins so far no commitment on the matter of what kind of characteristic — intrinsic, relational (if so, what are the terms of the relation?), etc. — the truth of a proposition is, nor on whether or to what extent its possession may be viewed as objective. Exactly those are the metaphysically substantial matters.

V

The third and last alternative to a correspondence account of the structure of truth is coherentism. Here is an expression of an old and sometime very influential objection to the coherence theory:

---

21 Compare the remarks of Horwich quoted in note 9.

the objection to the coherence theory lies in this, that it presupposes a more usual meaning of truth and falsehood in constructing its coherent whole, and that this more usual meaning, though indispensable to the theory, cannot be explained by means of the theory. The proposition "Bishop Stubbs was hanged for murder" is, we are told, not coherent with the whole of truth or with experience. But that means, when we examine it, that something is *known* which is inconsistent with this proposition. Thus what is inconsistent with the proposition must be something *true*: it may be perfectly possible to construct a coherent whole of *false* propositions in which "Bishop Stubbs was hanged for murder" would find a place. In a word, the partial truths of which the whole of truth is composed must be such propositions as would commonly be called true, not such as would commonly be called false; there is no explanation, on the coherence theory, of the distinction commonly expressed by the words *true* and *false*, and no evidence that a system of false propositions might not, as in a good novel, be just as coherent as the system which is the whole of truth.[22]

The Right Reverend W. Stubbs died of natural causes. Russell's point is that we may nevertheless envisage a comprehensive *fiction* part of which is that he was hanged for murder, and that in point of coherence such a fiction may very well stand comparison with what we take to be the truth. In order, then, to recover the idea that such a fiction *is* fiction, we need recourse to a notion of truth which the coherence account is powerless to explicate. Whatever "coherence" is taken to involve in detail, it seems likely that mutually incompatible, equally comprehensive, internally coherent systems of beliefs will be possible; more, *any* self-consistent proposition is likely to participate in *some* coherent system of belief with whatever degree of comprehensiveness you want. So the coherence theory cannot discriminate truth from falsehood — and it cannot justify principles like (non-contradiction):

if p is true, not-p is not true.

Yet surely any correct account of truth has to sustain such principles.

Notice that this objection in no way depends upon the detail of any particular proposed conception of coherence, and thus does not presuppose that the coherence account is being offered as an *analysis* of truth. The objection is purely structural. The driving thought is that whatever

---

22 Bertrand Russell, "On the Nature of Truth," *Proceedings of the Aristotelian Society* 7 (1906–7): 33–4.

coherence is taken to consist in, the suggestion that the truth of a proposition consists in its participation in a coherent system in effect falls foul of a dilemma: if *fiction* can constitute such a system, then participation in such a system is clearly insufficient for truth. If it cannot, then it appears that truth is not constituted purely in inter-propositional relations — the propositions in question have to meet some other condition, so far unexplicated, and Russell's hostile suggestion is that the only available such condition is: truth as ordinarily understood.

There are two possible lines of response. First, the coherentist may go relativist, conceding that there is indeed no *absolute* truth, and embracing the contention that, to the contrary, truth is relative to the system. Thus the proposition that Bishop Stubbs was hanged for murder can indeed be true, relative to a sufficiently coherent and comprehensive body of propositions which includes it. What we are pleased to regard as *the* truth merely reflects the actually entrenched such system. Principles, like non-contradiction, which seem to require that the truth cannot extend to every conceivable coherent system of propositions, are misconstrued when taken to have that implication. Sure, they are valid *within* systems: no proposition can participate in a coherent system for which its negation is already a member. But they have no valid application *across* systems.

Alternatively, a coherentist might try to avoid this extreme and rather unappealing form of relativism by earmarking certain propositions as in some way *privileged*, and construing truth not as participation in any old sufficiently comprehensive, coherent system of propositions, but as participation in such a system which is required in addition to include the privileged propositions. To be sure, thinking of truth as having such a structure does not by itself guarantee its uniqueness. But the resources may be available to do so if the theorist chooses the privileged base class cannily and interprets the relation of coherence in some correspondingly suitable way. For instance, the base class might consist of a large sample of our most basic beliefs. Then what might ultimately defeat the truth, conceived as by coherence, of the proposition that Bishop Stubbs was hanged for murder would be its inability to participate in a maximally coherent and comprehensive system of belief incorporating that particular membership.

This manoeuvre, however, appears open to an extremely powerful objection. The objection does, admittedly, make an assumption about the general character of the inter-propositional relationships which coherence, conceived as a structural proposal, might regard as important — albeit an assumption suggested by the very term "coherence," and validated by all the actual proposals which have been made under its head. That assumption is that the relations in question are *internal* relations: that the coherence, or otherwise, of a system of propositions is grounded *purely in their content*. The salient question is then: How can any proposal of this kind handle *contingency*? The general form of account proposed is that P's truth consists in its participation in a coherent system based on a specified base class, i.e., its coherence with the other propositions in that system. But that situation, when it obtains, should be a matter of relations of a purely internal character holding between P and the other propositions in the system. If P coheres with those propositions, it will therefore do so in *all possible worlds*. So how could the truth of P, when it is true, ever be a contingent matter?

There is only one possible line of response. If P, although true, could be false, and if its truth consists in its sustaining internal — necessary — relations to a system of propositions, then what contingency needs is the possibility of a switch in the system — a change in which are the propositions coherence with which determines truth — and the possibility that P may fail to cohere with the new system. If we say that a system is *dominant* if it is coherence with *it* that constitutes truth, then what contingency demands is flexibility in the matter of dominance. (Dominance might be interpreted just as a matter of incorporating lots of what we actually believe, and its flexibility would then be secured by the flexibility in the identity of our beliefs.)

Now, though, interestingly, we find we have come full circle with the re-emergence of a version of the Bishop Stubbs objection. All contingency is now being construed as turning on contingencies of dominance. So the obvious next question is: What properly coherentist account is to be given of the truth of a proposition of the form:

(K) S is dominant?

Naturally, the coherentist has to view the truth of an instance of K, like that of any true proposition, as a matter of its coherence with a system — but which system? Presumably any coherent system S will be such that it will cohere with S to suppose it is dominant even if it is not in fact so — if, for example, dominance is construed as a matter of what is actually believed, it ought in general to cohere perfectly with a system of beliefs that we do not in fact hold to suppose that we do hold them. So in general, for each comprehensive, coherent system S, whether dominant or not, the relevant instance of K will cohere with S with the consequence, first, that the fact of dominance — the actual truth-value of that instance — goes unrecovered; and second, that we remain powerless to explicate the contingency of a system's dominance, since the coherence of the relevant instance of K with the system in question will be a matter of necessity.

There is thus no prospect of explicating what it is for a proposition of the form "S is dominant" to be true in terms purely of relations of coherence if the truth in question is conceived as contingent — as it has to be, if contingency in general is to be recovered in terms of a coherentist account. What has to be said, it seems, is that for that proposition, like any other, truth is a matter of relations with *what is in fact* the dominant system. But then exactly the move has been made that Russell triumphantly anticipated: for this appeal to the notion of *what is in fact so* has not been, and apparently cannot be, explicated in terms of coherence.

The upshot is that coherentism, taken as a proposal about the general nature of truth-constituting relations, has no means — provided the relations in question are all internal — to recover the notion of contingent truth except at the cost of, one way or another, an appeal to a notion of what is in fact true of particular belief systems (that they are based on what we mostly believe, or otherwise dominant in some sense to be supplied) whose contingency is taken for granted and whose obtaining cannot be construed in terms of coherence. In brief, coherentism demands exceptions to its own account.[23] It thus has nothing to offer as a general account of the structure of truth.[24]

---

23 This moral is repeatedly emphasized in Walker's excellent study *The Coherence Theory of Truth* (see note 1 above).

24 The explicit argument has been against a response to the original Bishop Stubbs objection — the privileging manoeuvre — which was canvassed as an alternative to relativism about truth. Briskly, then, to review how a similar difficulty

VI

We have now reviewed each of the three possible structural alternatives to a correspondence conception of truth, and found that each is subject to seemingly decisive difficulties. It may seem to have been established, accordingly, that among the four paths on the original tree (p. 36 above), only the feathered path to the correspondence conception is viable — that, contra deflationism, our ordinary concept of truth requires us to think of a proposition's being true as, so to speak, a distinctive accomplishment, and that, contra intrinsicism and coherentism, we may not satisfactorily conceive of this accomplishment as an intrinsic property of a proposition or a characteristic conferred upon it by dint of its relation to other propositions. It would follow that even

---

afflicts the relativistic move: the relativist proposal has it that truth is always coherence with a system, but that there are thus as many versions of the truth as there are coherent comprehensive systems. Thus the proposition that Bishop Stubbs was hanged for murder, while unfit to participate in any comprehensive coherent system which is controlled by what we actually believe, may — presumably will — participate in other comprehensive and coherent systems. Well, we should now immediately press the question: What account has this relativism to offer of the truth of contingencies about belief — of propositions of the form "S is believed"? Again, it should cohere with any particular coherent comprehensive system to suppose that it is in fact believed — so such a proposition should be true relative to each particular system. So now the fact of actual belief seems fugitive. Suppose there is a single comprehensive and coherent system, S, incorporating (most of) what we actually believe, and that the proposition that Bishop Stubbs was hanged for murder is not a participant. Consider by contrast such a system, S', in which that proposition is a participant. Add to each the proposition that it is believed by most human beings. Clearly a Martian, presented only with axiomatizations of each system, would have no way of telling, just on the basis of facts about coherence, which, if either, we *did* believe. So the truth of the proposition that it is S we believe, if constituted just in facts about coherence, must reside in other such facts. The relativist-coherentist will offer, presumably, that it will be a matter of coherence with the Martian's own beliefs. But that is to appeal to a non-reconstructed notion of *what is in fact believed* by the Martian — and it was exactly the counterpart fact about us that the proposal seems to have no means to construe. So there is no progress.

if no satisfactory *analysis* of truth in terms of correspondence can be given, we are nevertheless squarely committed to a correspondence *conception* of truth — that there is no alternative but to thinking of the truth of a proposition as conferred upon it, in the general case, by its relations to non-propositional reality.

That is, in effect, the second main contention of the paper earlier advertised. But two very important qualifications are needed immediately. First, in the traditional debate, as we remarked, the correspondence theory was conceived as expressing a form of metaphysical *realism*, standing opposed to the idealism which kept company with the coherence theory. It merits emphasis that even if the effect of the foregoing arguments is indeed to impose a conception of truth as conferred on a proposition by aspects of non-propositional reality,[25] that conclusion certainly carries no direct implications for the realism debate in its modern conception. For example, nothing is yet implied about the *nature* of the relations in question, so there is consequently no immediate implication of the idea that the truth of a proposition consists in its successfully *representing* an aspect of reality, in any distinctively realist sense of "represent." There may in general be no alternative to thinking of propositions as made true, when they are true, by, *inter alia*, non-propositional matters. But there is so far no commitment to any specific general conception of the kind of relations that may be involved in truth, or of the nature of the non-propositional items in their fields. Any broad view which assigns a role in the constitution of truth to a domain outside the bearers of truth would be consistent with our findings; and that much most modern anti-realisms (for example, those canvassed by Dummett and Putnam) certainly do. In particular, nothing is implied about *cognitivism* — about whether the factors involved in appraising truth are invariably wholly cognitive — nor about *evidential constraint* — about whether it is possible for truth to outrun all evidence available in principle. Someone who thought, for example, of moral truth as broadly a matter of what *we* find acceptable in the light of a full appreciation of the non-moral facts and certain

---

25 Except in cases, naturally, where the proposition is actually about other propositions.

non-cognitive dispositions to moral sentiment would be making no demands on the notion to take him off the feathered path; on such a view, moral truth would be a complex matter, but one essentially implicating certain relations to aspects of the non-propositional world. Likewise, a proponent of a broadly Peircian conception of truth, that truth is what would be agreed upon by thinkers operating under epistemically ideal conditions, would be quite at liberty to think of the status of such propositions as owing in part to the impingements of a non-propositional world which such thinkers would feel. In sum, our findings at this point have almost no impact on the second of the great issues associated with the classical debate about truth: the issues of realism and objectivity.

However — this is the second necessary qualification — there ought in any case, I believe, to be no presumption in favour of a *monistic* view of truth.[26] If the difficulties which we have been exploring are to dispose of all the alternatives to correspondence once and for all, then it needs to be assumed that truth everywhere must possess a *uniform constitution*: that the truth of any true proposition always consists in the same sort of thing. Yet why should that be so? For instance, both intrinsicist and coherentist conceptions of truth fell into difficulty over the construal of contingent truth, but a proponent of either view could conceivably retrench if it could be argued that truth is only *sometimes* to be conceived as an intrinsic property of a proposition, or a property bestowed upon it by its relations of coherence with certain other propositions, while in other cases the structure of truth is best conceived as by correspondence. The upshot of the argument is that if truth has a single uniform constitution, then that constitution must be conceived along broadly correspondence lines. But what enforces the assumption of uniformity?

---

26 That is, in favour of the view that truth everywhere consists in the same thing. (This kind of "monism" about truth contrasts, of course, with that of Bradley and Joachim, for whom the thesis of monism is rather that reality is an intrinsically unified whole which is distorted when conceived as a totality of individual states of affairs, each apt to confer truth on a single proposition considered in isolation.)

I think the answer is: nothing. In fact, an opposed pluralistic outlook is intuitively quite attractive. It is quite appealing, for instance, to
think of the true propositions of number theory as those which sustain
certain internal relations — an appropriate kind of semantic consequence — to a certain base class of propositions — the Dedekind-Peano
axioms, for instance. Such an account, it should be noted, would extend to the axioms themselves (assuming the reflexivity of the relevant
internal relation). What it would not comfortably extend to would be
truths of the form: P is a Dedekind-Peano axiom (more generally, P is
a member of the relevant base class). But once coherentism forswears
the ambition to a *comprehensive* account of the structure of truth, that
limitation need not be a difficulty. An account along broadly similar
lines might also be attractive for truth as it applies to general moral
principles (as opposed to their applications).

A pluralistic conception of truth is also philosophically attractive
insofar as an account which allows us to think of truth as constituted
differently in different areas of thought might contribute to a sharp
explanation of the differential appeal of realist and anti-realist intuitions
about them. But I acknowledge, of course, that more detail and a
sharper theoretical setting is required for the proposal before it can
really be clear that it makes genuine sense, let alone possesses merit.
In particular, an account is owing of what would make it *truth* that
allowed of variable forms of instantiation in different areas — what
would make for the relevant *unity*. (This is not work that one might
excuse oneself from by pleading that truth is a "family resemblance"
concept, or whatever. Even that suggestion would at least require that
there be a network of marks of truth, any true proposition qualifying
as such by its exemplification of some sufficiently substantial set of
them; and the task of characterizing these marks would remain.)

In order to clarify the cast which a defensible alethic pluralism might
assume, it will help to revisit the conception, dominating the traditional
debate, that the winning position would be the provision of a satisfactory necessary-and-sufficient-conditions analysis of the concept. Earlier, I was concerned to point out that scepticism about that project
remained consistent with the interest of many of the questions, about
structure and objectivity in particular, which provided the driving force
of the traditional debate, and that these questions could survive in a
setting in which the idea of analysis of the notion of truth had been

abandoned altogether. Now, though, it is time to reconsider and qualify that scepticism. For misgivings about the project are driven by the particular conception we had in play of what a successful analysis — of truth, or anything — would have to accomplish. And on that score there is clearly some scope for relaxation. Such a necessary-and-sufficient-conditions analysis, after all, even if it could be provided, would only culminate in one particular *a priori* — presumably, conceptually necessary — claim. Why should not other such claims — even if not biconditional- or identity-claims — provide illumination of essentially the same kind? To be sure, if one wants conceptual clarity about what truth — or beauty, or goodness, etc. — is, then the natural target is an identity (or a biconditional). But perhaps the point of the inquiry can be equally if less directly served by the assembly of a body of conceptual truths which, without providing any reductive account, nevertheless collectively constrain and locate the target concept and sufficiently characterize some of its relations with other concepts and its role and purposes to provide the sought-for reflective illumination.

Faced, then, with the manifest improbability of an illuminating necessary-and-sufficient-conditions analysis of truth, there is still a different, more relaxed program of analysis which we might undertake before despairing of the whole business and falling back on the issues to do with structure. This more relaxed project will see us trying to build an overall picture of the concept of truth — of its contents and purposes — by the assembly and integration of as wide a variety as possible of basic *a priori* principles about it — "platitudes," as I've elsewhere termed them.[27] What would such principles be for the case of truth?

The method here should be initially to compile a list, including anything that chimes with ordinary thinking about truth, and later to scrutinize more rigorously for deductive articulation and for whether candidates do indeed have the right kind of conceptual plausibility. So we might begin by including, for instance,

---

27 The limitation to *a priori* cases effects, of course, a restriction on the standard lay use of "platitude," which applies to anything which no-one would dispute (and also carries an unwanted connotation of tedium).

: the transparency of truth — that to assert is to present as true and, more generally, that any attitude to a proposition is an attitude to its truth — that to believe, doubt or fear, for example, that p is to believe, doubt or fear that p is true. (*Transparency*)

: the opacity of truth — incorporating a variety of weaker and stronger principles: that a thinker may be so situated that a particular truth is beyond her ken, that some truths may never be known, that some truths may be unknowable in principle, etc. (*Opacity*)

: the conservation of truth-aptitude under embedding: aptitude for truth is preserved under a variety of operations — in particular, truth-apt propositions have negations, conjunctions, disjunctions, etc. which are likewise truth-apt. (*Embedding*)

: the Correspondence Platitude — for a proposition to be true is for it to correspond to reality, accurately reflect how matters stand, 'tell it like it is', etc. (*Correspondence*)

: the contrast of truth with justification — a proposition may be true without being justified, and vice-versa. (*Contrast*)

: the timelessness of truth — if a proposition is ever true, then it always is, so that whatever may, at any particular time, be truly asserted may — perhaps by appropriate transformations of mood, or tense — be truly asserted at any time. (*Timelessness*)

: that truth is absolute — there is, strictly, no such thing as a proposition's being more or less true; propositions are completely true if true at all. (*Absoluteness*)

The list might be enlarged,[28] and some of these principles may anyway seem controversial. Moreover, it can be argued that the Equivalence Schema underlies not merely the first of the platitudes listed — Transparency — but the Correspondence Platitude[29] and, as we have seen in discussion of deflationism, the Contrast Platitude as well.

---

28 One possible addition is reviewed in Section VII below.

29 For elaboration of this claim, see my *Truth and Objectivity*, 24–7.

There's much to be said about this general approach, and many hard and interesting questions arise, not least, of course, about the epistemological provenance of the platitudes. But such questions arise on *any* conception of philosophical analysis, which must always take for granted our ability to recognize truths holding *a priori* of concepts in which we are interested.

Let us call an analysis based on the accumulation and theoretical organization of a set of platitudes concerning a particular concept an *analytical theory* of the concept in question.[30] Then the provision of an analytical theory of truth in particular opens up possibilities for a principled pluralism in the following specific way: that in different regions of thought and discourse *the theory may hold good*, a priori, *of — may be satisfied by — different concepts*. If this is so, then always provided the network of platitudes integrated into the theory were sufficiently comprehensive, we should not scruple to say that truth may consist in different things in different such areas: in the instantiation of one concept in one area, and in that of a different concept in another. For there will be nothing in the idea of truth that is not accommodated by the analytical theory, and thus no more to a concept's being a concept of truth than its furnishing a model of the ingredient platitudes. In brief: the *unity* in the concept of truth will be supplied by the analytical theory; and the *pluralism* will be underwritten by the fact that the principles composing that theory admit of collective variable realization.

---

30 Readers familiar with Michael Smith's work will note a point of contact here with the conception of a *network analysis* which he derives from Ramsey and Lewis (see in particular Chapter 2, Section 10, of Smith's *The Moral Problem* [Oxford: Basil Blackwell, 1994]). The principal contrast with the approach to truth here canvassed is that a network analysis has to be based on a comprehensive set of platitudes whose conjunction so constrains the target concept that the replacement within them of all expressions for that concept by a variable and its binding by the description operator results in a definite description which is at the service of an analytically true identity,

Φ-ness is the property, F, such that {... F ... & ... F ... & ...}

which thus effectively supplies a reductive analysis of the concept Φ. An analytical theory, by contrast, need not — though it may — subserve the construction of such an analytically true identity.

One important question is whether any unmistakably coherentist conception of truth is indeed such a truth-realizer for a particular region of thought.[31] Another candidate I have explored elsewhere[32] is the notion of *superassertibility*. A proposition is superassertible just in case someone investigating it could, in the world as it actually is, arrive at a state of information in which its acceptance was justified, which justification would then persist no matter how much more relevant information was acquired. Clearly a notion of this kind must make sense wherever the corresponding notion of justification makes sense — wherever we have a concept of what it would be to justify a particular proposition, it will be intelligible to hypothesize the attainment of such a justification and its stability through arbitrarily extensive further investigation. It turns out that in any region of discourse meeting certain constraints, superassertibility will satisfy each of the platitudes listed above, so a *prima facie* case can be made that, with respect to those regions, the concept of superassertibility is a truth-concept.[33] In these areas, it is consequently open to us to regard truth as consisting in superassertibility. In other areas, by contrast, where the relevant background conditions arguably fail — in particular, where we can see that there is no essential connection between truth and the availability of evidence — then the concept of truth will not allow of interpretation in terms of superassertibility, and the constitution of truth must accordingly be viewed differently. It is perhaps superfluous to remark that a superassertibilist conception of truth chimes very nicely with the semantic anti-realism which Michael Dummett has presented as a generalization of mathematical intuitionism, whose cardinal thesis may indeed be taken to be that truth is *everywhere* best construed in terms of superassertibility.

---

31 For exploration of one local case, arithmetic, see the Appendix to this paper.

32 *Truth and Objectivity* Chapter 2; an earlier discussion is in Chapter 14, "Can a Davidsonian Meaning-Theory be Construed in Terms of Assertibility," of the second edition of my *Realism, Meaning and Truth* (Oxford: Blackwell, 1993).

33 For relevant details see the Appendix to this paper.

To be sure, the method of analysis incorporated in the analytic-theoretical approach is, as far as it goes, consistent with a monistic view of the target concept — but the approach cautions against prejudice in that respect since such an account may, in any particular case, prove to allow of multiple realization. That's a matter which will depend on the detail of the account, on whether it includes all relevant platitudes, and on whether the concept in question may justifiably be taken to have further components which are necessarily omitted by such an account (for instance, a component fixed by ostensive definition). Here, I have meant only to sketch how a principled pluralism about truth might conceivably emerge.

VII

I conclude by noting a different potential corollary of the analytic-theoretical approach to truth. If its satisfaction of the platitudes suffices for a concept to be a concept of truth, then wherever we can introduce a concept which is such a satisfier with respect to a particular class of contents, that fact on its own will justify us in regarding the contents in question as *apt for truth*. Or put another way: wherever the word "true" operates in a fashion agreeable to each of the theorems of a satisfactory analytical theory, then we should think of it as expressing a genuine concept of truth, and of the contents being expressed as genuinely truth-apt accordingly. And this will always be so just when we are dealing with contents which meet certain constraints of syntax and discipline. Roughly: the contents in question must allow for combination and recombination under the connectives — negation, the conditional, conjunction, disjunction — of ordinary sentential inference; they must allow of embedding within expressions of ordinary propositional attitudes; and their affirmation must be subject to recognized standards of warrant.[34] If that is right, then it falls out of the

---

34 How does it follow that a satisfier of the platitudes will be definable on such contents? Very straightforwardly. First, if we are dealing with a range of genuine contents — to the extent ensured by the hypothesis of discipline — for which

very analysis of the notion of truth that the aptitude for truth is a comparatively promiscuous property. Comic, moral, aesthetic, and legal discourses, for instance, all exhibit the requisite syntax and discipline and so presumably pass the test. The upshot is thus a tension with one traditional form of anti-realism about such discourses: the idea, typified by "expressivism" in ethics, that a target discourse whose surface exhibition of these features is not questioned may nevertheless not really be dealing in truth-apt contents — in "genuine" propositions — at all.

However, some recent critics[35] have objected that this upshot depends on focusing only on a selection of the platitudes which constrain the notions of truth and assertion, and ignoring in particular equally platitudinous connections of those notions with *belief*. Their thought is that one may be forced to look below the propositional surface of, e.g., ethical discourse if one takes it as a platitude that an assertion is a profession of belief[36] but also accepts, with Hume, that no belief can

---

we have the conditional construction, then nothing can stand in the way of the definitional introduction of a predicate, or operator, which is subject to the Equivalence Schema:

That P is Φ if and only if P.

As noted, that will then suffice for versions of Transparency, Contrast, the minimal degree of Opacity that attends contrast, and a Correspondence Platitude for Φ. It will further be open to us to insist that Φ be defined for all combinations of specified kinds of the contents in question and thereby secure Embedding. Assuming that the contents in question allow of tensed expression, Timelessness — effectively the principle that whatever may truly be thought or expressed at any particular time may, by appropriate variations of tense, be truly thought or expressed at every time — may be secured by stipulating that Φ is to be governed by analogues of the usual truth-value links between differently tensed counterparts. (If the contents in question are tenseless, then Timelessness will hold by default.) Absoluteness, for its part, will hold by default in any case unless we explicitly fix the use of a comparative.

35 For instance, Frank Jackson, Graham Oppy, and Michael Smith, in their "Minimalism and Truth Aptness," *Mind* 103 (1994): 287–302.

36 Of course, an assertion may be insincere. For an utterance to be a *profession* of a certain state means that one who accepts its sincerity must be prepared to ascribe that state to the utterer.

be, in and of itself, a *motivational* state and regards it as clear that whatever is professed by an ethical "assertion," it *is* such a motivational state.

One who advances this line of thought need not, it merits emphasis, be offering any criticism of the analytic-theoretical approach to truth as such. Moreover, the general point being made is obviously perfectly fair: conclusions drawn from a proposed analytic theory of a concept are, of course, liable to be vitiated if that theory omits to recognize what are in fact valid conceptual ties between the target concept and others. But what of the specific objection?

It might seem that the only clean way to dispose of it would be to controvert one of its two auxiliary premises; that is, to argue directly that certain kinds of belief *are* intrinsically motivational after all[37] or to make a case that the attitudes expressed by sincere ethical claims are, appearances notwithstanding, not *intrinsically* motivational.[38] However, it is not, on reflection, evident that it is necessary to take on either of those projects (even if either might very well succeed). Rather, the anti-expressivist may respond that, insofar as the questions whether a belief can be, in and of itself, a motivational state and whether the states professed by ethical utterances are indeed intrinsically motivational, are taken to be open, philosophically substantial questions, to that extent it is simply *not* a platitude that the assertion of any truth-apt content is a profession of belief. Or better: for one who accepts that those issues are open, *belief* is not the notion in terms of which to articulate the platitude which lurks in the vicinity. Instead, an alternative expression can be found by taking over for the purpose a term which Simon Blackburn conveniently introduces in his writings on these issues: *commitment*.[39] Blackburn's "commitments" are typically

---

37 This is a view often taken to be defended by John McDowell; see his "Are Moral Requirements Hypothetical Imperatives?" *Proceedings of the Aristotelian Society, Supp. Vol.* 52 (1978): 13–29.

38 Michael Smith himself eventually takes such a view in *The Moral Problem*.

39 See Blackburn, *Spreading the Word*, passim but especially Chapters 5 and 6.

expressed by indicative sentences; they may be argued for and against, reasoned to and from, accepted, doubted, and entertained. So the notion ought to provide everything here required: the relevant platitude is, in effect, that the assertion of any truth-apt content is the profession of a commitment. Since the two auxiliary premises are not simultaneously good for commitments, the objection accordingly lapses.

Someone who sympathizes with the view that only some commitments are pukka *beliefs* owes an account of what is distinctive of the narrower class. I know of no reason to reject out of hand the suggestion that a worthwhile such distinction may exist; and if it exists, the annexure of the term "belief" to the narrower class might conceivably be a well-motivated linguistic *reform*. Until then, the fact remains that our ordinary practice does not scruple to use "belief" across the range of cases where the expressivist would have us worry about it; and the anti-expressivist is free to respond to the objection by charging that it is only with this more generous notion that there is a platitudinous connection with assertion, and that the two auxiliary premises which the objection exploits cannot both be acceptable if it is the more generous notion of belief that is in play.

Appendix: Two Illustrative Satisfiers of the Platitudes for Truth

We shall reckon with just the seven platitudes proposed above: Transparency, Opacity, Embedding, Correspondence, Contrast, Timelessness, and Absoluteness. First, we note the following dependencies:

(i) *Transparency* is tantamount to the validity of the Equivalence Schema,

It is true that P if and only if P,

for all propositional contents, P, which in turn ensures that of the Disquotational Scheme,

"P" is true if and only if P,

assuming only the validity of the corresponding instance of

"P" says that P,

and the stipulation that the truth of a sentence is to enjoin and be enjoined by that of the proposition it expresses.

(ii) *Correspondence* is a platitude, whether for propositions or for sentences, only if suitably neutrally interpreted — that is, interpreted so as to be neutral on the status of the correspondence *theory*. As a platitude it thus carries no commitment to a real ontology of facts — "sentence-shaped" worldly truth-conferrers — nor to any seriously representational construal of "correspondence," but merely claims that talk of truth may be paraphrased by any of a variety of kinds of correspondence idiom. We may thus take the Correspondence Platitude for propositions to be, for example, this:

(CPP) It is true that P if and only if matters stand in conformity with the proposition that P.

CPP is an immediate consequence of the Equivalence Schema, together with the analogous equivalence controlling correspondence idiom itself:

 Matters stand in conformity with the proposition that P if and only if P.

Likewise the Correspondence Platitude for sentences may suitably neutrally be taken to be:

(CPS) "P" is true if and only if matters stand as "P" says they do.

Now wherever we have that

 "P" says that P,

it follows that

 Matters stand as "P" says they do if and only if P.

CPS is immediate from the last together with the Disquotational Scheme.[40]

(iii) *Contrast* — the contrast between truth and justification — is straightforwardly derived from the Equivalence Schema (or Disquotational Scheme) together with Embedding (specifically, its instance that every truth-apt content has a negation which is likewise truth-apt) and a very basic proof theory for negation. For propositions, the derivation runs as follows. Negation of both halves of the Equivalence Schema provides that

 It is not true that P if and only if not P,

while substitution of "not P" for "P" at each of its occurrences in the Equivalence Schema provides that

---

40 For parallel discussion, see my *Truth and Objectivity*, 25–7.

It is true that not P if and only if not P.

Transitivity of the biconditional then yields what I termed the Negation Equivalence,

It is not true that P if and only if it is true that not P,

— the commutativity of truth and negation. It then suffices for Contrast to reflect that, for any range of propositions for which neutral states of information are a possibility, negation does *not* commute with justification. For in such a neutral state, a lack of justification for P precisely does not convert into justification for its negation.

The upshot, then, is that our illustrations need address only the following: the Equivalence Schema, Opacity, Embedding, Timelessness, and Absoluteness.

Illustration 1: Pure Arithmetical Truth Conceived as Coherence

Assume a language, L, containing just the usual resources of first-order logic with identity plus the non-logical constants: Nx ("x is a natural number"), Sx ("the immediate successor of x"), and the decimal numerals, "0," "1," "2," "3" ... etc. Take as the coherence-base, **B**, the Peano axioms suitably formulated in this language, say as:

(i) $N(0)$
   : Zero is a number

(ii) $(\forall x)(Nx \rightarrow NSx)$
   : Every number is immediately succeeded by a number

(iii) $(\forall x)(\forall y)(\forall z)(\forall w)(Nx \& Ny \rightarrow (Sx=Sy \rightarrow x=y))$
   : Numbers are the same if their successors are the same

(iv) $(\forall x)(Nx \rightarrow \neg 0=Sx)$
   : Zero is not a successor

(v) $(F0 \& (\forall x)((Nx \& Fx) \rightarrow FSx))) \rightarrow (\forall x)(Nx \rightarrow Fx)$
   : Any characteristic possessed by zero and by the successor of any number which possesses it is possessed by all numbers

plus the standard recursive clauses for "+" and "×"

(vi) $(\forall x)\ x+0 = x$
(vi) $(\forall x)(\forall y)\ x+Sy = S(x+y)$

(vii) $(\forall x)\ x \times 0 = 0$
(viii) $(\forall x)(\forall y)\ x \times Sy = (x \times y) + x$

and axioms to govern the definition of the regular decimal numerals from "1" onwards in terms of iterations of "S" on "0."

The proposal, then, is that a statement's being a *pure arithmetical truth of first-order* may be identified with its *cohering with* **B**. How is coherence here to be understood? Intuitively all the significant statements of first-order number theory fall into one of two classes: a *simple-arithmetical* base class whose members draw on no expressive resources save the numerals, the expressions for addition, multiplication and identity, and expressions for other operations which may be (recursively) defined in terms of those notions; and a remainder, each of which can be formed by (iterated) introductions of the logical constants into sentences of the base class in accordance with the standard first-order formation rules. From a classical point of view, it is quite intuitive that the truth-value of every first-order pure arithmetical sentence *supervenes upon* the truth-values of sentences in the base class: specifically, determine the truth-value of each of the latter and you have implicitly settled the truth-value of every pure arithmetical thought which may be expressed at first-order. (The crucial point, of course, is that simple arithmetic has the resources to name every element in the domain of quantification of full first-order arithmetic.) A natural version of truth as coherence, which should be attractive to those of broadly formalist disposition, simply follows through on this intuition, characterizing the coherence of simple-arithmetical sentences in terms of their syntactic derivability from ingredients in **B**, and that of the remainder in accordance with the sort of recursive clauses familiar from standard truth-theories. It could run like this:

(i)   If A is a simple-arithmetical sentence of L, then A coheres with **B** just if A may be derived from elements of **B** in standard (classical) first-order logic with identity.

(ii)   If Ax is any open sentence of L in one free variable, x, and A is $(\forall x)Ax$, then A coheres with **B** just if each of $A0, A1, A2, \ldots$, coheres with **B**.

(iii) If Ax is any open sentence of L in one free variable, x, and A is $(\exists y)(Ay)$, then A coheres with **B** just if at least one of $A0, A1, A2, \ldots$, coheres with **B**.

(iv)   If A is B&C, then A coheres with **B** just if both B and C cohere with **B**.

(v)   If A is B∨C, then A coheres with **B** just if either B coheres with **B** or C coheres with **B**.

(vi)   If A is B→C, then A coheres with **B** just if it is not the case that A coheres with **B** and C does not.

(vii) If A is ⌐B, then A coheres with **B** just if B does not.

To the platitudes, then. First does this proposal validate the Equivalence Schema? Can it be affirmed, for all first-order expressible pure arithmetical statements, P, that

(E^C) P coheres with **B** if and only if P?

Dialectically, the status of a positive answer is somewhat akin to that of Church's Thesis, that all effectively calculable arithmetical functions are general recursive. A formal proof of Church's Thesis would demand some independent formal characterization of the effectively calculable functions — the very thing that Church's Thesis purports to provide. Likewise a proof of (E^C) would demand some independent characterization of the first-order arithmetical truths. So, as with Church's Thesis, it seems it cannot be definitely excluded that *intuitive* counterexamples to (E^C) might be forthcoming: sentences of the relevant kind which intuitively ought to rank as true yet which there is no reason to regard as cohering with **B** in the light of the stated clauses; or conversely, sentences which intuitively ought *not* to count as true, yet which do apparently so cohere. What can be said to make it plausible that there are no such cases?

Well, if (E^C) did have counterexamples, then — assuming the consistency of **B** — they could not come from within simple arithmetic, which comprises a complete and consistent system which is axiomatized within **B**. So their provenance would have to be of one of two kinds. *Either* truth in first-order arithmetic does not supervene upon simple-arithmetical truth — so that some arithmetical truths are determined by factors beyond the truth-value assignments in simple arithmetic and the semantics of the constants. That is surely excluded by the fact that "0," "1" and their suite collectively name everything in the domain. *Or* conversely, coherence as characterized outruns arithmetical truth (as it would if **B** were inconsistent or if, say, some quite different — perhaps intuitionistic — account of the truth-conditions of universally quantified arithmetical sentences was thought appropriate than that which informs clause (ii)). Prescinding from the scenario of inconsistency, then, it does seem reasonable to doubt — or at least that one of realist inclination should doubt — that intuitive counterexamples of either kind will be forthcoming.

Of course, some kinds of arithmetical realist will doubtless regard truth, so characterized, as at best merely *extensionally equivalent* with the real thing. But even for such a realist, the coincidence in extension would be necessary. What, if anything, is wrong with the coherentist account would not be its extensional inaccuracy.

(ii) How much Opacity should be required of a truth predicate is controversial, but the arithmetical coherentist proposal is generous on this score. Matters of syntactic derivability, even though effectively decidable, can be mistaken or unknown by any single competent judge, or group of judges, in practice. And the presence of clause (ii) ensures that coherence in effect follows the Omega Rule, so that the proposal is hospitable to the idea that some arithmetical truths may be unknowable in principle.

(iii) Embedding: any statement couched purely in first-order arithmetical vocabulary can be regarded as in the relevant sense apt to cohere with the Peano axioms. Since the logical constants are part of that vocabulary, aptitude for coherence with the Peano axioms is thus conserved under the usual logical operations.

(iv) Timelessness: relations of coherence as defined are eternal.

(v) Absoluteness: relations of coherence as defined do not admit of degree.

Illustration 2: Truth Conceived as Superassertibility

Recall that a statement is superassertible just in case it is justified by some accessible state of information and will continue to be so justified no matter how that state of information is improved. (When *I* is such a state of information with respect to a statement, S, I shall say that *I* is S-stable.) Superassertibility models the truth-platitudes under three assumptions concerning the region of discourse, D, with which we are concerned:

(i)   that it is *a priori* that all truths of D are *knowable*;
(ii)   that the states of information which specifically bear on the characteristic claims of D are of a timelessly accessible kind;
(iii)   that it is a necessary condition of knowledge (at least of the subject matter of D, if not in general) that it exists only where a claimant does not thereby lay himself open to a charge of irrationality.

(i) is a repudiation of evidence-transcendent truth for D. (ii) has the effect that the opportunity for justification of a particular claim within D is never ephemeral but remains eternally open in principle for any suitable enquirer, no matter what her circumstances. (Note, however, the qualification: *suitable* enquirer. Suitability may demand, in particular, a certain innocence. It may be impossible for one who *knows too much* to justify a certain statement, even though evidence speaking defeasibly on its behalf is timelessly available.) (ii) also implies that states of information may be conceived as *additive* — accessing one such state never costs you in principle the opportunity to access another (though again, since warrant is a function of one's *total* state of information, the import of a body of information under addition may naturally be different from what it would have been in isolation). (iii) imposes a boundary on externalist conceptions of knowledge: let it be that, at least with respect to certain subject matters, knowledge should be viewed as grounded purely in the exercise of what are in fact reliable cognitive powers and stands in no need of further internal qualification: still, it should not be open to internal *dis*qualification. There is no knowledge, even of such subject matters, in any case where persistence in a knowledge claim would commit a subject to disregarding the balance of the available evidence and so convict her of irrationality.

Pure mathematics and issues of moral and aesthetic principle may arguably be thought to supply examples of discourses meeting these conditions under only relatively modest idealizations of the powers of their practitioners. Discourse concerning the spatially and/or temporally remote would do so, if at all, only under more elaborate idealizations — maybe of dubious coherence, like the possibility of time travel.

The platitudes of Opacity, Embedding, Timelessness, and Absoluteness are all straightforward under these assumptions. To take them in that order:

First, it is clear that the superassertibility of a statement can *in practice* elude any single competent judge, or group of judges. On the other hand, it cannot be undetectable *in principle*: if a statement is superassertible, then that fact will show in the S-stability of the relevant — superassertibility-conferring — state of information and hence will be detectable, albeit inconclusively, in just the same way that such S-stability is detectable. But that is no objection under the assumption (i) that we are operating in a region where it is *a priori* that all truths are knowable. For that is to suppose that the truths are detectable in any case.

Second, any statement is apt to be superassertible which is apt to be warranted in the first place, since its superassertibility is merely a matter of the S-stability of some warrant-conferring state of information. But aptitude for warrant itself is, of course, inherited under embedding within the standard logical operators. So such embeddings conserve aptitude for superassertibility.

Next, since one of our assumptions is exactly that states of information are accessible timelessly, it follows that superassertibility is, likewise, an eternal characteristic of any statement that has it.

Last, the definition of superassertibility — though the notion must inherit any vagueness in the notion of (all-things-considered) warrant — manifestly makes no provision for degrees: one statement may be more warranted than another, but if both are nevertheless all-things-considered warranted, and if their warrants are respectively stable, then they are equally and absolutely superassertible.

The key issue is accordingly the status of the Equivalence Schema with "true" interpreted as "superassertible,"

(E^S) It is superassertible that P if and only if P.

There are some subtleties here[41] but our discussion is simplified by

---

41 See my *Truth and Objectivity*, Chapter 2, Section V.

the announced assumption (i), that we are working in a region where the schema,

$P \rightarrow$ It is knowable that P,

holds good *a priori*.

We consider each direction of (E^S) in turn. First, suppose that it is superassertible that P but that it is not the case that P. Then, by (i), it can be known that it is not the case that P. But that is absurd. For whatever state of information was possessed by one who had that knowledge, it would have — by the implication of additivity in (ii) — to be able to co-exist with the enduring all-things-considered warrant for P ensured by its superassertibility. And no-one could be said to know that not P whose total state of information warranted, to the contrary, a belief in P unless — contrary to (iii) — the belief that not P can be an example of knowledge even when irrationally held.

Now suppose that P but that it is not superassertible that P. Since P is not superassertible, we have it that there is no P-stable state of information — that any warrant for P can be defeated. So any subject who claims to know that P is nevertheless destined to lose a debate with a sufficiently resourceful agnostic; for — by additivity — the agnostic will always be able to come up with some consideration which will spoil whatever case the believer advances for P. It follows that it will not be possible rationally to sustain a belief in P. So, by (iii), P cannot be known; whence by (i) it cannot be that P, contrary to hypothesis.

CANADIAN JOURNAL OF PHILOSOPHY
Supplementary Volume 24

Peirce's Double-Aspect Theory of Truth*

MARK MIGOTTI
The University of Calgary

The idea of a double-aspect approach to a philosophical conundrum is familiar in metaphysics and the philosophy of mind and has been recently introduced as well into epistemology.[1] As a class, double-aspect theories attempt, as it might be put, *reconciliation by reorientation*. Matter and mind, for double-aspect theorists, are not independent substances, whose co-presence in a single entity such as a human person might be deeply mysterious; they are different aspects of a single substance — a person in modest versions of the theory like Strawson's, the universe as a whole in Spinoza's more ambitious case. Similarly, according to Susan Haack, the epistemic justification of a belief of a given subject is not something conceptually isolated from a causal explanation of its presence, but rather epistemic justification has two aspects, a causal one concerned with *what* a subject's evidence for a belief is, and an evaluative one concerned with *how good* the subject's

---

* I would like to thank Susan Haack and Howard Burdick for discussions that inspired the writing of this paper, and in the former case for characteristically helpful comments on an earlier draft as well. I am grateful, too, for comments on that earlier draft from Cheryl Misak, Paul Forster, and the members of the Hamilton College Philosophy Department Discussion Group, especially Betty Ring.

1 And also into the philosophy of action and moral psychology. Christine Korsgaard takes Kant to have held a "'double-aspect' theory of motivation," according to which "the motive of a chosen action has two aspects: the aspect under which the action is presented to the agent as something she might do and the aspect under which she actually chooses to do it" (*The Sources of Normativity* [Cambridge: Cambridge University Press, 1996], 243).

evidence is.[2] The degree to which the subject is justified in holding a belief depends equally upon the identity of his or her evidence for it and on the quality of that evidence.

The dual purpose of this paper is to argue, first, that Peirce held a double-aspect theory of truth (though not, of course, under that name), and second, that this theory, contrary to much received wisdom, is compatible with a robustly "realist" acknowledgment that the realm of truth might well outstrip the realm of possible human knowledge.

The truth, for Peirce, is by nature both independent of us and yet accessible to us; that, I maintain, is the chief burden of his theory. The theory is double-aspect in attributing to truth each of two properties that have (like matter and mind, or causation and justification) often been assumed to be immiscible; namely, essential *independence* and equally essential *accessibility*. In the paper's first three sections, I develop an account of Peirce's theory of inquiry and of the Pragmatic Maxim that shows how the double-aspect theory emerges from them, and in the remaining two sections I set out to refute objections to the theory generated by the conviction that it unacceptably compromises the independence of truth itself from our human attempts to determine the truth.[3]

---

2 Haack, *Evidence and Inquiry* (Oxford: Basil Blackwell, 1993), 29–30, 73–81; "A Foundherentist Theory of Empirical Justification," typescript, to appear in *The Theory of Knowledge*, ed. L. Pojman (Belmont, CA: Wadsworth, 1998), 6–15.

3 The view that accessibility and independence cannot possibly be happily married in the way that I am going to argue they can be is widespread. Amongst philosophers who are not Peirce scholars, but have occasion to refer to his work, it leads to almost comically discrepant estimates of his outlook. For example, on the basis of 5.416 ("Your problems would be greatly simplified if, instead of saying that you want to know the 'Truth', you were simply to say that you want to attain a state of belief unassailable by doubt," cf. page 78 below), J.J.C. Smart rashly (and falsely) concludes that "Peirce was not really interested in truth" ("Realism v. Idealism," *Philosophy* 61 [1986]: 303); while Thomas Nagel, on the basis of the sharp distinction between the theoretical and the practical made in Peirce's 1898 Harvard lectures, published as Peirce, 1992, takes him to be so exclusively interested in truth at the expense of belief as to be "more of a Platonist" than "a pragmatist in the currently accepted sense" (*The Last Word* [New York: Oxford University Press, 1997], 128).

I   Inquiry and the Settlement of Belief

Around 1906 Peirce declared in passing that "pragmatism is scarce more than a corollary" of Alexander Bain's definition of belief as "that upon which a man is prepared to act" (5.11).[4] Bain's definition posits an internal connection between belief and readiness to act; if S believes that p, then S must in appropriate circumstances be *guided* by the assumption that p. Belief is also internally connected to the concept of truth in that to believe is to accept as true. It is this connection that, as Peirce points out in notes on logic from 1873, makes it "absurd to suppose a mind which should say this is the truth but I do not believe it" (W3:79). The concept of inquiry, meanwhile, is taken to be internally connected both to the concept of truth and to that of belief: "Nor," insists Peirce, "is there any matter of fact involved in saying that the truth is the object aimed at in investigation, for investigation implies that the conception of truth is developed" (ibid.), and, several sentences earlier in the same long paragraph, "investigation and reasoning is but a particular case of that struggle which is occasioned by the irritation of doubt, and ... the final cause of that struggle is nothing but a settled belief" (W3:78).

Summarizing, I suggest that the following four principles have, for Peirce, the status not of empirically controvertible matters of fact, but rather of conceptual explications.

1(a)   To believe is to be disposed to act.
1(b)   To believe is to accept as true.
2(a)   To inquire is to seek the truth.
2(b)   To inquire is to seek to convert doubt into settled belief.

---

4   I refer to the Hartshorne-Weiss edition of the *Collected Papers* (*Collected Papers of Charles Sanders Peirce* [Cambridge, MA: Belknap, 1931–35]) by an Arabic numeral for the volume number followed by an Arabic numeral for the paragraph number within the volume, and to the Fisch et al. chronological edition (*The Writings of Charles Sanders Peirce* [Bloomington, IN: Indiana University Press, 1982–]) by "W" followed by volume number and page number.

At the heart of Peirce's theory of truth is the idea that the concept of truth is to be clarified by way of the concepts of inquiry and of settled belief; that, in terms of the principles above, 2(b) should be regarded as an elaboration or specification of what is meant by 2(a). As he puts it with deliberate provocation in an article of 1905 intended to explain to its readers what pragmatism is:

> if by truth and falsity you mean something not definable in terms of doubt and belief in any way, then you are talking of entities of whose existence you can know nothing, and which Ockham's razor would clean shave off. Your problems would be greatly simplified, if, instead of saying that you want to know the 'Truth', you were simply to say that you want to attain a state of belief unassailable by doubt. (5.416)

For Peirce, apparently, to seek the truth is to seek nothing other than settled belief.

To a host of critics, the allegedly evident falsity of this alleged consequence of Peirce's view is sufficient reason to dismiss it out of hand. Harry Frankfurt, for example, in a pointed critique of "On the Fixation of Belief," argues that while 2(a) respects what he calls the "cognitive significance" of inquiry, 2(b) does not. Frankfurt contends that accepting 2(b) would commit one to granting that an individual who "invited some subtle psychologist or advertising wizard to induce him to believe some proposition" was thereby engaged in inquiry. As it is clear from Peirce's homage to the scientific method of fixing belief at the close of "Fixation" and from many other passages that Peirce would resist the suggestion that indoctrination or any other form of evidence-indifferent belief formation should qualify as a mode of inquiry, Frankfurt draws the harsh conclusion that Peirce's discussion is simply rife with "inconsistencies that render [it] incoherent."[5]

Peirce himself became aware that the rhetoric and argument of "Fixation" could easily give rise to the sort of objection pressed by Frankfurt. Writing some thirty years after the publication of that essay, Peirce explains that it

---

5 Frankfurt, "Peirce's Account of Inquiry," *Philosophical Review* 55 (1958): 590.

assumes, for no better reason than that real inquiry cannot begin until a state of real doubt arises and ends as soon as Belief is attained, that 'a settlement of Belief', or, in other words, a state of *satisfaction*, is all that Truth, or the aim of inquiry consists in. The reason I gave for this was so flimsy, while the inference was so nearly the gist of Pragmaticism, that I must confess the argument of that essay might with some justice be said to beg the question. The first part of the essay, however, is occupied with showing that, if Truth consists in satisfaction, it cannot be any *actual* satisfaction, but must be the satisfaction which *would* ultimately be found if the inquiry were pushed to its ultimate and indefeasible issue. (6.485)

Peirce here provides an interpretation of what it means to say that the fixation of belief is the goal of inquiry that speaks directly to Frankfurt's criticism; no merely "actual" and perhaps fleeting settlement of belief is intended as inquiry's "final cause," but rather an unbudgeable doxastic satisfaction, which, it is claimed "would be found if ... inquiry were pushed to its ultimate and indefeasible issue" (6.485).

Since we are at this point explicating the concept of inquiry, the occurrence of that very concept in the clause just quoted raises a threat of vicious circularity; but this can be parried easily enough by spelling out what is meant in the terms of 2(b) itself. Doing so yields the following refinement of 2(b):

2(b)':   To inquire is to seek that settlement of belief that would be found if the pursuit of settled belief were pushed to its indefeasible limit.

2b' will not condone what Frankfurt calls "capricious" methods of belief formation. To believe capriciously, according to Frankfurt, is to fix belief "without exercise of intellectual sovereignty."[6] But to seek belief as such, without regard for anything outside its attendant satisfactions as belief, its capacity to provide what might be called the comfort of apparent cognition, is not to inquire by the standards of 2b'. That principle demands of inquirers that they seek a special sort of belief-settlement — one that *would* be found if the pursuit of settled belief were pushed to its indefeasible limit — and it is hard to imagine that anyone whose beliefs are prompted or sustained by non-intellectual, extra-

---

6 Ibid., 591.

evidential causes could plausibly be construed as aiming at this goal.[7] Routes to belief that bypass intellectual sovereignty, in other words, cannot be routes whose intended terminus is the indefeasible limit of the search for settled belief.[8]

In "Fixation," Peirce had urged the importance of "the proposition that the settlement of opinion is the sole end of inquiry" on the grounds that it "sweeps away, at once, various vague and erroneous conceptions of proof" (5.375). In particular, he explained, it entails:

1.   That without the stimulus of "real and living doubt ..., all discussion is idle";

2.   That demonstration need not rest on "some ultimate and absolutely indubitable propositions," requiring instead only premises that "are not in fact doubted at all";

and

3.   That "when doubt [on a topic] ceases, mental action on the subject comes to an end; and, if it did go on, it would be without a purpose" (5.376).

Each of these claims, however, is significantly qualified by later remarks intended to deflect just the sort of criticism made by Frankfurt.

With regard to the first point, Peirce (in effect) acknowledges an ambiguity in the notion of "real and living doubt." On the interpretation suggested by many passages in "Fixation," real doubt means some-

---

7 I say "hard to imagine," not "impossible," because of the difference between a capriciously held belief in Frankfurt's sense, and a belief for which, objectively speaking, there is little or no evidence. If one believed that the advertising wizard was peculiarly knowledgeable, and so looked to him for answers to questions on all subjects, one might well be inquiring by the standards of 2b'; for such a case does not necessarily present us with an abdication of intellectual sovereignty, as opposed to a feeble use of intellectual capacity. Genuinely capricious belief is belief caused by non-evidential factors, such as (barring exceptional cases) desire, hope, and fear.

8 The strongest piece of textual evidence in favor of Frankfurt's interpretation is Peirce's notorious stipulation that by "inquiry" he will mean "the struggle to attain belief caused by the irritation of doubt" (5.374, grammar altered). It is instructive, however, that he immediately follows this statement by admitting that "this is sometimes not a very apt designation."

thing like "state of cognitive disquiet caused by a recalcitrant or surprising experience," but on the view favoured by later reflections, real doubt need not be caused by an actually disruptive experience. Instead, it can, for example, be prompted by undertaking "a general review of the causes of our beliefs" and discovering thereupon that "most of them have been taken on trust and have been held since we were too young to discriminate the credible from the incredible" (5.376 n. 3).[9] On this latter account, as Susan Haack notes, the scope of genuine doubt has increased so as to coincide with the scope of acknowledged uncertainty.[10] With regard to the second point, Peirce admits that premises that are not currently doubted may become subject to doubt in the future (5.376, n. 1), and this means that the premises of a demonstration can after all enjoy a status more satisfactory than that of simply being immune to current doubt: they can also prove doubt resistant over the long haul, i.e., they can be *true* (according to Peirce's own conception of truth). Finally, with respect to the last point, Peirce notes, in 1903, that mental action on a topic with respect to which doubts have as of now been settled could still be pointfully undertaken with the aim of "self-criticism" (5.376, n. 2).

In the wake of these qualifications, the question wherein lies the philosophical significance of the allegedly crucial proposition that the settlement of belief is the sole end of inquiry becomes acute. The answer, or at least one answer, is that the proposition can serve as the cornerstone of a promising theory of truth and meaning.

---

9 Notice the echo here of the opening sentence of Descartes' "First Meditation": "Some years ago I was struck by the large number of falsehoods that I had accepted as true in my childhood, and by the highly doubtful nature of the whole edifice that I had subsequently based on them" (*Meditations on First Philosophy*, trans. John Cottingham [Cambridge: Cambridge University Press, 1996], 12).

10 Haack, "The First Rule of Reason," in *The Rule of Reason: The Philosophy of Charles Sanders Peirce*, ed. (Toronto: University of Toronto Press, 1997), 247.

II Nominal Definition and the Pragmatic Maxim

"That truth is the correspondence of a representation with its object," Peirce writes in 1906, "is, as Kant says, merely the nominal definition of it" (5.553). The "merely" in this sentence signals a conviction that a correspondence formulation of this sort is far from satisfactory as it stands. In the terms of the sequel to "Fixation," "How to Make Our Ideas Clear," to have a merely nominal definition of a concept or idea is to have a definition of it "in abstract terms," and it is a large part of the burden of the second of the 1877 papers to "formulate the method of attaining to a more perfect clearness of thought [than that achieved by familiar use and abstract distinctness on their own]" (5.390). According to Peirce, logicians have traditionally recognized only the first two of three levels of clarity of which ideas are susceptible. When logicians speak of a clear (as opposed to an obscure) idea, Peirce observes, they seem to mean nothing more than "a subjective feeling of mastery" or "lack of hesitancy in recognizing [the idea] in ordinary cases," and when they speak of a distinct idea (as opposed to a confused one), they mean "one which contains nothing that is not clear," i.e., one that can be given "a precise definition ... in abstract terms" (5.390). It is Peirce's contention that this traditional two-place hierarchy is inadequate and that we cannot really "know what we think [and] be masters of our own meaning" (5.393) unless we reach "a clearness ... of higher grade than the 'distinctness' of the [traditional] logicians" (5.394).

Peirce begins the clarification of our ideas by reflecting on the identity conditions of our beliefs. Relying upon Bain's principle that to believe is to be prepared to act, he argues that "different beliefs are distinguished by the different modes of action to which they give rise. If beliefs do not differ in this respect, if they appease the same doubt by producing the same rule of action, then no mere differences in the manner of consciousness of them can make them different beliefs, any more than playing a tune in different keys is playing different tunes" (5.398). Relying upon the conclusion defended in "Fixation" that the settlement of belief is the goal of inquiry, he maintains that anything to do with a thought that is irrelevant to the purpose of settling belief — which is to say irrelevant to the purpose of establishing habits of action — "is an accretion to [the thought], but no part of it" (5.400).

Putting these two points together yields the thesis that "we come down to what is tangible and conceivably practical, as the root of every real distinction of thought, no matter how subtle [*sic*] it may be; and there is no distinction of meaning so fine as to consist in anything but a possible difference in practice" (5.400). This thesis, reformulated, becomes the well-known Pragmatic Maxim: "Consider what effects, that might conceivably have practical bearings, we conceive the object of our conception to have. Then our conception of these effects is the whole of our conception of the object." This, Peirce claims, is "the rule for attaining the third grade of clearness of apprehension" (5.402).

"How to Make Our Ideas Clear" closes with the application of the Pragmatic Maxim to the following half-dozen concepts: transubstantiation, hardness, weight, force, reality, and truth. Peirce's theory of truth, then, is reached by applying the Pragmatic Maxim to the concept "truth" in an effort to acquire for it a grade of clearness superior to that afforded by "merely nominal" definitions such as the correspondence formulation cited above. Within the argument of that essay, however, the need to apply the Pragmatic Maxim to the concept "truth" arises, not of its own accord, but in the course of applying the maxim to the concept "reality."

Peirce opens his discussion by remarking that "reality" is a conception entirely familiar to all competent speakers of English, one that "every child uses ... with perfect confidence, never dreaming that he does not understand it." As far as the first grade of clearness is concerned, there is nothing unclear about this concept. "As for clearness in its second grade, however, it would probably puzzle most men, even among those of a reflective turn of mind." All the same, Peirce proposes a solution to this definitional puzzle that relies upon specifying "the points of difference between reality and its opposite, fiction." The definition arrived at is that "the real [is] that whose characters are independent of what anybody may think them to be" (5.405).[11]

---

11 Cornelis de Waal notes that Peirce owes this definition to Duns Scotus. (De Waal, "Peirce's Nominalist-Realist Distinction: An Untenable Dualism," *Transactions of the Charles S. Peirce Society* 34 [1998], 180)

Of course, Peirce has formulated an abstract definition of reality only to highlight its ultimate insufficiency. If we want a more perfect apprehension of what we mean by "reality," we must apply to it the Pragmatic Maxim, and the first thing we notice when we do this is that "the only effect which real things have is to cause belief, for all the sensations which they excite emerge into consciousness in the form of belief." It is here that truth enters the picture, for, claims Peirce, "the question now becomes "how is true belief (or belief in the real) distinguished from false belief (or belief in fiction)." These opening steps in the pragmatic clarification of the idea of reality are followed by a highly condensed and enigmatic allusion to "Fixation": "Now," Peirce maintains, "as we have seen in the former paper, the ideas of truth and falsehood, in their full development, appertain exclusively to the experiential method of settling opinion" (5.406). This talk of "the ideas of truth and falsehood, in their full development" is puzzling. Is "in their full development" supposed to be equivalent to "at the third grade of clearness"? If so, why does the idea of truth not, officially anyway, get put to the pragmatic test for another two pages? Indeed, if the pragmatic clarification of truth has already been carried out by the end of "Fixation," then why repeat the exercise in "How to Make Our Ideas Clear"?

But if "full development" here does *not* mean "full pragmatic clarification," then what does it mean? Though Peirce does not tell us in so many words, he does provide clues. In the long paragraph that introduces the notion under examination (and which immediately precedes the application of the Pragmatic Maxim to the ideas of truth and reality), he offers condensed arguments against the adequacy of the conceptions of truth associated with each of the three non-experiential methods of settling opinion canvassed in "Fixation." The key claims are these:

1. Regarding the method of tenacity:
    "A person who arbitrarily chooses the propositions which he will adopt can use the word truth only to emphasize the expression of his determination to hold on to his choice."
2. Regarding the method of authority:
    "It is noticeable that where different faiths flourish side by side, renegades are looked upon with contempt even by the party

whose belief they adopt, so completely has the idea of loyalty replaced that of truth-seeking."

3.   Regarding the *a priori* method:
"[Followers of this method] seem to think that the opinion which is natural for one man is not so for another, and that belief will, consequently, never be settled." (5.406)

Since, as in "Fixation," these three unsatisfactory methods of fixing belief are nevertheless ordered in respect of increasing adequacy, it is plausible to suppose that the conceptions of truth that apparently flow from them are similarly ordered. Assuming that this is so, I propose to interpret the relationship between the "development" of an idea and its pragmatic clarification as follows: only when an idea has been fully — or, better (I think): sufficiently — developed is it a serious candidate for pragmatic clarification. The "development" of an idea, in this sense, is, I conjecture, something that occurs *in between* the second and third grades of clearness. Let me try to make this clear by example.

Consider the claim that a tenacious believer, one whose beliefs are arbitrarily formed, "can use the word truth only to emphasize the expression of his determination to hold on to his choice." It does not seem necessary to insist (implausibly) that such a believer *thinks* the word "truth" can only be used to express his determination to hold onto the beliefs of his choice. The point is rather that emphasis is the only use such a believer can *actually have* for the words "true," "truth," and their ilk. For a tenacious believer, to say that "*p* is true" is, in effect, to do nothing other than offer a rhetorical variant on "I believe that *p*." If, as I would like to conjecture, the tenacious believer might well have an adequate grasp of the concept "truth" at the second grade of clearness, then Peirce's claim is perhaps this: for such a believer there is tension, perhaps even incompatibility, between what he thinks is meant by the word "truth" and the *actual role* the concept plays in his life and language.[12] The tension is not so stark for those whose characteristic

---

12   I think that it is in fact necessary that the tenacious believer be credited with some grasp of the difference between *p*'s being true and *p*'s being believed by him. Otherwise it is hard to see how he could find any use for the word "true" even as an "expression of his determination to hold on to his choice [of belief]."

method of belief fixation is that of authority or the use of *a priori* reason, but it is eliminated only within the context of the experiential method.[13] It is, then, the elimination of this tension that constitutes

---

Presumably, Peirce has in mind the popular practice of defending the epistemic standing of a belief by appealing to its truth, insisting that, e.g., "I believe it because it is true." This sort of appeal sounds more useful than does the flatly tautological "I believe it because I believe it," but because believing that it is true is a conceptual consequence of believing it in the first place, the former turn of phrase is always in danger of degenerating into a merely rhetorical variation of the latter. This danger is avoided only when "because it is true" is elliptical for something such as "on such and such unimpeachable grounds" or "because of such and such incontrovertible evidence." The tenacious believer, however, qualifies as such precisely because of the willful character of the relationship he has to his beliefs, and this willfulness precludes those beliefs from responding in an appropriate way to epistemically respectable sources of belief such as sense-experience, valid inference, and so on.

13 With regard to the method of authority, Peirce identifies the tension as that between loyalty and truth-seeking, and offers as evidence for it the tendency on both sides of a conflict of faiths to regard renegades with contempt. I conjecture that Peirce sees in such contempt the betrayal of an obscure sense that loyalty to the faith is in fact, though not in theory, valued independently of the faith's claim to have a lock on the truth. If one were wholehearted in the view that one's faith was superior to all others in virtue of its being a superior means of reaching the truth, one should welcome converts who see the light. That one is instead contemptuous of them because they were willing to betray the other side shows that one harbours the view that loyalty to the cause has value, and indeed paramount value, independently of the cause's ability to defend its claim to being a privileged vehicle of the truth. And that view compromises the degree to which one's allegiance to one's own side can genuinely express or coincide with one's commitment to discovering the truth.

With regard to the *a priori* method, Peirce's complaint is that its followers prize internal consistency above harmony with perceptual experience. Again, Peirce is not, I suggest, supposing that *a priori* metaphysicians will admit that they have no faith in the ultimate settlement of opinion, but rather that "they *seem* to think that the opinion which is natural for one man is not so for another, and that belief will, consequently, never be settled (emphasis added)." It is the intellectual behavior of the a priorist, his favouring systematic cohesion over experiential anchoring, that betrays his indifference to the ultimate settlement of opinion; which indifference amounts, in Peirce's terms, to an indifference to the truth, however much the *a priori* metaphysician will protest to the contrary.

the full development of the ideas of truth and falsity and renders them suitable for being raised to the third grade of clearness promised by the Pragmatic Maxim.

Let me describe the defect from which the non-experiential methods of settling opinion are said to suffer as a tension between verbal and epistemic commitments or practices. Verbally, the tenacious believer acknowledges that truth requires correspondence to reality and that it is essential to reality to be as it is independently of what anyone takes it to be. By universal instantiation, the second verbal commitment entails that the nature of reality is independent of what I in particular take it to be, and it follows from this that my believing something to be so cannot, of itself, (barring exceptional cases) make it so. But as we have seen, the epistemic behaviour of the follower of the method of tenacity is such as precisely to equate "my believing that p" with "its being the case that p."[14] Adherents of the experiential method, by contrast, are, insofar, inquisitive rather than dogmatic. They too are committed to the truth of what they believe for as long as they believe it. But they do not think that the truth about something can be unearthed by the simple expedient of forming a belief about it. Instead they hold that genuine inquiry requires "an activity of thought by which we are carried, not where we wish, but to a fore-ordained goal"

---

14 On the evidence of some fascinating experiments in developmental cognitive psychology, the stage of development reached by the average three year old exemplifies the tenacious method of belief formation to a remarkable degree. For example, three-year-old subjects shown a closed candy box will say that they think the box contains candy. The box is then opened and revealed to contain only pencils. When the subjects are asked what they had originally believed about the contents of the box, they will claim to have "known all along" that the box had pencils inside. It is not until age four or five that subjects admit to their initial mistake. (See Alvin Goldman, "Empathy, Mind, and Morals," *Proceedings and Addresses of the American Philosophical Association* 66.3 (1992): 25 for a description of the experiments and references to the literature.) The consonance of the results of these experiments with Peirce's well-known claim (from 1868, at 5.233) that children begin to form a conception of themselves as distinct selves only when they become aware of their ignorance and error is remarkable.

(5.407), and they manifest this conviction by submitting their beliefs to the test of further experience and severe scrutiny.

So: only in the context of the experiential method are the conceptions of truth and reality sufficiently developed as to make it worthwhile to try to render their meaning pragmatically, as well as verbally clear. At the end of the two and a half pages it takes Peirce to divulge the meaning of truth and reality at the third grade of clearness is the famous sentence "The opinion which is fated to be ultimately agreed to by all who investigate is what we mean by the truth, and the object represented in this opinion is the real" (5.407). The chief practical consequence of truth is, therefore, that it is "fated" to yield to genuine inquiry, prosecuted over the indefinitely long haul with sufficient patience, ardour, and intelligence; and the pragmatic meaning of reality is that the real is that which is represented in a true opinion.

"But," observes Peirce, "it may be said that this view is directly opposed to the abstract definition we have given of reality, inasmuch as it makes the characters of the real depend on what is ultimately thought about them" (5.408). Does it not appear, in other words, that the pragmatically clarified conception of truth itself falls victim to a version of the tension that disqualified the conceptions of truth associated with the three non-experiential methods of settling belief, in this case a tension between verbal and pragmatic definition, between reality at the second grade of clearness and reality at the third grade? That appearances are revealing in this respect: that Peirce's pragmatically clarified "truth" foists upon the concept features incompatible with the genuine article — with what any sensible person will (or at least should), upon reflection, agree is meant by the word "true" — is the conviction of philosophers concerned to preserve the independence of truth and reality themselves from all human attempts to determine them. To thinkers of this cast, a double-aspect theory of truth in the Peircean mold is fatally flawed, since the two aspects, independence and accessibility, are essentially discrepant. Real truth, such opponents of Peirce will claim, is characterized precisely by its independence of anything to do with accessibility. Peirce disagrees.

III The Fate of Genuine Inquiry

In "How to Make Our Ideas Clear," Peirce replies thus to the charge that the idea of reality at the third grade of clearness turns out to be dependent upon thought in a way at odds with the independence of thought enshrined in its verbal definition of the idea:

> The answer is that, on the one hand, reality is independent, not necessarily of thought in general, but only of what you or I or any finite number of men may think about it; and that, on the other hand, though the object of the final opinion depends on what that opinion is, yet what that opinion is does not depend on what you or I or any man thinks. (5.408)

To the question "Are truth and reality independent of thought or not?" Peirce proposes here to respond: "They are and they aren't." They are independent of the vagaries of how or what you or I or the whole of humanity happen to think, but their experiential meaning has the consequence that genuine inquiry, an exercise of thought, is *destined* to come to rest in the true and the real, so what it means to say that something is true or real is not (pragmatically) definable independently of all reference to thought. Let me for the sake of argument grant that Peirce's acceptance that there is a sense in which truth and reality are dependent upon thought in general commits him to some sort of idealism. It is sometimes held — or assumed, or stipulated — that this consequence precludes Peirce from espousing a correspondence theory of truth, since that theory is metaphysically realist in character, and so incompatible with any form of idealism. This claim, however, is true only for a suitably circumscribed class of correspondence theories, ones that, as Susan Haack puts it, "have teeth,"[15] and the evident incompatibility of Peirce's theory with a correspondence theory of this ambitious sort cannot, without question-begging, support a negative answer to the question whether Peirce's pragmatically clarified truth fully respects truth's independence of the vagaries of human thought. The debate, in a word, concerns whether Peirce (or Kant for that mat-

---

15 Haack, "Realism," *Synthese* 73 (1987): 288–89.

ter) is entitled to claim that a metaphysically neutral correspondence formulation, nominal and less than fully adequate though it may be, nevertheless states an uncontroversial truth about truth.

So far, using the language of the double-aspect interpretation, we have arrived at the following: the *independence* of truth *from* thought is captured in the claim that if something is true, then "it is so, whether you or I or anybody think it is so or not ... [and] no matter if there be an overwhelming vote against it" (2.135); and the *accessibility* of truth *to* thought is captured in the claim that honest inquiry, carried out sufficiently far, is fated to arrive at the truth. I shall on occasion refer to the first claim as the independence thesis, and the second as the accessibility thesis.

In an undated footnote added to the original text of "How to Make Our Ideas Clear," Peirce expands upon what he means by claiming that inquiry is "fated" to arrive at the truth:

> Fate means merely that which is sure to come true, and can nohow be avoided. It is a superstition to suppose that a certain sort of event are ever fated, and it is another to suppose that the word fate can never be freed from its superstitious taint. (5.407, n. 1)

It is at first glance unfortunate to find the word "true" used in this explanation of what is meant by the word "fate," since the latter had been introduced to help explain the meaning of the former, but there is in fact no vicious circularity involved. Peirce's point could be made equally well by any of several phrases not containing the word "true"; for example, "that which is sure to come about," or "that which must happen." The point, I take it, is that the eventual upshot of genuine inquiry is *constrained*, and that it is in virtue of this constraint that there is at the limit no room for intelligible disagreement amongst inquirers as to what is the case. This is why reality and truth, though utterly independent of any vagaries of actual thinking, are not independent of thought *überhaupt*, or "thought in general." If Peirce is right, there is a necessary connection between the nature of the real and the nature of (a certain kind of) thought; namely, that "the reality of that which is real depends upon the real fact that investigation [the exercise of inquisitive thought] is destined to lead, at last, if continued long enough, to a belief in it" (5.408).

In line with what Robert Almeder calls the "received view" of the matter, I think it important to emphasize the subjunctively conditional character of Peirce's accessibility thesis. *If* inquiry *were* persisted in long enough, its deliverances *would be* true: That is what Peirce thinks follows from applying the Pragmatic Maxim to the concept "true," and it would be fallacious to think that this conditional entails or requires that inquiry will be persisted in long enough in fact to turn up the true answer to any particular question. Almeder asserts that the received view interprets Peircean truth "as an ideal product, rather than the destined product of scientific inquiry,"[16] and he disputes it on the grounds that Peirce remained convinced that inquiry somewhere in the universe will continue indefinitely, so that "the truth *will* come on any answerable question" (ibid., 88). The implied contrast between truth as an ideal and truth as destined product is unhelpful. Peirce, it seems to me, holds that truth is *both* an ideal product *and* the destined product of genuine inquiry persisted in long enough. It is ideal, rather than actual, since it may transcend or contravene what is actually believed at any given point in time; and it is the destined rather than the accidental upshot of inquiry, since inquiry, *if it is persisted in long enough*, can "nohow" avoid coming to rest in the truth. The fatedness of truth's discovery, in other words, applies only to the consequent of Peirce's accessibility conditional, not, as Almeder seems to assume, to its antecedent.

Eliminating the red herring of the fate of actual inquiry brings into relief the pertinence of the following question: What right does Peirce have to be so confident that investigation, even if persisted in unto all eternity, is destined to issue in opinions that get matters right, rather than, for example, in the universal acceptance of stubborn prejudice, or a limited view, or undetectable error? With regard to the first of these suggested contrasts, the answer, I shall argue, lies in the unavoidability of experienced external reality. With regard to the second, it lies in the fact, as I shall show it to be, that Peirce's theory, properly understood, does not commit him to the view that inquiry is

---

16 Almeder, "Peirce's Thirteen Theories of Truth," *Transactions of the Charles S. Peirce Society* 21 (1985): 87.

destined to light upon all the truth that there is. On the third contrast, though, I will in the present work be silent.

Genuine inquiry, we recall, uses the experiential method and seeks to "determine [belief] by nothing human, but by some external permanency — by something upon which our thinking has no effect" (5.384). Something external in this sense, "something upon which our thinking has no effect," is also something real, but for Peirce not everything real is *eo ipso* external. The distinction, he explains in the 1872–3 Logic Notebook, is that "that is external to the mind, which is what it is, whatever our thoughts may be on any subject; [while] that is real which is what it is whatever our thoughts may be concerning that particular thing" (W3:29). Any reality, in other word, is such that it has a character that is independent of what we think about *it*, while an external reality has a character that is independent of anything we think *period*. Suppose, for example, that Smith dreams that he succeeds in climbing Mount Everest. It thereby becomes a real fact that he so dreamt on the night in question; the events in the dream are as they are independent of what Smith or anybody else takes them to be. But the dream is not an external reality; it has the character it has only because Smith thought (in the mode of dreaming) as he did. Had he dreamt differently, a different real fact would have resulted, so the content of Smith's dream is not independent of thought period, for its existence is constituted by Smith's dream thoughts on that night. Were Smith instead actually to succeed in climbing Mount Everest, the fact that he did so would be both real and external. For that fact to have been otherwise, no mere change of *thinking* on the part of Smith or anybody else would be sufficient; only (given the nature of the external reality in question) a change in *action* could have accomplished that.

What Peirce calls the final opinion, the destined upshot of genuine inquiry indefinitely pursued, is a reality, but not an external one. It is not an external reality because an opinion is itself a kind of thought. "If there were no thought," notes Peirce, "there would be no opinion, and therefore, no final opinion" (W3:29); but it is nevertheless real because, since "it is not changed if [people] think otherwise ... it is quite independent of how any number of men think" (W3:46). It is the prerogative of external realities, Peirce argues at length in the Logic Notebook, to account for the reality, the fixity and fatedness, of the final opinion. In order to dissipate the "strangeness" of the fact that inquiry that follows the experiential method "seem[s] fated to come to the final conclusion," he declares:

> we adopt the conception of external realities. We say that ... observations are the result of the action upon the mind of outward things, and that their diversity is due to the diversity of our relations to these things; while the identity of the conclusion to which the mind is led by them is owing to the identity of the things observed, the reasoning process serving to separate among the many different observations that we make of the same thing the constant element which depends upon the thing itself from the differing and variable elements which depend on our varying relations to the thing. (W3:44)

We can, for Peirce, be exactly as confident in the fatedness of inquiry to get matters right eventually as we can be confident that there are external realities. Experientially speaking, to say that inquiry is fated to get things right and to say that there are external things to get right is to say the same thing in different words: "Therefore," he concludes, "when we say that there are external things, and that observations are only the appearances which these things produce upon sense by their relations to us, we have only in an inverted form, asserted the very same fact and no other which we assert when we say that observations inevitably carry us to a predetermined conclusion" (W3:47).

Not only, then, does Peirce reject the contention that an adequate understanding of truth cannot grant equal status and importance to its independence *and* to its accessibility; he maintains, moreover, that the independence and the accessibility share the same root, namely the fact that experience forces itself upon us. On the one hand, according to Peirce, experience is the source of truth's essential independence, the source of our correct belief that truth and reality are independent of us, because it includes an element of compulsion. "Experience," he explains, "is that determination of belief and cognition generally which the course of life has forced upon a man." Though "one may lie about it, ... one cannot escape the fact that some things *are* forced upon his cognition." We thus form the notion that certain things are as they are independently of how we take them to be because we are the subjects of a mode of consciousness, experience, in which things are thrust upon us willy-nilly; and it is in this "element of brute force" that we discover something that exists "whether [we] opine it exists or not" (2.138). In Peirce's doctrine of the Categories, this brute-force-from-outside aspect of experience is called its secondness.

On the other hand, because the experience that forces itself upon us presents itself as indicative of an intelligible world — not a Kantian or Platonic "intelligible world," defined by contrast to the world of sense, but rather a world (the one in which we live) conveyed via the senses (cf. "Fixation," 5.384) that conforms to numerous intelligible patterns and laws — we come to realize, at the third grade of clarity, that it makes no sense to define truth and reality in a way that renders them potentially incognizable altogether. (The intelligibility and law-like character of experience is, according to the doctrine of the Categories, a consequence or condition of its thirdness.) If we agree with Peirce that "the essence of truth lies in its resistance to being ignored" (2.139), then it follows from an application of (so to speak) quasi-double-negation that its essence lies equally in its fatedness to reveal itself to a sufficiently persistent inquiry that uses the experiential method. So it is because experience presents itself to us as an intelligible constraint on our lives — something that is both intelligible to us and yet constraining (and so independent) of us — that truth and reality, experientially defined, must be just as *independent* of what we happen to think as they are *accessible* in principle to genuine inquiry persisted in over the indefinitely long haul (I will be returning to this notion of experience as intelligible constraint in this essay's concluding pages).

Inquiry, therefore, is guaranteed to overcome prejudice and arbitrariness in the indefinitely long run in virtue of its commitment to learning from experience. Peirce allows that "Our perversity and that of others may indefinitely postpone the settlement of opinion; it might even conceivably cause an arbitrary proposition to be universally accepted as long as the human race should last"; but adds that "even that would not change the nature of the belief, which alone could be the result of investigation carried sufficiently far; and if, after the extinction of our race, another should arise with faculties and disposition for investigation, that true opinion must be the one which they would ultimately come to" (5.408). Plainly, the final opinion to which inquiry is (allegedly) destined to lead is not to be equated with a universally accepted opinion, just as such, no matter how long the universal acceptance lasts. It is genuine investigation, conducted in accordance with the method of experience, that needs to be continued "sufficiently far" in order to generate a final opinion, and whether or not genuine investigation is going on is quite independent of whether or not human beings are in existence and in the habit of forming opinions. Genuine inquiry cannot come to rest in a universally accepted prejudice because a prejudice, by definition, owes its existence not to an experienced external reality, but to a misguided disposition, a "perversity" of the prejudiced mind.

IV The Problem(s) of Buried Secrets

Peirce understood that the arguments so far presented provide insufficient defence of the double-aspect theory against the objections of realist opponents. Grant for the sake of argument that we have been given reason to think that inquiry, in virtue of its connection to experience, has the resources to prevent itself, in the limit, from licensing arbitrariness and prejudice. There remains the question of inquiry's capacity to uncover *all* the truth and reality that there may be in the universe, or even on our modestly sized planet.

> But [he writes] I may be asked what I have to say to all the minute facts of history, forgotten never to be recovered, to the lost books of the ancients, to the buried secrets
> "Full many a gem of purest ray serene
> The dark unfathomed caves of ocean bear;
> Full many a flower is born to blush unseen,
> And waste its sweetness on the desert air."
> Do these things not really exist because they are hopelessly beyond the reach of our knowledge? And then, after the universe is dead (according to the predictions of some scientists), and all life has ceased forever, will not the shock of atoms continue though there will be no mind to know it? (5.409)

That Peirce quite rightly takes the possibility of buried secrets to be a serious problem for the accessibility face of the double-aspect theory is shown by the fact that he broaches the issue immediately after stating a version of the accessibility thesis; namely that "the reality of that which is real does depend upon the real fact that investigation is destined to lead, at last, if continued long enough, to a belief in it" (5.408).

What sort of "dependence" can Peirce have in mind here? It would seem at first as if he ought to be committed to the thesis that for all x, if x is real then sufficient inquiry is destined to lead to a belief in it. But if he is committed to this, the possibility of buried secrets threatens to pose more than a mere problem; it looks instead like an outright refutation. Insofar as buried secrets are well and truly *buried*, inquiry can hardly be *destined* to uncover them; but insofar as they are *secrets*, they are not figments or fictions, and so, by Peirce's abstract definition of reality, they are real. Therefore, it seems, if buried secrets are possible, so are realities whose reality consists in something other than the fact that investigation is destined to lead to a belief in them.

"How to Make Our Ideas Clear" offers the following response to the threat presented by the possibility of buried secrets:

> though in no possible state of knowledge can any number be great enough to express the relation between the amount of what rests unknown to the amount of the known, yet it is unphilosophical to suppose that, with regard to any given question (which has any clear meaning), investigation would not bring forth a solution of it, if it were carried far enough" ... Who can guess what would be the result of continuing the pursuit of science for ten thousand years, with the activity of the last hundred? And if it were to go on for a million, or a billion, or any number of years you please, how is it possible to say that there is any question which might not ultimately be solved? (5.409)

That this reply cannot stand on its own seems to have been suspected by Peirce even at the time of writing it. Immediately after making it he: (a) raises an objection to it (that its appeal to "remote considerations" is at odds with his "principle that only practical considerations make a difference"); (b) asserts — what he was later almost unambiguously to recant — that propositions about buried secrets "concern much more the arrangement of our language than they do the meaning of our ideas"; (c) insists that "it seems to [him], however, that we have, by the application of our rule reached so clear an apprehension of what we mean by reality, and of the fact which the idea rests on, that we should not, perhaps, be making a pretension so presumptuous as singular, if we were to offer a metaphysical theory of existence for universal acceptance among those who employ the scientific method of fixing belief"; and (d) reassures his readers that "as metaphysics is a subject much more curious than useful, the knowledge of which, like that of a sunken reef, serves chiefly to enable us to keep clear of it, [he] will not trouble [them] with any more Ontology at this moment" (5.409–10). By 1905, he had become positively coy about the position on buried secrets and not-yet-actualized possibles adopted in "How to Make Our Ideas Clear," beginning a sentence with the confident assertion that it "endeavoured to gloze over [the matter] as unsuited to the exoteric public addressed"; and concluding it with the quite different possibility that "perhaps the writer wavered in his own mind" (5.453). Either way, Peirce as much as admits that his pragmatically clarified account of truth and reality cannot solve the problem of buried secrets without a more searching inquiry into both the scope and purport of the theory and the precise nature of the problem than was provided in the brief paragraphs devoted to the subject in "How to Make Our Ideas Clear."

The nub of that essay's reply to the problem of buried secrets is that we can't know that there are any, and this reply fails to meet the objection squarely. The idea animating the objection is that the mere *possibility* of buried secrets tells against Peirce's theory. To Peirce's "if inquiry went on long enough, all secrets might be revealed," the objector will counter: "But then again some might not, and the identity of a fact as fact is quite independent of whether or not it is ever discovered, which is to say that its reality is independent of whether 'investigation is destined to lead … to a belief in it.'" This alleged independence of fact as such from the upshot of investigation in the indefinitely long run can take a weaker or a stronger form. On the one hand, there is the apparent possibility that inquiry, carried out for as long as you like with the utmost wholeness of heart and acuity of mind, might miss out on some of the truth; and on the other hand, there is the more radical apparent possibility that inquiry might come to rest in unrectifiable mistakes. In the first case, we are talking about irremediable ignorance — inquiry might be destined to remain in the dark about certain things — while in the second case we are talking about irremediable error — inquiry might be destined to get certain matters wrong.

An example of Hartry Field's brings the character of these two possibilities nicely into view. Field asks us to consider the simple question "How many dinosaurs were there?" and then invites us to agree that it is undeniable (1) that the question is perfectly meaningful, and (2) that exactly one of the positive integers answers it correctly.[17] The

---

17 Field, "Realism and Relativism," *Journal of Philosophy* 79 (1982): 553–67.

objection to Peirce from potentially irremediable ignorance appeals to the thought that the evidential traces of the dinosaurs may prove too meagre unto all eternity for inquiry ever to discover which whole integer it is that correctly answers the question how many of them there were. Remember that Peirce had insisted that "it is unphilosophical to suppose that, with regard to any given question (which has any clear meaning), investigation would not bring forth a solution of it, if it were carried far enough." So, if inquiry were to prove *un*able to number the dinosaurs, this remark seems to commit Peirce to denying clear meaning to the question "How many dinosaurs were there?," and that contradicts the apparently uncontentious assumption (1) above.

The objection from irremediable error presupposes the soundness of that from irremediable ignorance and makes the further claim that, as J.J.C. Smart puts it, "truth might do more than *outrun* [the settled opinion of inquiry indefinitely pursued], it might *conflict* with it."[18] Smart's example of a case in which inquiry would be doomed to settle on a falsehood involves "suppos[ing] that what we think of as our four-dimensional space-time universe is a cross-section of a larger five-dimensional universe, with another four-dimensional universe as another cross-section."[19] The point can be made in a slightly more prosaic way apropos of our friends the dinosaurs. Suppose that, remarkably, inquiry turns up enough evidence pertaining to the population of the dinosaurs to enable inquirers to think that its exact size has been determined. Now suppose that one or two dinosaurs were gobbled up by predators moments after seeing the light of day, so that no traces of their existence survived more than a short period after their demise. In such a case, inquiry might, on unimpeachable grounds, deem the number of the dinosaurs to have been, say, 10^{10}, whereas their actual number was 10^{10} plus one or two. Consequently, says the objector, the correct answer to the question "How many dinosaurs were there?" and the answer that inquiry in the long haul is destined to settle on, supposing it settles on a particular number, are not necessarily identi-

---

18 Smart, "Realism v. Idealism," 307.

19 Ibid., 309.

cal; and the truth of the matter in such a case would, of course, be provided by the correct answer, not the only nearly correct one arrived at by inquiry indefinitely continued.

Neither of these objections can be countered by appealing to the point, correctly emphasized by Cheryl Misak,[20] that chief among Peirce's concerns in this area is a regulative principle to the effect that if inquiry into a given topic is to be a coherent enterprise, inquirers have no choice but to presuppose that their best possible efforts would be sufficient to disclose the truth of the matter. The soundness of such a principle can be granted by the sort of objector I am envisaging, who will go on to insist that the sheer *existence* of a truth about the matter has nothing to do with the soundness of the principle. Even if we must assume that our best efforts will get it right, it is still possible that those efforts will fall shy or wide of the mark, and that possibility, according to the objection, suffices to show that the problems of buried secrets give rise to a more robust tension between Peirce's abstract definition of reality as independent of us and his pragmatically clarified account of truth as the fated final opinion than did the problem of firmly entrenched prejudice.

V The Meaning of Pragmatic Meaning

I said above that the objection from irremediable error presupposes the cogency of the objection from irremediable ignorance, and it is clear why this must be so. Where there is error, there too there must be ignorance of the error as such; to become aware that one has made a mistake is *ipso facto* to free oneself from it (this, indeed, is a consequence of the internal connection between belief and acceptance as true noted in Section I above). It is not immediately apparent, though, that there is a relation of entailment or presupposition running in the other direction. Why might it not be *in*defensible to insist that inquiry carried out long enough could not possibly fail to capture *everything* that is

---

20 Misak, *Truth and the End of Inquiry* (Oxford: Clarendon, 1991), 137–61.

true, but *defensible* to maintain that inquiry is guaranteed never finally to settle on what is false? In fact, I think that the chief of Peirce's lessons in this area is just this: that while it makes sense to concede that the truth might *outstrip* the destined upshot of inquiry, it does not similarly make sense to suppose that the truth could *make a mockery* of the destined upshot, that genuine inquiry could be doomed to abject failure, even in the limit. At present I am not going to try to establish this double-barreled thesis, but aim instead to defend only the more modest claim that the objection from irremediable ignorance can be successfully rebutted within a distinctively Peircean framework. What I will argue is that, while the objector is right to maintain that there is no *a priori* guarantee that inquiry must uncover all that there is, he is wrong in thinking that this admission strikes at the heart of Peirce's theory, for it does not undermine the core claim that pragmatic meaning deepens and clarifies linguistic meaning

The issues raised by buried secrets invite discussion in terms of the meanings of concepts, words, and sentences rather than as in "How to Make Our Ideas Clear," in terms of the clarity of ideas. For it is the apparently evident meaningfulness of a question such as "How many dinosaurs were there?" that provokes resistance to Peirce's suggestion that our understanding of what it is for something to be true is deepened and clarified by realizing that to call something true is to say that inquiry indefinitely continued would come to rest in that something. What, though, does it mean to say that a question is "evidently meaningful"? Presumably, it means at least (and perhaps at most) that the question is readily understandable; that, philosophical subtlety aside, no competent speaker of English would be unclear about what was being asked. I shall call this sort of meaning, the sort conferred by ready intelligibility to competent speakers, linguistic meaning, and will contrast linguistic meaning with pragmatic meaning in just the way that Peirce contrasts abstract-verbal clarity with experiential-pragmatic clarity.

Now: the point of articulating the Pragmatic Maxim, of identifying a layer of meaning more substantial than the purely verbal-linguistic, is to help us get clearer about the contents of our thoughts and enable us to become "masters of our own meaning" (5.393). One way we can get clearer about a word, a concept, a sentence, or something of that sort, is by understanding more perspicuously and explicitly than before what we can and do mean by it; this is what Peirce in "How to Make Our Ideas Clear" tries to do for the concepts of hardness, weight, reality, and truth. Another way is by being brought to recognize that we *cannot* mean something that we might (confusedly and mistakenly) have thought we did. This is what Peirce does in the same essay when he maintains that "talk of something as having all the sensible characters of wine, yet being in reality blood, is senseless jargon" (5.401), and that "[to state] that we understand precisely the effect of force, but what force itself is we do not understand ... is simply a self-contradiction" (5.404). In this capacity, the Pragmatic Maxim is in the business of unmasking empty verbiage, showing certain words or concepts to be void of "intellectual purport," however much otherwise intelligent people may carry on as if the items in question had a clear and legitimate meaning.[21] The problem of buried secrets then is this: statements about entities that may once have existed, but whose traces have disappeared entirely, are not plausibly classified as empty verbiage.

Peirce himself would surely have had reason to agree that a statement such as "There have been exactly 10^{10} dinosaurs on earth" should not be equated with a statement about transubstantiation or a force-in-itself-wholly-separate-from-its-effects as far as pragmatic meaning is concerned. For the ingredients of the statement in question — the existential quantifier, the concept of a class of objects with cardinality 10^{10}, the concept of a dinosaur, and the concept of the planet earth — have pragmatic meaning. A buried secret is not something with no effects at all, but something whose effects are irretrievably lost. That

---

21 It is when it is functioning in this capacity that the Pragmatic Maxim can seem most strongly to anticipate the Verification Principle of the Vienna Circle. Yet even when Peirce comes closest to the Vienna positivists in the tenor of his language — as when he proclaims that the Pragmatic Maxim "will serve to show that almost every proposition of ontological metaphysics is either meaningless gibberish ... or else is downright absurd" — it remains perfectly clear that the demolition of metaphysics was never his primary objective: "instead of merely jeering at metaphysics, like other prope-positivists, whether by long drawn out parodies or otherwise, the pragmaticist extracts from it a precious essence, which will serve to give life and light to cosmology and physics" (5.423).

every dinosaur that ever lived manifested its existence by means of certain effects — for example, that of being visible to other dinosaurs, of eating, excreting, and so on — seems as evident as anything else we think we know about dinosaurs. The apparent problem for the Peircean is that it is also plausible to maintain that too many of the countless traces of the dinosaurs have been obliterated by subsequent events and their effects to leave us any justified assurance that even the best possible inquiry is destined definitively to establish their exact number. More precisely, the problem is that while we lack assurance that inquiry must succeed in correctly numbering the dinosaurs, we have assurance that there was a determinate number of dinosaurs; which shows, it seems, that what it means to say that exactly *n* dinosaurs roamed the earth is not deepened and clarified, but falsified, by applying the Pragmatic Maxim and coming to the conclusion that it means that inquiry is destined to settle on *n* as the correct answer to the question "How many dinosaurs were there?"

Another way of posing the difficulty is this: it is one thing to hold that alleged objects with no effects whatsoever are impostors — pseudo-objects, non-things — and that language that purports to talk about such nonentities is "senseless jargon." It is quite another thing to deny that there could possibly be objects that *once had* effects but no longer *have* them, i.e., to deny the coherence of buried secrets. To lump buried secrets together with wholly effect-less (non-)things is, in effect, to insist that the existence of an object *at any time* depends upon its effects lasting *throughout* time. Much better to say that as long as an object had effects at some time, its existence as such is secured and our conception of the object is our conception of whatever effects it had. Much better to say this, and also closer to Peirce's intentions, as evidenced by the following passage from about 1904:

> The intellectual meaning of a statement is precisely the same whether it refers to past or future time. To say that a piece of porcelain is soft before it is baked is equivalent to saying that if anybody during that period tries to scratch it with a knife he will succeed, and to say this is again equivalent to saying that every experiment which is logically necessitated, if this be true, to turn out in a certain way, will turn out in that way; and this last statement has a corresponding equivalent, and so on endlessly. But of this endless series of equivalent propositions there is one which my situation in time makes to be the practical one for me, and that one becomes for me the primary meaning. As long as the porce-

lain is not yet baked, I mean by calling it soft that if anyone tries to scratch it with a knife he will readily succeed. But after it has been baked, and nobody has taken occasion to try that experiment, it is a different experiment among the endless series of equivalents that now expresses my primary meaning. The nature of the fact does not change; but my relation to it and consequent mode of conceiving do change, although I all the time recognize the equivalence of the different meanings. (8.195)

Peirce here argues that although *all* singular facts or events in the past are "buried" in the sense of no longer available for present inspection, this does not mean that they cannot be uncovered by inquiry; the inquiry will just have to be more ramified and wider in scope than it would be if the singular fact or event in question was still available for straightforward testing. If the porcelain has not yet been baked, we test for softness by taking out a knife and scratching. If the porcelain has been baked untouched, we infer its prior softness from evidence about how porcelain behaves in general and evidence that this is and was normal porcelain.

"Pragmaticism," Peirce insisted at around the same time as the writing of the passage above, "could hardly have entered a head that was not already convinced that there are real generals" (5.503). We can now see one clear reason why he would say this, for the solution just offered to the problem of the pragmatic meaning of statements about singular past facts and events requires a web of connections between the *singular* facts and events and the relevant *general* kinds and patterns. The pragmatic meaning of saying that *this* porcelain was soft *then* is, Peirce tells us above, not specifiable independently of the pragmatic meaning of "porcelain" as such. Just so, again about midway through the first decade of this century, did he repudiate the suggestion of nominalism in "How to Make Our Ideas Clear" by maintaining that the hardness of a never-touched diamond is a real fact about it, a fact that consists in its possessing just those properties of diamonds as a class of really similar objects "from [which] hardness is believed to be inseparable" (5.457).

The same strategy can be applied to cases in which no instances of the relevant natural kinds are any longer available for present experimentation. Take a patch of territory once highly conducive to such-and-such species of dinosaur, which flourished at the time elsewhere in the region to which the patch belongs; on that patch a large asteroid lands, obliterating all traces of whatever organisms had flourished on it beforehand. Though all direct traces of the dinosaurs that once lived on the territory in question are gone, nevertheless inquiry could legitimately infer their existence, and thus grant pragmatic meaning to statements asserting (or denying) their existence, on the basis of the many traces of essentially related matters that remain available: for example, the effects of the asteroid's landing and the remains of dinosaurs from neighbouring areas. Considered in isolation, the existence of these dinosaurs would be a buried secret. But for Peirce, "there is no such thing [as] an isolated fact" (5.457), and that allows for the possibility that, considered in conjunction with the rest of what we know, much that would otherwise be lost can yet be found.

But perhaps not all. Perhaps a fact as minute as the precise number of dinosaurs that lived on that asteroid-plagued piece of earth will resist determination, even in the final opinion. In that case, this resistance itself should figure in the final opinion, along with the reasons for its obtaining. The fact that the final opinion will lack any claim of the form "Exactly n dinosaurs lived here," with some whole number substituted for "n," will not be isolated or surd; a complex mesh of considerations found in the final opinion will positively *exclude* any such commitment. As Cornelis de Waal puts it, "Answering a question is not the only way in which opinion regarding that question can be settled. Opinion can be settled also by finding a question unanswerable."[22]

De Waal does not think that the possibility of a final agnosticism with respect to certain questions is sufficient to answer the objection from irremediable ignorance, and in this I agree with him. For suppose that inquiry finally settles on the view that the exact number of dinosaurs that roamed the earth is an unrecoverable fact. It still seems as meaningful as ever to say that the number was such and such, say 10^{10}, and one wonders what on Peircean grounds this meaning could consist in, given that, *ex hypothesi*, it can no longer be explicated by reference to inquiry's coming to settle on it as the answer to the ques-

---

22 de Waal, "The Quest for Reality: Charles S. Peirce and the Empiricists," doctoral dissertation, University of Miami, 1997, 203.

tion how many dinosaurs there were. The meaning consists, I suggest, in the *residue* of the pragmatic meaning that the statement had as long as inquiry into the subject was a live option. Just as, on the ontological side of the coin, a buried secret is something with *erstwhile* effects, so, on the linguistic side of the coin, a statement to the effect that such and such is the case as regards a permanently buried topic is something with *erstwhile* pragmatic meaning. The key point in either case is that something with erstwhile effects or meaning need not be run together with something with no effects or nugatory meaning.

In the relatively easier case of singular facts or events locked in the past, Peirce argued that statements asserting their existence could be ascribed pragmatic meaning in virtue of a battery of general truths about the substances involved. He insisted that, for example, the pragmatic meaning of *"that* porcelain was soft before it was baked" is fundamentally the same as that of "porcelain is soft before it is baked," although different experiments express the statement's "primary meaning" according as we are dealing with baked or unbaked porcelain. The hard case, in which inquiry settles on unanswerability as the answer to a question, can, I want to argue, be treated as a limit case in which we have not just a different primary meaning, but no more primary meaning. Nevertheless, lack of primary meaning notwithstanding, statements that convey possible answers to not positively answerable questions can still be regarded as meaningful, as distinct from empty or self-contradictory. Following the line of thought implicit in Peirce, this residue of meaning might be called "secondary meaning"; in the terminology I have adopted it will be called "linguistic meaning." As long as evidence pertaining to dinosaur populations might be forthcoming, the pragmatic meaning of "Exactly 10^{10} dinosaurs roamed the earth" consists in a commitment to inquiry's settling on 10^{10} as the exact number of the dinosaurs *if it settles on a particular number in answer to the question* "Exactly how many dinosaurs were there?"[23] If it is stipulated that a point has been reached at which it is

---

23 Cf. Peirce's 1905 suggestion that "truth" be defined as "that to a belief in which belief would tend if it were to tend indefinitely to absolute fixity" (5.416).

finally evident that no further evidence is to be had, then the statement will have been drained of pragmatic meaning; its linguistic meaning, though, remains, and remains the same as it ever was.

How can this be? Recall the Pragmatic Maxim: "Consider what effects, that might conceivably have practical bearings, we conceive the object of our conception to have. Then our conception of these effects is the whole of our conception of the object"; and notice that the initial instruction (to consider effects that might conceivably have practical bearings) is ambiguous between a present tense and a tenseless reading. In the 1905 passage cited above, Peirce makes it clear that it is the present-tense reading that captures the intent of the maxim.

> A practical attitude of mind concerns itself primarily with the living future, and pays no regard to the dead past or even the present except so far as it may indicate what the future will be. Thus, the pragmaticist is obliged to hold that whatever means anything means that something will happen (provided certain conditions are fulfilled), and to hold that the future alone has primary reality. (8.194)

My solution to the problem posed by irremediable ignorance is to take the tenseless reading of the Pragmatic Maxim, according to which we consider not only effects that (as of now) might conceivably *have* practical bearings, but also any effects that (at any time) might *conceivably have had* practical bearings, to provide a way of explaining how, in the limit case, linguistic meaning can turn out to exceed pragmatic meaning, yet ultimately remain beholden to the latter for whatever intellectual-experiential clarity it has.

My proposal in a nutshell is that possession of pragmatic meaning *at any time* suffices for possession of legitimate linguistic meaning *for the rest of time*. It is only failure *ever* to have pragmatic meaning that renders a purported case of linguistic meaning illegitimate and void of intellectual-experiential content. This suggestion opens up the possibility that at the hypothetical end of inquiry the class of sentences with legitimate linguistic meaning will be larger than that of sentences with current pragmatic meaning. On the plausible assumption that all declarative sentences with legitimate linguistic meaning are thereby endowed with a Tarskian truth-condition, the proposal countenances the possibility that the realm of actual truth turns out to exceed the realm of possible knowledge.

To allow the possibility of irremediable ignorance in the way suggested is, I grant, to admit that the independence of truth has a certain priority over its accessibility. For the independence thesis brooks no violations whatsoever, whereas cases of irremediable ignorance are precisely cases of inaccessible truth. I do not, though, take this admission to compromise the fully fledged double-aspect character of the theory, since in another sense, it is the accessibility thesis that "underpins" the independence thesis. It is still pragmatic meaning that determines the presence or absence of legitimate linguistic meaning; and according to the current proposal, it is part of the pragmatic meaning of truth that the extension of the predicate "true" might exceed the extension of the predicate "settled on by genuine inquiry over the indefinitely long haul"; though of course one could never establish the point by *identifying* a particular truth that inquiry had missed out on.

And why should the pragmatic meaning of "true" include such a robust commitment to the independence of truth from knowledge, even as it insists on truth's essential accessibility to knowledge? Because, I think Peirce would say, that wealth of intelligible experience that crowds in on us daily contains within it an element of "brute force which is decidedly anti-intellectual," an "idea of brute-thereness — or whatever best names it — ... quite distinct from any concept" (8.195). It is, I noted above, characteristic of discourse about possibly buried matters that it is built up of components each of which on its own has a pragmatic meaning of an ordinary kind. As Hilary Putnam has observed, it is "with the aid of quantifiers and other logical constants" that "our conceptual powers [can be extended] beyond the range of the verifiable."[24] In Peirce's terms, it is in the nature of secondness to convey to us an idea (perhaps better: an impression) of existential otherness, and acknowledging the possibility of permanently buried secrets is simply one way of acknowledging the ultimate ineradicability of this otherness. This is why it is so natural to appeal (overtly or covertly) to the existential quantifier in formulating putative counter-example s to Peirce's pragmatically clarified conception of truth. For (to reiterate) it is not what it is to be a dinosaur, nor what it is to be a set of objects with cardinality 10^{10}, nor what it is to roam the planet earth that resists prag-

---

24 Putnam, "Pragmatism," *Proceedings of the Aristotelian Society* 95 (1995): 297.

matic clarification; it is the sheer having-been-thereness on earth of (maybe) exactly 10^{10} dinosaurs that poses the apparent problem.

The full context of the remarks about brute force and brute-thereness quoted above help to make my point clearer:

> "Then you maintain, do you," [Peirce imagines someone objecting to his views on the reality of the past] "that when you directly act upon a thing in making an experiment, this direct action consists entirely in the fact that subsequent investigators will ultimately be led to the conclusion that you did act upon it?" "Ah, that I have not said, but have carefully guarded against such an interpretation by saying that it is only of conceptions, that is, of the intellectual part of meaning that I was speaking. The pragmaticist need not deny that such ideas as those of action, of actual happening, or individuality, of existence, etc., involve something like a reminiscence of an exertion of brute force which is decidedly anti-intellectual, which is an all-important ingredient of the practical, although the pragmat[ic]istic interpretation leaves it out of account. Yet while he may admit that this idea of brute thereness — or whatever best names it — is quite distinct from any concept, yet he is bound to maintain that this does not suffice to make an idea of practical reality. (8.195)

Because it leaves out of account the element of brute force involved in "such ideas as those of action, of actual happening, or individuality, of existence," the pragmaticist conception of truth appears at first blush to make life difficult for itself by allowing the problems of buried secrets to take on the air of formidable objections. But, as I have tried to show, and as Peirce makes clear above, the pragmaticist is not obliged to leave the element of brute existence out of account altogether; he simply does not locate it in the intellectual part of the meaning of "true." Where that element finds its place in the overall theory, I have argued, is at the linguistic level of meaning, the level at which the meaning of "true" is compatible with the possibility of irremediable ignorance. So, in a small nutshell, my view is that the intellectual-pragmatic aspect of the meaning of truth underwrites its essential accessibility to inquiry carried out over the indefinitely long haul, while the existential-linguistic aspect underwrites its essential independence from what you or I or anybody thinks. The independence of truth from thought, though it extends all the way to the possibility of irremediable ignorance, the possibility of truths that can never be turned up by any amount of inquiry whatever, does not compromise the thoroughly double-aspect character of Peirce's theory. And that, I think, is a good thing, for the theory has much to recommend it, and it may well prove to be true!

CANADIAN JOURNAL OF PHILOSOPHY
Supplementary Volume 24

Truth and Ends in Dewey's Pragmatism

HENRY S. RICHARDSON
Georgetown University

I

Dewey's voluminous writings, spanning decades and reflecting the contrasting national moods of different historical periods, abound with tensions, not to say contradictions. In highlighting and working with a conflict within Dewey's commitments, then, I do not mean to be catching him out or correcting a mistake. The tension on which I focus is one with which he struggled for most of his philosophical career and one that he never satisfactorily resolved, yet it is also one that goes to the heart of what it is to be a pragmatist. It involves the role of final ends in a philosophy that places practical reasoning at the heart of all knowledge. I will argue that while Dewey had powerful philosophical prejudices that prevented him from adequately dealing with this problem himself, a solution is nonetheless forthcoming that maintains, and perhaps even deepens, the main themes of his pragmatism. Setting out this solution will lead me, in the end, to a novel formulation of the pragmatist theory of truth.*

In simplest terms, the question over which Dewey vacillated and equivocated was whether it is possible to reason about final ends, ends sought for their own sakes. I postpone until the next section my explanation of the compatibility between final ends and Dewey's important

---

* I am grateful to Chad DeChant, Emily Hoechst, Joseph Kakesh, and Matthew McAdam for helpful discussion and to Cheryl Misak for detailed comments on an earlier draft.

view that the only ends worth considering are ends-in-view, ends that orient action in a given context of action and that stand in a continuum (of a kind we must explore) with the means to be employed. Common sense will suffice, for now, to convince us that Dewey, too, must have thought of action as oriented towards ends, and conceived of these ends as playing a central role in practical reasoning. The question, again, is whether reasoning can establish the ends of action, or whether it is limited to selecting means to ends that are fixed in advance. About this question, as I say, Dewey spoke out of both sides of his mouth.

On the one side, Dewey eloquently attacked narrow instrumentalism, decrying the obsessive focus on mechanical efficiency that had reached a fever pitch at the turn of the century in the work of industrial engineer Frederick W. Taylor. Given the aim of producing the greatest number of bolts in the shortest time with a fixed pool of workers, Taylor would study how to divide the labour to minimize wasted motion. That this blinkered focus on the means to an industrial goal resulted in treating workers as animals was an implication that Taylor seemed sometimes to relish.[1] Reacting against this dehumanizing movement, Dewey powerfully championed intelligence as against mechanical efficiency:

> The pragmatic theory of intelligence means that the function of mind is to project new and more complex ends — to free experience from routine and from caprice. Not the use of thought to accomplish purposes already given either in the mechanism of the body or in that of the existent state of society, but the use of intelligence to liberate and liberalize action, is the pragmatic lesson. Action restricted to given and fixed ends may attain great technical efficiency; but efficiency is the only quality to which it can lay claim. Such action is mechanical (or becomes so), no matter what the scope of the pre-formed end, be it the Will of God or *Kultur*. But the doctrine that intelligence develops within the sphere of action for the sake of possibilities not yet given is the opposite of a doctrine of mechanical efficiency. Intelligence *as* intelligence is inherently forward-looking; only by ignoring its primary function does it become a mere means for an end already given. The latter *is* servile, even when the end is labeled moral,

---

1 Cf. Robert Kanigel, *The One Best Way: Frederick Winslow Taylor and the Enigma of Efficiency* (New York: Viking, 1997), reviewed by George F. Will in the *New York Times Book Review*, June 15, 1997.

religious, or esthetic. But action directed to ends to which the agent has not previously been attached inevitably carries with it a quickened and enlarged spirit. A pragmatic intelligence is a creative intelligence, not a routine mechanic.[2]

The liberating possibility that pragmatism holds out here seems to be clearly drawn: intelligence will lead us to attach ourselves to new ends, including more complex or specific ends, thus freeing us from the heteronomous imposition of ends by sources independent of the will. Dewey here strikes a neo-Kantian chord.

On the other side, however, stands the persistent impression that Dewey was a friend of technocracy. Throughout his life, Dewey remained qualifiedly optimistic that properly applied empirical science would be the tool needed to liberate action from the bonds of routine and caprice.[3] The account of intelligence, as he elaborated it, stressed experimental method rather than insight into the ends of action. In contrast, say, to his one-time disciple and more pessimistic rival Walter Lippmann, who eventually attempted to revive ancient Greek conceptions of human nature, Dewey put his faith in public policy experts.[4] For Dewey, reliance on policy experts — albeit experts who are well

---

2 I employ the following abbreviations in citing Dewey, often citing both a popular edition and the collected works:
   MW: The Middle Works, 1899–1924, ed. Jo Ann Boydston (Carbondale, IL: Southern Illinois University Press, 1976–83)
   LW: The Later Works, 1925–1953, ed. Jo Ann Boydston (Carbondale, IL: Southern Illinois University Press, 1981–91)
   HNC: Human Nature and Conduct (New York: Modern Library, 1930)
   Logic: Logic: The Theory of Inquiry (New York: Irvington, 1982 [1938])
   PP: The Public and Its Problems (New York: Henry Holt, 1927)
   PW: John Dewey: The Political Writings, ed. Debra Morris and Ian Shapiro (Indianapolis, IN: Hackett, 1993)
   TOV: The Theory of Valuation (Chicago: University of Chicago Press, 1939)
       The quotation in the text is from Dewey, "The Need for Recovery of Philosophy" (1917) in *PW* 6–7. See also *HNC* 198, *MW* 14:138.

3 Cf. *HNC* 277, *MW* 14:189.

4 On Lippmann and his relation to Dewey on this issue, see John Patrick Diggins, *The Promise of Pragmatism* (Chicago: University of Chicago Press, 1994), Chapter 8.

informed about public needs — was essential to a scientific approach to policy. When framing the appeal to science, Dewey drew differently than in the passage just quoted the contrast between the enlightened and the benighted:

> When we say that thinking and beliefs should be experimental not absolutistic, we have then in mind a certain logic of method [which implies] that policies and proposals for social action be treated as working hypotheses, not as programs to be rigidly adhered to and executed.[5]

In carrying through this experimental approach, which was definitive of Dewey's pragmatism in general, what mattered was "the use of intelligence to judge consequences."[6]

This consequentialist appeal does not yet cycle us back to a narrow instrumentalism. Dewey is indeed rejecting policy reasoning that starts out from a single fixed and absolute end. Further, his invocation of the notion of judgment implies, in his philosophical usage, that the inferences to be drawn are not merely mechanical or technical.[7] Nonetheless, Dewey is here at the very least playing into the hands of the modern instrumentalist who recognizes the importance of trading off and ranking the various things we seek. If, further, we combine this invitation to consequentialism with Dewey's negative remarks about final ends, the side of Dewey that embraces a restriction of reasoning to instrumental reasoning — albeit a flexible and broad instrumental reasoning rather than a rigid and narrow one — will come clearly into view. "End-in-itself," he wrote in *The Theory of Valuation*, is a contradictory term.[8] There seems no point, then, in trying to set forward a conception of final ends, worth seeking for their own sakes. Rather, it would be sufficient to uncover the consequences of a policy proposal and to engage in such trade-offs as this empirical information prompts.

---

5 Dewey, *PP* 202–3. See p. 208 for the proviso about informed experts.

6 *PP* 45.

7 See, e.g., Dewey, "The Logic of Judgments of Practice," *MW* 8:47.

8 Dewey, *TOV* 41, *MW* 13:228. Cf. *Logic* 175–76, *LW* 12:179.

At one point he even approves of the view, which he takes to be Aristotle's, that "we never deliberate about ends, but only about means."[9] If we press Dewey for the standard to which such practical judgment should direct itself, he is consistently evasive, and surely deliberately so. He gives different descriptions of the overall standard in different places: as he himself says, "in quality, the good is never twice alike."[10] In various places, he characterizes it as "growth," "the cultivation of interests," or "a coordination or unified organization of activities."[11] All three of these formulations share their most striking feature with Aristotle's initial identification of *eudaimonia* as the ultimate end in Book I, Chapter 5, of the *Nicomachean Ethics*, namely: they represent a merely verbal achievement and offer no practical guidance whatsoever. If one was looking for a "new and more complex" final end, being offered *success* would leave one searching.

What had seemed to be truly liberating, then, in Dewey's rhetoric about intelligence has here vanished, and we are left with an uninspiring and uninspired consequentialism. Instead of a contrast between accepting fixed final ends and forging new ones, we have something much closer to Max Weber's distinction between the "absolutistic" pursuit of a *single* final end and the "responsible" trading off of one's many ends.[12] While the latter may allow for revising ends, it does not,

---

9 Dewey, "The Logic of Judgments of Practice," *MW* 8:38. Cf. *Logic, LW* 12:17: "Rationality as an abstract conception is precisely the generalized idea of the means-consequence relation as such." It does seem clear that Aristotle's *bouleusis*, normally translated as "deliberation," is limited to the selection of means (including constitutive means) to given ends: cf. Thomas Tuozzo, "Aristotelian Deliberation Is Not of Ends," in *Essays on Ancient Greek Philosophy*, vol. 4: *Aristotle's Ethics*, ed. J. P. Anton and A. Preus (Albany, NY: SUNY Press, 1991). The question, however, is whether Aristotle would allow for practical reasoning about final ends.

10 *MW* 14:146.

11 "Growth": *MW* 14:194. "The cultivation of interests": *LW* 7:208. "Coordination or unified organization": *TOV* 49, *LW* 13:234.

12 I refer to Weber's contrast between *Wertrationalität* and *Zweckrationalität* in *Economy and Society* 1.2 (Berkeley: University of California Press, 1968), 24–26.

on this sort of consequentialist picture, allow for establishing new final ends.[13] It is perhaps for this reason, then, that one recent critic has concluded that "Dewey saw no troubling dualism between means and ends because he regarded ends as given."[14] Certainly, if exercising intelligence essentially involves setting forth and defending new and more complex ends, Dewey spent far more time preaching the importance of intelligence than exercising it himself.

In this essay, without being romantic about it, I seek to recover the liberating promise of Dewey's pragmatism. I will develop that side of Dewey that would allow for the forging of new ends in deliberation while correcting the narrowness of philosophical vision that leaves us with the impression, at the end of the day, that Dewey was a boring technocrat whose consequentialism undercut his attachment to progressive politics and neutralized his call for deliberative democracy. I have no interest in claiming that my Dewey is the essential Dewey. Perhaps the technocratic side of him looms larger in his corpus and explains more of his view. What motivates this project is, rather, a conviction that there are important and true insights in Dewey's pragmatism which require this revision to other parts of his view if they are not to be lost. In thus playing the revisionist with Dewey's view, I can at least claim to be heeding his plea not to be trapped by the authority of the past.

I will begin with diagnosis, putting forward in the following section a somewhat speculative construal of the reasons for Dewey's misguided resistance to the notion of final ends. Section III will then detail the disastrous implications, in Dewey's own terms, of his failure to develop a more robust view of the employment of intelligence to generate new ends. I will argue that the central defects of Dewey's view, those which have caused it to be largely abandoned today, are traceable to this one failing. This accordingly poses a problem of reconstruction for the friend of Deweyan pragmatism. In Section IV, I consider a

---

13 In *Aufgeklärtes Eigeninteresse* (Frankfurt a. M.: Suhrkamp, 1992), n. 36, Stefan Gosepath notes that Weber's initial definition of *Zweckrationalität* in *Economy and Society* 1.2 allows for weighing ends against each other.

14 Diggins, *The Promise of Pragmatism*, 242.

relatively conservative response, one which proceeds by trying to graft onto Dewey an independent account of final ends. I mention this hybrid approach largely as a foil to the more integrally pragmatist account developed in Section V, which takes its cue from the fact that pragmatism gives primacy to practical reasoning in a more pervasive way, even, than did Kant. For the pragmatist, all inquiry is practical, but also fallible. I will sketch a pragmatist theory of truth that indicates how a cognitivist approach to reasoning about ends may be combined with the robust fallibilism that particularly characterized C. S. Peirce's seminal pragmatism. Once this reinstatement of truth and fallibilism to their central places is in view, I will be in a position, in Section VI, to explain how a consistent Deweyan pragmatist can wholly avoid technocracy.

II

Dewey's statement that a "final end" is an oxymoron was a sophomoric way of making one of his most important points about practical reasoning. The sense in which no end can be "final," for Dewey, is that as situations unfold and as we attempt imaginatively to review the consequences of a proposed action, we will, if our intelligence is engaged, constantly remake and refashion our ends. No end is ever specified in final form at the outset of deliberation. But traditional defenders of final ends could easily accept this as a point about the limits and tentativeness of our insight. It will be my task in this section to disentangle Dewey's useful observations about deliberation from his excesses of rhetoric, and to show that final ends, in another and more substantial sense, are in fact fully compatible with his view.[15]

Dewey is well known for his view that end and means stand in a continuum.[16] While this view is often cited, it seems but poorly un-

---

15 The material in this section revisits some points made in my *Practical Reasoning about Final Ends* (New York: Cambridge University Press, 1994), Section 23.

16 See, for example, *The Quest for Certainty*, LW 4:124, 222–28; TOV 40–50, LW 13:226–36.

derstood. One possible source of confusion is the related claim that Dewey made for the special case of political reform. As the title of one of his late essays put it, "Democratic Ends Need Democratic Methods for Their Realization."[17] In this case, the means must be congruent with the end. Given Dewey's own proclivity for summing up his views on end and means by saying that he is denying the "dualism" between them, it is natural that even as sensitive a commentator as John Patrick Diggins should take the empirical failure of this special point about democracy to cast doubt generally upon "Dewey's belief in the unity of means and ends."[18] Yet the point of the continuum of end–means lies elsewhere. In introducing it, Dewey used Charles Lamb's example of burning down the house to roast the pork. Clearly, Dewey is not insisting that pork be roasted only by means of burning pork fat. Rather, he is making three related observations that flow from the fact, as he sees it, that ends are not rightly viewed as strongly separable from the context of action.

To begin with, Dewey is building on his characterization of deliberation as working with what he calls "ends in view." These are ends framed by the agent in relation to a context of action. Rather than being timelessly given by human nature or *a priori* theory, they are formed in reaction to some problem, obstacle, or want of fulfillment that the agent has experienced.[19] While sometimes Dewey's presentation of this point sounds positively anti-theoretical, presaging recent attacks on abstraction in ethics, his arguments for taking context seriously do not actually exclude a complementary reliance upon abstractions.[20]

---

17 First published in *New Leader*, October 21, 1939; reprinted in *PW* 205–6.

18 Diggins, *The Promise of Pragmatism*, 272.

19 Dewey develops this notion of an end-in-view in *TOV* and *HNC*.

20 By itself, then, the context-embeddedness of deliberation does not rule out, for example, natural-law views of human ends, which might simply hold that all rational ends-in-view are contextualized specifications of essential human goods. That abstractions are allowed and indeed indispensable despite contextuality is well argued by Onora O'Neill in *Towards Justice and Virtue* (Cambridge: Cambridge University Press, 1996).

Second, and somewhat more prescriptively, Dewey inveighs against ends that are wholly separate as well as remote in time from the context of action. He notes that both the idealist and the practical person fall prey to this error.

> The "idealist" sets up as the ideal not fullness of meaning of the present but a remote goal. Hence the present is evacuated of meaning. It is reduced to being a mere external instrument, an evil necessity due to the distance between us and significant valid satisfaction ...
>
> Meanwhile, the practical man wants something definite, tangible and presumably obtainable for which to work ... In his utopian search for a future good he neglects the only place where good can be found.[21]

Both utopianism and a fetish for "things" come under Dewey's censure, here. But how can an end not be separated from the context of action, as either a normative goal to be fulfilled or a thing to be obtained? Dewey's answer echoes Aristotle: the end, the "meaning," should be regarded as lying in the present activity itself. This is "activity" (*praxis*) in something like Aristotle's technical sense, undertaken for its own sake.[22] It is not required to neglect the future, but only to see it through the lens of present activity controlled by intelligence. In the case of someone building a house, for instance,

> the more he considers the future uses to which his house will probably be put the better he will do his present job which is the activity of building. Control of future living, such as it may turn out to be, is wholly dependent upon taking his present activity, seriously and devotedly, as an end, not as a means.[23]

Dewey should allow, then, that one might have a remote end, such as being able eventually to enjoy a peaceful retirement fishing from one's porch; it is just that present activity will not be rightly oriented towards this goal unless one undertakes that present activity as itself

---

21 *HNC* 274, *MW* 14:187–88.

22 Aristotle, *Nichomachean Ethics* 1139a35–b4. For good reason, Dewey departs from Aristotle in suggesting that even productive actions may be treated as activities valuable for their own sake: see *HNC* 271, *MW* 14:186.

23 *HNC* 269, *MW* 14:184.

meaningful. Intelligent activity will never be merely instrumental, will never be done solely for the sake of something else. Even if it is a means to a remote end, it will also be sought for its own sake, and in such a way that the remote end gets shaped by the meaning of present activity. Dewey's Aristotelian point here, therefore, gives additional depth to the dependence of ends upon the present context of action.

The first point is a general one about the contextuality of ends, while the second notes that actions that appear to be merely instrumental are properly understood as ends in their own right, and hence as activities in Aristotle's sense (*praxeis*). Each of these conclusions lends support to a third, which is that end and means ought to be revised in light of each other. An abstract goal needs to be understood in light of a context that sets the costs of ways of achieving it and suggests ways of achieving it. Means to an end are to be transformed, in context, by incorporating them into activity that is worth doing for its own sake. In the context of tenure, for instance, the writing of articles can be converted from being a mere means to job security to being an integral part of the disinterested search for truth, with the result that the articles themselves become less brash and more thoughtful (*can be*, I said). In this sense, end and means are on a "continuum" of mutual influence in deliberation: neither is cordoned off from the other in deliberation.[24]

I accused Dewey of using sophomoric rhetoric in attacking final ends. My reason should now be plain. If, with Aristotle, we understand a final end to be one sought for its own sake, it is clear that Dewey's conception of deliberation invokes final ends. The ones upon which he insists are those found in present activity; but so long as any further final ends are viewed from within the contextual point of view of worthwhile but temporarily frustrated activity, he says nothing to exclude them. If "final" in qualifying ends meant "not subject to revision," he would have a case against them; but this is not what "final" means in this context.

Why might Dewey have been led to trade on this bad pun, if that is what it is? The deeper reason, I think, is the widely shared tendency to

---

24 See my "Beyond Good and Right: Toward a Constructive Ethical Pragmatism," *Philosophy & Public Affairs* 24 (1995): 108–41.

conflate what I suggest we call "the order of finality" with the order of justification. The "order of finality" arises once we allow — as Dewey, in his resistance to there being just one end relevant to each deliberative problem, surely would — that we can iterate the relationship of seeking something for the sake of an end. In particular, qualitative distinctions arise involving chains of finality, of being sought for its own sake. For example, some ends-in-view are not final ends at all, as they are not sought for their own sakes. We sometimes, as Dewey notes, aim at the North Star not so as to get there but so as to travel north.[25] But even final ends can be chained. Thus, building a house, which, if I follow Dewey's advice, I will engage in as an activity choiceworthy in itself, I also pursue for the sake of producing a satisfactory house. The meaning of "a satisfactory house," Dewey insists, ought in turn to be analyzed by reference to the future activities that the architecture will enable and encourage. Thus, I pursue one activity as a final end but also for the sake of other activities I shall engage in as final ends. This possibility that a final end, sought for its own sake, might also be sought for the sake of something else was recognized and analyzed by Aristotle.

Now, Dewey claims that *all* ends are also means.[26] Since final ends may be chained, this claim does not imply that there are no final ends. It does, however, imply that there are no unqualifiedly final ends, as Aristotle would call them: ends sought *only* for their own sake. In particular, it implies that there is no "most final" or "ultimate" end (*telos teleiotatos*), which is an unqualifiedly final end unrivalled by any others.[27] Dewey has various grounds for resisting the claim that there is any ultimate end of human action. Some of his points are well taken and some not. The common conflation of finality and justification, which he employs, unfairly slops opprobrium over onto the notion of

---

25 *HNC* 226, *MW* 14:156.

26 *HNC* 226, *MW* 14:156.

27 I develop these distinctions more at length in *Practical Reasoning about Final Ends*, Section 7, and interpret the relevant text of Aristotle in "Degrees of Finality and the Highest Good in Aristotle," *Journal of the History of Philosophy* 30 (1992): 327–52.

an ultimate end. Many have mistakenly thought that if there is an ultimate end, it must be the source of all practical justification. Dewey, in particular, linked belief in an ultimate end to humankind's perennially misguided quest for certainty.[28] In another place, he declares that the idea of an end sought only for its own sake is empty, the vestige of belief in an end fixed by essential human nature and discoverable *a priori*.[29] Yet, as I have argued elsewhere, an end may be ultimate because it serves satisfactorily to regulate the manner and degree of all subordinate pursuits, even though the justification or establishment of this end draws holistically on many particular grounds.[30] Rightly understood, then, the idea of an ultimate end implies neither certain knowledge nor the possibility of *a priori* discovery. It is compatible with a pragmatist's strong fallibilism and experimentalism.

We should, accordingly, set aside all of Dewey's resistance to ultimate ends that derives from his mistakenly equating the order of justification with the order of finality. His remaining grounds for skepticism about the existence of an ultimate end are serious. They centre on his understanding of deliberation as proceeding from problematic aspects of ever-changing context. Although we may try to follow his advice and undertake our actions as activities worth doing for their own sakes, they will never reach a self-sufficient stasis of the kind described most vividly by the Stoics. "'Endless ends,'" he writes, "is a way of saying that there are no ends — that is[,] no fixed self-enclosed finalities."[31] Note, however, that this is a substantive claim, now, about the values in human life, rather than an analytic claim about the meaning of "final end." If there is no activity worth doing for its own sake and capable of rightly regulating all subordinate activities in a way that is stable against contextual perturbations, then there is no ultimate end. While these substantive claims provide some reason to doubt

---

28 *HNC* 236, *MW* 14:162.

29 *HNC* 223–24, *MW* 14:154–55.

30 I argue this point in *Practical Reasoning about Final Ends*, Part 4.

31 *HNC* 232, *MW* 14:159.

that there is any ultimate end, once we set aside mistaken claims we see that Dewey does not provide a conclusive case.

Accordingly, Dewey's analysis of deliberation, as arising out of a concrete context and as oriented to ends-in-view which ought to be understood in relation to present worthwhile activity, is not incompatible with a robust account of final ends. Indeed, the notion of worthwhile activity that it embeds depends upon the concept of a final end. While Dewey presents some independent grounds for doubting that there is any ultimate end, his account of deliberation could be developed in a direction that would allow robust enough deliberation about ends so that the possible existence even of an ultimate end could at least be a live question. In the next section, I will argue that good Deweyan pragmatists should welcome this sort of development.

III

There are many reasons that Dewey's pragmatism needs to be supplemented by a more robust account of deliberation about final ends. Some of these reasons are internal to his view, while some arise from external criticisms. All are connected to difficulties that stem from attempting to build normatively critical conclusions on an account of practical reasoning without drawing on reasoning about ends. The difficulties show up in Dewey's account of the good and in his moral theory, and have unfortunate consequences there as well as in his attitude towards political reform.

Dewey does seek to build on practical reasoning. A central theme of Dewey's pragmatism is his attempt to break down the traditional dichotomy between theoretical and practical reasoning. Scientific reasoning, on his understanding, must be understood in terms of science as a form of purposive activity. C.S. Peirce, the founder of pragmatism, insisted for this reason that the meaning of a statement must be found in the difference it makes to practice.[32] Similarly, for all of the

---

32 Cf. C.J. Misak, *Truth and the End of Inquiry* (Oxford: Oxford University Press, 1991), Chapter 1.

pragmatists, truth was to be understood in relation to our practices of inquiry. Even by those pragmatists (notably Peirce) whose account of truth idealized the practices of inquiry, truth was conceptually linked to the purposive human activity of inquiry. With his neo-Hegelian hostility to "dualisms," Dewey pushed the *rapprochement* of theoretical and practical reason the hardest, insisting that science serves human values and that ethical and political reasoning about human values must be scientific. This does not mean that he was a crude instrumentalist who equated what's true with what's pleasing to believe. For one thing, the pragmatists remained fallibilists who resisted any such sure formula for ascertaining truth.[33] For another, we have already seen that Dewey was no instrumentalist about practical reason. But we can say that, in an important sense, for Dewey all reasoning is practical reasoning. This overall pragmatist tenet is what makes Dewey's reticence about reasoning about final ends so awkward.

The dilemma that Dewey faces is simple. Let me summarize it abstractly before we look at some of its instances: he seeks to take a deeply critical stance, one with the potential of showing that existing desires or common actions or prevailing political institutions are bad or wrong. Having stressed the primacy of practical reason, it seems that he would need to refer to an ultimate end, or at least to higher-order final ends, in order to ground this criticism. The ground on which he rests does, indeed, seem to resemble an ultimate end as I have characterized one; Dewey, however, refuses to admit that it is. What, then, is the ground on which he stands? He never makes clear. This is one reason that he can be easily co-opted by Richard Rorty's more skeptical or relativist neo-pragmatism, which brags about having nowhere to stand.[34]

Dewey's account of the good presents the simplest case of this dilemma. In the first edition of his *Ethics* (1908), he is at pains to reject crudely hedonistic analyses of the good. He prefers desire-satisfaction accounts. Beyond that, he seeks, like the ancients, to discriminate between what is desired and what is desirable, between apparent happi-

---

33 Cf. Hilary Putnam, *Pragmatism* (Oxford: Blackwell, 1995), Lecture 1.

34 See, e.g., Richard Rorty, *The Consequences of Pragmatism* (Minneapolis: University of Minnesota Press, 1982).

ness and true happiness. He encourages individuals, as we have seen, to exercise their intelligence to determine what is worth seeking. Yet he also rejects subjectivism or relativism about the good. The good for any one individual is not to be equated with what he or she thinks is good. Accordingly, Dewey is pressed into giving an account of objective judgment about the good. He concludes this part of his discussion by raising a "final question":

> The final question of happiness, the question which marks off true and right happiness from false and wrong gratification, comes to this: Can there be found ends of action, desirable in themselves, which reenforce and expand not only the motives from which they directly spring, but also other tendencies and attitudes which are sources of happiness? Can there be found powers whose exercise confirms ends which are stable and weakens and removes objects which occasion only restless, peevish, or transitory satisfaction, and ultimately thwart and stunt the growth of happiness? Harmony, reenforcement, expansion are the signs of a true or moral satisfaction.[35]

What is it to be a "sign" of true or moral satisfaction? Let us postpone answering this question until we have considered the chapter "The Good of Activity" from Dewey's *Human Nature and Conduct*, published two decades later (1929). This chapter reflects a Hegelian's acrobatic ability to combine antithetical statements. Much of the chapter is devoted to castigating the view, which Dewey takes to have been exploded by the devastating experience of the Great War, that humanity is or ought to be oriented to "an exhaustive, stable, immutable end or good."[36] While he admits that his position puts him closer to an Epicurean hedonism than to the absolutist views of Plato, Aristotle, or Spinoza, he again insists on taking a more critical stance, on sorting among desired activities. Summing up his conclusions about this, he writes that "the welfare of others, like our own, consists in a widening and deepening of the perceptions that give activity its meaning, in an educative growth."[37] The point that I have to make about

---

35 Dewey, *Ethics* (1908): *MW* 5: 259.

36 *HNC* 287, *MW* 14:198.

37 *HNC* 293, *MW* 14:202.

Dewey's theory of the good is a simple one, and is indifferent as between this later, more educationally focused account and his earlier one centred on relations of mutual support among the objects of desire (among ends-in-view). It is that these notions play the role, in Dewey's theory, of an ultimate end. They stand as highest-order standards for the practical regulation of conduct, as the highest-level criteria of practical judgment.

Dewey clearly thought otherwise; but his reasons are mistaken. One of them I have already exposed: his saddling the idea of an ultimate end with the needless further assumption of *a priori* status. Another emerges from his discussion of the good. At one point he concedes that one might express his theory in terms of a "categorical imperative": "So act as to increase the meaning of present experience." But this formula, he insists, is "sterile," and has no concrete implications unless it is supplemented by situational knowledge.[38] The formula, nonetheless, is not wholly empty; and if we add the elements of harmony and mutual reinforcement more potential implications for practice are added. If an ultimate end had to serve as a sufficient basis for generating a decision procedure to decide concrete cases, then this could not be an ultimate end; but there is no need to demand this. An ultimate end can orient and regulate a system of subordinate final ends that help, in conjunction with situational facts, to provide guidance for action.[39]

The dilemma for Dewey, here, is this: he must either admit that he has contradicted his denial of any possible role for ultimate ends or else depart from the pragmatist's primacy of practical reason. How might the latter move work? On what footing might harmony, mutual reinforcement, and growth be defended, if not on a practical one? There are various philosophical possibilities. One which has been attributed to Dewey is to rely upon the distinction between analytic claims about ethical concepts and synthetic claims about that to which they apply. One might treat Dewey as offering an analysis of "good" that was meant to compete directly with, say, Stevenson's emotivist analysis.

---

38 *HNC* 283, *MW* 14:196.

39 See my "Degrees of Finality and the Highest Good in Aristotle" for an interpretation of the *Nicomachean Ethics* along these lines.

"Good" might be equated with "would be desired by an intelligent person mindful of the relations of mutual support among her ends and of the potential for future growth."[40] But accepting the analytic/synthetic dualism would compound the general break with the pragmatist spirit caused by separating out a purely theoretical basis for the criterion of ethical judgment.[41]

A similar dilemma for Dewey reappears at the next level of his theory, that of ethics proper. Dewey's answer to his own "final question" as to whether anything bears the marks of true happiness is that the "social good" does. Thus arises, at the heart of his ethical theory, an immediate and intimate connection between the individual good and the social good. How is this connection established? Axel Honneth has recently pursued this question probingly, and has persuasively argued that Dewey never resolves a tension in his view between a more Kantian approach, according to which such a result might derive from procedural constraints on practical reasoning, and a more Aristotelian approach, according to which it would flow from natural teleology.[42] A Kantian transcendental argument, like an appeal to the analysis of ethical concepts, would mark a departure from pragmatism, while an open embrace of Aristotelian teleology would contradict Dewey's rejection of ultimate ends. It is no wonder that this tension remains unresolved.[43]

Unable to admit that he was defending a pragmatic account of the ultimate end of human action, Dewey faltered in providing concrete

---

40 I modify the sort of interpretive suggestion made by James Rachels in "Dewey and the Truth about Ethics," in *New Studies in the Philosophy of John Dewey*, ed. Steven M. Cahn (Hanover: University Press of New England, 1977), 149–71.

41 Dewey himself was hostile to the linguistic turn of mid-century Anglo-American philosophy. Cf. Jennifer Welchman, *Dewey's Ethical Thought* (Ithaca: Cornell University Press, 1995), 1.

42 Axel Honneth, "Between Proceduralism and Teleology: An Unresolved Conflict in Dewey's Moral Theory," *Transactions of the Charles S. Peirce Society* 34 (1998): 689–711.

43 Dewey's reluctance to admit any role for ultimate ends thus explains why he was not able to embrace the sort of "constructive ethical pragmatism" for which I argue in "Beyond Good and Right."

guidance for practice. The apostle of attending to the specifics of situation was remarkably unspecific and vacillating in his ethical and political advice. Nor was this simply because he wasn't good at giving it. Start with the individual good. Unwilling to treat harmony, growth, or mutual reinforcement as constituent elements of a complex ultimate end, Dewey never developed a strong basis for the criticism of desires. He was not interested in producing a modern counterpart of the classical theory of virtue. In ethics proper, his vagueness about the good translated into a lax optimism about the coincidence of individual and social good. He rests too much weight on what "intelligent" people will think, and too little on the substantive theory of the human good. In his politics may be seen two further unfortunate corollaries of his inability to face his implicit commitment to a conception of an ultimate end. First, his resistance to developing a strongly critical theory of virtue prevented him from making any place in his view for anything like a classical republican theory of civic virtue. Second, his vacillation between more procedural and more substantive ethical approaches had its parallel in his wavering between radically reformist stances in politics and his relatively optimistic and complacent embrace of technical expertise in the making of policy.[44]

Dewey's inability to confront the dilemma that pits his resistance to the notion of an ultimate end against his overall pragmatism, therefore, had serious repercussions for his ability to follow through on the promise of that pragmatism by constructively addressing practical problems. As I hope to show in later sections, it also undercut the presentation of his views about truth. The question for a present-day Deweyan, then, is how better to respond to this dilemma.

IV

I will be arguing that a Deweyan pragmatist's best response to the dilemma posed by his reluctant reliance on a conception of an ultimate end would be to develop a more robust account of deliberation about

---

44 The tensions mentioned in this paragraph are well set out by Diggins.

ends and to incorporate an explicit role for final and ultimate ends in practical inquiry. Since this proposal may seem needlessly radical, let me first devote this section to describing a more concessive response, one that a pragmatist should, ultimately, find unsatisfactory.

This alternative response has two parts. It begins by noticing that Dewey's forte is to characterize the process and procedures of inquiry. Dewey would contradict himself if he embraced final and ultimate ends. Accordingly, this line of thought would go, let his talk about harmony, mutual reinforcement, and growth be counted as suggestions for the continuing process of deliberation rather than as substantive recommendations for how one ought to live. After all, it might be argued, one cannot claim both that it is rational to pursue those ends upon which intelligence will decide *and* that intelligence is to be defined by reference to certain final ends. Harmony and coherence must have a status as something besides ends on a view that gives reasoning as broad a role as does Dewey. If they were treated as ends, then one would indeed have a regress of ends.[45] Accordingly, they must be given a basis that counts them as defining elements of rational procedure rather than themselves as ends.

This point about establishing the importance of harmony, mutual reinforcement, and growth is a deep and serious one. Although this is not the place to attack its presuppositions, let me just note that at work, here, is again the conflation of the order of justification and the order of finality.[46] Many, however, will persist in taking this methodological worry seriously. For them, the more concessive response to Dewey's dilemma about ends will have the added attraction of setting this worry to rest.

---

45 I am indebted to Elijah Millgram for the thought in this paragraph. See also James Dreier, "Humean Doubts about the Practical Justification of Morality," in *Ethics and Practical Reason*, eds. Garrett Cullity and Berys Gaut (Oxford: Oxford University Press, 1997), 81–99.

46 I develop the case against the presuppositions of this worry in *Practical Reasoning about Final Ends*, Sections 20 and 29, in the course of defending the importance of coherence.

The response, then, would concede on Dewey's behalf that his account of inquiry is simply an account of *how* we ought to think and deliberate, one that makes no attempt to legislate *what* we ought to think or do.[47] On this interpretation, we should not be surprised that Dewey does not clearly set out what the individual good is, that he is vague about the moral principles he supports, or that he vacillates regarding particular political reforms. We should not expect him to concentrate on taking such stands. Rather, we should recognize that he is simply trying to inspire us to think about these matters in a way that would enable us to integrate scientific method with practical commitment. To arrive at a view about *what* to do, the second part of this concessive response holds, we need to supplement Dewey's account of rational procedure with final ends drawn from some other source.

This two-part response is not my invention. It was more or less the approach taken by political thinker Walter Lippmann.[48] In his youth a protege of William James, Lippmann wrote books which initially exuded a pragmatist's confidence in the liberating and empowering potential of science. In the aftermath of the First World War, however, Lippmann's tone became more somber and contemplative. He came to believe that the principles underpinning legitimate government and civility among individuals required a firmer basis than could be provided by the pragmatists' procedures of inquiry. Without rejecting those, he turned to natural law for a grounding of these principles and to Plato and Aristotle for a conception of the human essence purportedly capable of grounding objective final ends.

Does this supplementation of Dewey amount to a total transformation? There is at least one later essay in which he indicates that it was never his ambition to extend his pragmatist understanding of truth to practical commitments such as final ends. While this essay takes a noncognitivist line — quite the opposite of a natural law position — it does at least draw a distinction, a dualism, if you will, between facts

---

47 Dewey's tendency to proceduralism is emphasized by, e.g., Diggins, *The Promise of Pragmatism*, and Honneth, "Between Proceduralism and Teleology."

48 I draw my description of Lippmann from Diggins, *The Promise of Pragmatism*, esp. 331–42.

and values, of the kind that the two-part response exploits. In "Philosophy and Civilization" (1927), he wrote:

> Meaning is wider in scope as well as more precious in value than is truth, and philosophy is occupied with meaning rather than with truth. Making such a statement is dangerous; it is easily misconceived to signify that truth is of no great importance under any circumstances; while the fact is that truth is so infinitely important when it is important at all, namely in records of events and descriptions of circumstances, that we extend its claims to regions where it has no jurisdiction.[49]

In its concern with meaning, Dewey here wrote, philosophy is forward looking rather than backward looking. It is concerned with "prophecies rather than records," prophecies that "proclaim that such and such *should* be the significant value to which mankind should loyally attach itself."[50] In light of Dewey's lifelong attempt to reconcile science and values, this non-cognitivist passage is astonishing. For the friend of ethical objectivity, the two-part concessive response to the dilemma about ends offers a way to limit the damage that this split between description and prescription, records and prophecy, threatens. Dewey would at least have given us a unified method of inquiry, substantively anchored on the descriptive side by experiment, substantively grounded on the prescriptive side by natural law.

From the characterization of pragmatism that I have given above, however, it should be plain that I consider this two-part view a complete abandonment of pragmatism's most exciting project, its unified account of reasoning, which invests primacy in practical reason and assures a place for truth throughout by means of a thorough-going fallibilism. Accordingly, there is strong reason for a Deweyan pragmatist to resist this response if another is available that is more compatible with this central project. There is, and it is built around keeping that project centre stage rather than hidden in the wings.

---

49 *PW* 33.

50 Ibid., 35.

V

The more pragmatist response to Dewey's dilemma about ends employs his understanding of inquiry as action in order to develop a more robust account of deliberation about final ends. Doing so will require moving in a direction directly counter to the non-cognitivism discussed in the last section. It will mean taking truth to be of "infinite importance," or at least central importance, in future-oriented deliberation as well as in backward-looking description. Indeed, the crucial move will be to recognize that deliberation about ends extends to deliberation about truth, considered as the end of inquiry. I will develop this response dialectically. I start by taking more seriously than is usual the pragmatist idea that inquiry is a mode of action. This implies that it is oriented by some end or ends. The overall end of inquiry is truth. Yet how can this end be conceived as anything other than a fixed and remote ultimate end, of the kind that Dewey most wanted to avoid? The answer, the pragmatist should insist, is that there is room deliberatively to specify the end of truth and that we must remain open to doing so anew. This section will first set out these steps in the abstract. It will then proceed to show how this conception resolves some perennial problems that dog the pragmatist theory of truth. The final section will explain how this conception would allow a Deweyan pragmatist to avoid a technocratic approach to politics.

While it is obvious that inquiry is a mode of human cooperative activity, it is not so obvious what the significance of this fact is for philosophical reconstructions of truth and knowledge. Hilary Putnam brings out an initial aspect of this significance. Putnam usefully contrasts Peirce's and Dewey's conceptions of inquiry, which emphasize the active, experimental manipulation of the environment, with Carnap's more logicized notion:

> Scientific theories are confirmed by "evidence", in Carnap's systems of inductive logic, but it is immaterial (that is to say, there is no way to represent the difference in the formalism) whether that evidence — those "observation sentences" — is obtained as a result of intelligently directed experimentation, or it just happens to be available ... Fundamentally, the standpoint is that of a single isolated spectator who makes observations through a one-way mirror and writes down observation sentences.

Dewey's and Peirce's views of inquiry, Putnam notes, contrast on both counts: they emphasize intelligent interaction with the environment and cooperation within a community of inquirers. Whereas Carnap's approach leads to modelling the scientific method as the computation of a function, the approach shared by Peirce and Dewey resists any such abstraction away from real interaction among human beings.[51] In the final section, I will return to the cooperative aspect of inquiry. For now, I concentrate on the point that inquiry is active.

As Dewey put it in his *Logic*:

> All controlled inquiry and all institution of grounded assertion necessarily contains a *practical* factor; an activity of doing and making which reshapes antecedent existential material which sets the problem of inquiry.[52]

We should not overinterpret this role for experiment in Peirce and Dewey. It is not that they advocated turning every exercise in government policy-making, for instance, into an opportunity for controlled experimentation. As a recent commentator points out, for the early Dewey, at least, "experiment" was roughly a synonym for "experience."[53] Yet the fact remains that his conception of experience builds in a more active aspect than does a view like Carnap's. As Dewey wrote,

> Experience in its vital form is experimental, an effort to change the given; it is characterized by a projection, by reaching forward into the unknown; connection with a future is its salient point.[54]

Thus, inquiry is no passive palimpsest that merely records the passing show. Like all human action, it is a future-directed and active effort.

---

51 Putnam, *Pragmatism*, 69–70.

52 Dewey, *Logic* 160, *LW* 12:162; emphasis Dewey's.

53 Welchman, *Dewey's Ethical Thought*, note 5.

54 Dewey, *Creative Intelligence: Essays in the Pragmatic Attitude* (New York: Rhinehart, 1945 [1917]), 7; as quoted in Diggins, *The Promise of Pragmatism*, 262f.

These observations about inquiry return us to a slogan for the more pragmatist solution to Dewey's dilemma about final ends that I am now beginning to unfold. It is this: all reasoning is practical reasoning. This is not simply because, as Putnam has emphasized, theoretical inquiry constitutively contains normative commitments, and hence blends the cognitive and the conative. It is also because theoretical or scientific inquiry is a mode of practical activity, reaching forward and changing the world. Accordingly, it also blends the receptive and the directive.[55]

While this latter point may be disputable as regards Peirce, it is central in Dewey. A cardinal theme of the latter's "instrumentalism" is the directive aspect of all inquiry. As Diggins puts it:

> Whereas [James] maintained that inquiry arises from an state of psychological tension and culminates in a new state of belief, Dewey insisted that inquiry aims to alter not only mental states but actual conditions, and it does so by rendering an "indeterminate situation" determinate in order to achieve not only emotional comfort but intelligent control. Unlike James, Dewey became interested in knowledge that could contribute to a public good and not only individual success; unlike Peirce, he saw the thinker moved to inquiry not only by an "irritation of doubt" but also by an encounter with a "problematic situation" whose resolution required cooperative effort.[56]

The last point is worth highlighting: to the facts that inquiry is active and directed towards the future, we must add that it also arises out of concrete problems in just the way that all deliberative problems do. If so, then inquiries will have ends-in-view.

From the fact that each episode of inquiry has an end, it does not follow that there is one end shared by all episodes of inquiry. Nonetheless, it is traditional to think that inquiry does have an overall end, one which helps mark it off from other sorts of activity. While it is not,

---

55 This pair of distinctions is well laid out by J. David Velleman, "The Possibility of Practical Reason," *Ethics* 106 (1996): 694–726, note 721. Velleman's lucid article spurred my thinking at many points, often ones at which I disagree with him.

56 Diggins, *The Promise of Pragmatism*, 227, citing Dewey, *Experience and Nature*, 87–89, and *The Logic of Inquiry* (New York, 1938), 8.

indeed, an ultimate end, it is a strongly regulative one. Seeing how this final end functions in pragmatist inquiry will facilitate our attempt to resolve Dewey's dilemma by integrating within his view a robust account of deliberation about final ends. This account of deliberation will remain at once truly cognitive in its orientation and deeply pragmatist. The final end toward which inquiry is oriented is truth.[57] This orientation helps differentiate inquiry from other types of practical activity, such as playing charades or splitting wood. This is not to say that inquiry may be usefully *defined* as activity directed towards truth, any more than chess may be usefully defined as a game directed towards checkmate (for what is checkmate?). Nonetheless, an orientation towards truth is as characteristic of inquiry as an orientation towards checkmate is of playing chess.

Dewey did not always give prominence to truth, sometimes shifting to "warranted assertability."[58] Then again, he also, as we have seen, shied away in general from talk about regulative ends. We have seen in general why the latter stance was a mistake. I suggest that his occasional reluctance to talk about truth was also a mistake, one stemming from his not having seen how openness to deliberation about the end of truth presents an alternative to both correspondence and coherence views.

In order to arrive at an understanding of this third alternative, we need first to discuss how it is that truth can function as a final end for inquiry. After all, it is fatuous to say, "I aim to arrive at true beliefs and nothing but true beliefs." Sure, you do; but how will you act so as to

---

57 I say "truth" rather than "truths" or "true beliefs" in order to signal that the idea of truth has some structure, to which I will come shortly. The aim is not a quantitative one of amassing atomistic truths. The role of this end is rather that of orienting and regulating than of describing something to be maximized. For parallel reasons, I would speak of "the good" rather than "good actions." On the regulative function of final ends, see my *Practical Reasoning about Final Ends*, Section 7.

58 Cf. Diggins, *The Promise of Pragmatism*, 229. I give conceptual (not textual) grounds, below, for thinking that a good Deweyan would not elide truth with that of which the evidence warrants the assertion.

achieve that aim? How may we conceive of truth, such that it could function as the end of the practical activity of inquiry? It is on its way to answering this question, as Dewey rightly perceived, that the traditional conception of truth as correspondence falls flat on its face. Perhaps — the point is disputed — we can meaningfully conceive of an object, the True, to which successful belief corresponds. We cannot, however, meaningfully construct a relationship between any particular truth and any part of that object.[59] Accordingly, the philosopher's idea of correspondence cannot offer any practical guidance to the concrete inquirer. But this is to say that truth understood as correspondence with reality cannot function as a final end for practical reasoning.

A coherence account of truth fares no better. To make this point vivid, let us consider a caricature of Peirce's view of truth, which we may take to be the relevant form of a coherence view. This identification is a shortcut, one that makes immediately apparent what might be shown by a longer route, namely that "coherence" is no simple idea, logically definable apart from context and from our practices. Rather, it is a complex idea meaningfully definable only within a set of practices of inquiry. The cartoon Peirce, then, defines truth as that result to which an idealized set of inquirers would, with infinite time, converge. (This proposal does violence to Peirce, who refrained from *defining* truth in this way. Rather, he offered his account as a *partial* analysis of the notion.[60] The proposal does, however, well represent the spirit of coherence theories of truth.) Now we can again ask whether truth-as-coherence, so understood, can serve as the final end that differentiates inquiry from other forms of activity. The answer is no, for its characterization depends upon a prior understanding of inquiry. If we attempted to cast truth, so interpreted, as the end of inquiry, we would be putting forward what Velleman has called a merely "formal aim" of the activity. As he notes, the "conception of truth as the eventual

---

59 Cf., e.g., Hilary Putnam, "Realism and Reason," in *Meaning and the Moral Sciences* (Boston: Routledge & Kegan Paul, 1978), 123–40; Donald Davidson, "The Structure and Content of Truth," *Journal of Philosophy* 87 (1990): 279–328.

60 This point is well set out by C.J. Misak in *Truth and the End of Inquiry*.

deliverance of rational activity ... renders theoretical reasoning vacuous, like a [competitive] game whose only object is winning."[61]

Dewey's understanding of practical reasoning suggests a specifically pragmatist understanding of truth. Although it is neither a correspondence nor a coherence theory, setting it out requires combining the elements of correspondence and of coherence in the right way. The decisive objection to coherence theories is that they understate our fallibility, for there is no characterization of coherence which blocks the possibility of untruth. The decisive objection to correspondence theories is that because we have no theory-independent access to the facts or the world, there is no meaningful way to characterize the relation of correspondence on which they rely. The pragmatist understanding of truth that emerges from our present discussion avoids both of these problems, for it neither puts forward a final epistemic ideal nor avoids doing so by positing an object to which truths mysteriously correspond. Instead, the pragmatist inquirer seeks (1) to get things right, but recognizes that to reduce the indeterminacy of this aim, she must also (2) be open to specifying the aim of truth by reference to epistemic or coherence desiderata. In order not to fall back into the coherentist camp, however, she must insist on her fallibility with regard to her specification of the end of truth. That is, she must also aim (3) to get the specification of the aim of truth right. At step (1), the truth enters as an end or object, but merely in a formal way that does not yet exclude either correspondence or coherence readings. The idea of specifying truth at (2) does exclude correspondence theories by introducing a constitutive epistemic element; but the openness to further specification at (3) in turn departs from coherence theory and restores the aspect of fallibility which, correspondence theorists charge, the coherence theorist forgets. This pragmatist is, in short, both a cognitivist and a fallibilist all the way down.[62]

---

61 Velleman, "The Possibility of Practical Reason," note 706. Velleman is confident that truth, otherwise understood, can serve as a substantive end for theoretical reasoning. He does not, however, explain his alternative interpretation of truth.

62 In *Pragmatism*, 20f., Putnam suggests that this combination of anti-scepticism and fallibilism is pragmatism's most distinctive feature.

Truth may be conceived as the regulative end of the activity of inquiry without truth thereby becoming cast in stone or erected as a fixed or remote end. It remains possible to re-specify this end of inquiry in light of reasons that arise in some particular context of action. As Dewey writes, truth has,

> like all genuine ideals, a limiting and directive force. But in order to exercise [its] genuine function [it] must be taken as [a] reminder [...] of the concrete conditions and operations that have to be satisfied in actual cases. In serving as such [a] generalized instrument [...], [its] meaning is exemplified in [its] use. The *abstract* meaning of *truth*, of *being* true, for example, has changed with the development of experimental inquiry.[63]

Let me explain. One may begin with an interpretation of the end of truth along roughly the following lines: the inquirer ought to aim at results that cohere with the other things that we know about the world and are supported by our best research methods. A particular effort at inquiry, however, may generate particular reasons for revising what we had held about the world (and not just on the open question that was the subject of the inquiry), what we consider a proper method of research, or how we understand coherence. Consonantly with the pragmatist's general emphasis on revisability, any of these modes of revision should be allowed.

As I have argued elsewhere, specifying of ends in light of more concrete commitments is an important way that rational deliberation may extend to establishing final ends, to ultimate ends.[64] This is possible even for ends regulative of a whole domain of activity, as we will easily see so long as we keep in mind the distinction between the order of finality and the order of justification. While an end may be regulative of a whole domain, its justification, and hence its possible revision, may hang on more concrete considerations. To take an analogy: while the goal of success may regulate a domain of individual business executives' actions, the specification of success might reasonably shift in

---

63 Dewey, *Logic* 178, *LW* 12:179; emphasis Dewey's.

64 *Practical Reasoning about Final Ends*, esp. Chapters 4 and 10.

response to changes in the concrete possibilities for arranging daycare for those executives' children.

It may be objected that truth is a primitive, and such a fundamental one that it is silly to speak of specifying it. For the same reason, some may also doubt that it can serve as the end of any practical activity, as it is too abstract and general an object at which to aim. In response to these worries, an analogy may help. My comparison is to the role of happiness, *eudaimonia*, in Aristotle's *Nicomachean Ethics*. Similar worries have been raised about this end. Some doubt that it can serve to orient practical deliberation at all.[65] Others deny that it is open to continual specification, and instead insist that the deliberation that it leaves open is narrowly instrumental.[66] Contrary to both these views, I would support a picture of what goes on in the *N.E.* according to which Aristotle begins by identifying "happiness" as the label for the ultimate end, and then proceeds, throughout the body of that work, to specify its content, first by listing the virtues of character that are necessary components of happiness and then (in Book X) by characterizing the good of contemplative activity that is to regulate this overall package of virtues within a happy life.[67] Happiness, on this reading of Aristotle, is a complete life in which the virtues of character are actualized in such a way that contemplative activity is well served. This process of specifying the end of happiness represents a way of proceeding that is far more attractive and fruitful than that of many present-day consequentialists, who do take "happiness" (or "welfare") as a primitive that they are unwilling or unable to specify and go on to derive implications from this fixed but abstract end.[68] Aristotle's own results in the *N.E.*, on the picture I have so briefly just sketched, illustrate what

---

65 Cf. Sarah Broadie, *Ethics with Aristotle* (New York: Oxford University Press, 1991), 198. I criticize Broadie's view in *Practical Reasoning about Final Ends*, 194, 217.

66 See note 9 above.

67 I defend this interpretation of the *N.E.* in "Degrees of Finality and the Highest Good in Aristotle."

68 I defend this judgment in "Beyond Good and Right."

can be accomplished via taking such an abstract aim as a regulative end to be specified.[69]

Much the same structure could apply to the specification of the end of truth. Instead of the virtues of character as elements of a conception of happiness, we have various intellectual virtues (or cognitive desiderata) as elements of a working conception of truth. For the practical purpose of guiding inquiry, in other words, truth will be understood as cohering with most of what else we (think we) know, as being simple enough to be graspable by human expressive capacities, and so on. We thus arrive at a picture of what Putnam has called "human cognitive flourishing."[70] Yet there is also an analogue to Aristotle's Book X contemplation, the component end that is *primus inter pares*. The cognitive aim that plays this role is the practical counterpart of the correspondence idea, namely, the general ideal of fidelity to the facts. This functions, within inquiry, to require the participant to be flexible enough to consider revising any previous conclusion that one may come to have reason to abandon or shift, and even to revise one's conception of evidence or justification (for this reason, this ideal of fidelity to the facts cannot be equated with that of fitting with the evidence). We know that various cognitive ends (simplicity, elegance, coherence, and so on) need to be specified and woven together to define a conception of inquiry. The picture I have just sketched, which involves specifying the cognitive ends that shape the way truth is concretely understood and specifying their relative place within the overall aim of inquiry, provides a basis for saying that when cognitive ends are specified, truth is specified.[71]

One more point on the basis of the analogy with Aristotle's ethics. In the pragmatist conception that I am sketching, there would be as

---

69 That the specification could have been undertaken in a practical setting, and not just in the philosopher's armchair, I argue in *Practical Reasoning about Final Ends*, Section 32.

70 Hilary Putnam, *Reason, Truth, and History* (Cambridge: Cambridge University Press, 1981), 134.

71 I here aim to close a gap in the argument of *Practical Reasoning about Final Ends*, at p. 267.

little sense in asking whether truth is "really" coherence or "really" correspondence as there is in asking, about Aristotelian right action, whether it is "really" the action that would flow from good character or the action that would be discerned as such by practical wisdom. The answer, in Aristotle, is that right action is action that proceeds from good character in the way in which the person of practical wisdom would modulate it. On the pragmatist interpretation of truth that I propose, to aim at truth is to aim at exercising the cognitive virtues in a way that is throughout responsive to the facts, or to such considerations as arise.

Armed with this conception of truth as an end subject to constant re-specification, the pragmatist can steer between the rocks of skepticism and positivism.[72] Skepticism, at least of some kinds, may be avoided, as there is some basis on which to state standards of inquiry, namely the various cognitive virtues that are supported by our present practices of inquiry. Positivism, of the kind typified by Carnap, Popper, and their followers, may also be avoided, for this provisional account of rationality is explicitly not erected as a final criterion of truth. Rather, the "correspondence" element, the virtue of fidelity to the facts, blocks any suggestion that the working conception of truth, interpreted in terms of the other cognitive virtues, provides us with anything like a decision procedure or method of computation.

By the same token, this complex interpretation of truth would enable the pragmatist to avoid two further, related traps. One is the trap of a crude relativism that would flow from conjoining a criterial conception of rationality (the cognitive virtues as criterial of truth) with the observation that in different cultures, or on different sides of a "paradigm shift," different sets of cognitive virtues reign. In resisting this picture, the pragmatist may appeal to the catch-all virtue of fidelity to highlight what remains fixed even across deep shifts of paradigm or deep cultural differences. This is not to say that what remains fixed will *be* some precise understanding of this umbrella virtue, only that whatever continuities that may exist may be ranged under that

---

72 My thoughts in this paragraph owe a long-term debt to Putnam's *Reason, Truth, and History*.

virtue. Instead of a relativism to two hermetically isolated set of criteria, we will end up with a — perhaps difficult — disagreement about how best to specify the end of inquiry. The last trap that this hybrid understanding of the end of truth allows us to avoid is that of crude instrumentalism. This is the sort of misunderstanding of Dewey and his pragmatism that was long rife: truth, it was thought, was equated by the pragmatists with whatever works. (Never mind that they never said, precisely, what it is for something to "work"!) As an antidote to such misunderstandings, the present proposal, instead of casting truth as a highly abstract but fixed end remote from the continuum of end-means, regards truth as an end subject to revision. While other practical considerations may enter into its precise specification, the principal elements in the conception of truth are the cognitive virtues. Inquiry is action, and aims at success, but success at inquiry is essentially different from success at charades or wood-splitting.

Many contemporary philosophers will object to this loose talk about the interpretation of truth, for they do regard truth as a formal primitive, and one that could be wholly dispensed with were it not for its usefulness in application to a whole range of sentences (as in "Everything Joe said just now was true").[73] But the pragmatist understanding of inquiry as action points us to a countervailing piece of linguistic evidence. Ordinary usage distinguishes between the conversational implications of the following two statements:

(1)   "We should not pass this piece of legislation."

and

(2)   "It is true that we should not pass this piece of legislation."

I concede that these two statements are semantically equivalent. Notice, however, that in conversational context one would expect (2), but not (1), to be said concessively ("It is true ..., but ..."). What is being conceded? That there is some reason, some (at a minimum) intersubjectively cognizable reason that the legislation should not be

---

73 See, e.g., Paul Horwich, *Truth* (Oxford: Basil Blackwell, 1990).

passed. The second statement is thus put forward as a move in a practice of giving and accepting reasons (to use Brandom's phrase).[74] In implicitly recognizing the existence of competing considerations, such a statement is less conclusory, and more open to rebuttal and the possibility of error, than is (1). The first statement, by contrast, has no such connotation of reason-giving, and could well be put forward sincerely by someone who did not believe that such statements have truth values.

These facts about the linguistic role of "true" have perhaps been overlooked by philosophers who have focused solely on semantics and ignored the pragmatics of inquiry. "Truth," as an end of inquiry, plays just this practical role of underlining our ever-present fallibility. That is why its component virtue of fidelity to the facts, or responsiveness to such reasons as may arise, requires an openness to re-specifying even our working understanding of the component cognitive virtues of well-conducted inquiry.

I suggest that this is a fact about our practices of inquiry, that they are oriented to truth in just this way. If I am right, we will get no handle on the question whether our practices of inquiry ought to be open about our commitment to this revisability, too — whether we ought to be willing to revise our commitment to revisability in light of reasons. This question is philosophically nice, but effectively unanswerable. I set out on this path of argument by considering how the end of truth might help differentiate the activity of inquiry from other activities; but of course we cannot begin this enterprise unless we already know a lot about what inquiry is.

VI

We have arrived at this pragmatist understanding of truth as the end of inquiry by emphasizing one side of Dewey, a side which offers the materials better to resolve the difficulties about the good, about ethics,

---

74 Robert B. Brandom, *Making It Explicit: Reasoning, Representing, and Discursive Commitment* (Cambridge, MA: Harvard University Press, 1994), xiv and passim.

and about politics into which he fell on account of his inhospitality to deliberation about final ends. Since I have sketched such a constructively pragmatist approach to ethics elsewhere,[75] I will here set out how this could work for politics. Since I haven't space to push from these abstractly philosophical considerations all the way to concrete political advice, I will instead concentrate on showing how Dewey could avoid the charge of technocracy I mentioned at the outset of this essay. While my suggestions will remain procedural, the procedures I sketch have a better chance at yielding concrete results than did Dewey's own. His main obstacle in this regard was this: while he consistently emphasized that political inquiry should be undertaken in a pragmatic spirit, with an active effort to project future consequences and to judge what would be the best option, he steadfastly refrained from saying anything about the final ends of politics. Instead, he wrote vaguely about "success." This vagueness seemed to leave the door invitingly open for narrowly instrumentalist forms of policy reasoning. These provide some schematic, but fixed, interpretation of "success" such as the maximization of wealth or of preference satisfaction, and interpret the weighing of consequences as a measurement of their score according to that index. In short, Dewey seemed to welcome through the back door a form of narrowly instrumental reasoning that he officially despised.

The unified conception of inquiry sketched in the last section provides a way of retaining the vague talk about success while resisting this narrow instrumentalism. The core idea of that conception was that inquiry is practical activity oriented towards the end of truth. Contrary to what this formula might seem to imply, this does not convert inquiry into a narrowly instrumental activity, for the bare end of truth does not suffice to guide action, while the commitment to fallibilism that orientation to truth involves implies that one must remain open to re-specifying it. This inquiring attitude will, in turn, factor through one's other final ends: as an inquirer, one should remain open to reconceiving them should reasons for doing so arise. For this reason,

---

75 See my "Beyond Good and Right."

then, taking political deliberation seriously as a form of inquiry will discourage viewing it as narrowly instrumental.

Does it make sense to view political decision-making as a form of collective inquiry? There are strong reasons to think that the ideals of democracy, at least, require understanding politics as involving joint deliberation, in which mutual exchange of reasons and collective judgment over alternatives, rather than merely the pulling and tugging of forces, are determinative of collective decisions.[76] Further, it is, I think, needful and possible for us jointly to deliberate about the ends of policy, even under conditions of pluralism.[77]

Dewey himself wavered on these questions. Resistant, as he was, to seeing an important role for final ends, he did not always describe truth as the end of practical inquiry. As in the non-cognitivist moment mentioned in Section IV, he sometimes spoke of truth as the end of inquiry, the good as the end of conduct, and the beautiful as the end of creation — seemingly implying that truth is not the end of practical deliberation.[78] We have seen, however, that this non-cognitivist moment ought to be rejected in favour of a more unified, more pragmatist understanding of inquiry as activity. I have also mentioned that in relation to that activity, truth is not an ultimate end, but only a strongly regulative final end. This is because, like any activity, it must be somewhat sensitive to the other demands on our time and resources and to the other final ends to which we are committed. Truth, then, on the sort of Aristotelian possibility mentioned in the last section, would be an element of the good; and practical

---

76 See, e.g., Joshua Cohen, "An Epistemic Conception of Democracy," *Ethics* 97 (October 1986): 26-38; Jürgen Habermas, *Between Facts and Norms*, trans. W. Rehg (Cambridge, MA: MIT Press, 1996); David Estlund, "Who's Afraid of Deliberative Democracy? On the Strategic/deliberative Dichotomy in Recent Constitutional Jurisprudence," *Texas Law Review* 71 (1993): 1437-77; and my "Democratic Intentions," in *Deliberative Democracy*, eds. J. Bohman and W. Rehg (Cambridge, MA: MIT Press, 1997) 349-82.

77 I defend this claim in "Democratic Deliberation about Final Ends," in progress.

78 Dewey, *Logic* 178, *LW* 12:179.

deliberation, or deliberation about conduct, would be distinctive in taking the whole good as its concern.[79] Nonetheless, as inquiry, practical deliberation would remain oriented towards the truth, the truth about what ought to be done or, in politics, the truth about the public good. On this constructively pragmatist view, then, an important task of public deliberation will be continually to try to provide better specifications of the schematic aim, the public good. This is not the central task of this deliberation, which is, rather, to resolve the various concrete problems that arise. It is, nonetheless, an inescapable job that must be accomplished on the way to fulfilling this concrete role.

While the philosophical contrast between instrumental reasoning and reasoning about ends provided one support for the suspicion that Dewey was drawn to a technocratic conception of policy-making, another is the more institutionally focused worry about his willingness to welcome an army of social science experts into democratic dialogue. Thus, when he writes, movingly, that *"the* problem of the public" is "the improvement of the methods and conditions of debate, discussion, and persuasion," he does so in the middle of a discussion of the role of policy experts. Not only does he not reject them: he hangs his hopes on them. The improvements of which he there writes mainly involve increased awareness on the part of the experts of the needs and interests of the citizenry. Without an important place for deliberation about ends, this looks to be a form of technocracy, albeit a beneficent one. He writes that the crucial expertise needed "is not shown in framing and executing policies, but in discovering and making known the facts upon which the former depend."[80]

Yet there is no reason to resist this role for experts within a democracy, so long as their work is not seen as sufficient to provide the minor premise (the premise of the possible) to complete some practical syllogism that begins with some fixed policy end (the premise of the good). And Dewey insists in these same pages that any such

---

79 Compare Dewey's view of the social good as the "substance" of the most inclusive good: e.g., *Ethics* (1908), *MW* 5:261.

80 Dewey, *PP* 208.

"subsumptive" view of policy reasoning must be avoided. Accordingly, this finding of facts and projection of likely consequences must, rather, be viewed as part of the continuum of end-means in which the ends-in-view are subject to being intelligently refashioned. Regarding policy-making as a form of inquiry oriented towards the truth about the public good reinforces this general lesson from the continuum of end-means, for it places all of public deliberation within a broader effort that refashions final ends in the course of collective deliberation.

Compensating for Dewey's occasional tendency not to range practical deliberation under inquiry is his view that democratic deliberation is inquiry *par excellence*. His reason for holding this is his view that all inquiry requires certain democratic conditions. At this point, we return to the collective aspect of inquiry mentioned (but not discussed) in the last section. Presaging Habermas, Dewey held that all inquiry, including scientific inquiry, should conform to certain standards of openness, publicity, and impartiality, standards of the kind paradigmatically realized by a legitimate democracy. As Putnam notes, Dewey's case for this conclusion spans the continuum from end to means.[81] It is partly an instrumental case — so organizing inquiry promotes its success — but it is also partly an intrinsic case — so organized, inquiry better realizes its intrinsic value as an activity. Democratic inquiry is good because democratically governing is good.

"To save science from the sins of bureaucracy," Diggins writes, "Peirce insisted that the community of inquirers must remain independent of society and its demands."[82] If we stress that all inquiry is practical inquiry and the democratic inquiry is inquiry *par excellence*, however, then we can hardly expect to insulate inquiry from society's practical demands. Instead, we must find a way to reconcile the responsiveness to individual sovereignty (a Jeffersonian commitment that Peirce also resisted[83]) with a cognitive understanding of inquiry. The key to resolving this problem philosophically, as I have argued else-

---

81 Putnam, *Pragmatism*, 72–74.

82 Diggins, *The Promise of Pragmatism*, 193.

83 Ibid., 192.

where, is to combine the two moments of correspondence and coherence, as in the interpretation of truth put forward in the last section.[84] We must recognize, in other words, that while "correspondence," or process-independent standards or constraints, partly determine the truth about what we ought to do, it is true that process-dependent, democratic aspects involving individualized popular sovereignty also partly determine the truth about what we ought to do.

To resolve this problem philosophically, however, is not yet to resolve it institutionally or concretely. To say that the political inquirer *ought* to listen to the needs of the public is not yet to say anything about how to avoid the dangers that bureaucracy entails. We have seen what a legitimate bureaucracy, for a reformed Deweyan pragmatist, is not: it is not a body of narrowly instrumental reasoners reaching policy decisions in rigid, *zweckrational* ways. We have glimpsed a view of what it is, namely a part of the broader public enterprise at refashioning public ends in the course of selecting among alternative means. But why ought we have bureaucracies at all?

The answer that emerges from the reconstruction of Dewey undertaken here is that the public enterprise of specifying the ends that guide policy is so complex that it is best carried out in layers and stages. It is a matter in which we must divide our labour. While no end should be taken as epistemically fixed, some ends need to be institutionally fixed for the purpose of orienting the deliberative work of those policy-makers in a position to guide the experts' efforts at projecting consequences. Institutionalized pockets of special concern and focused expertise of this kind, despite the potentials for abuse they represent, do not necessarily clash with democracy.[85] Rather, they are an unavoidable part of a democratic effort to inquire about the complex problems that face us.

Many crucial questions remain about how this sketch of democratic inquiry about the ends and means of political action could best be filled in. Let me just mention two. First, as Dewey emphasized, and as I have

---

84 I argue this point in "Democratic Intentions."

85 Mark E. Warren makes this case persuasively in "Deliberative Democracy and Authority," *American Political Science Review* 90 (1996): 1–15.

elsewhere argued myself, deliberation that is responsive to the continuum of end-means is essentially reflective.[86] Lacking a criterion external to it, it consciously reviews, in the ideal, all of the reasons that bear on any question before it. This will include some reasons that are impossible completely to articulate, and instead have their home in our emotional reactions. It is in part in order to elicit these emotional responses that Dewey recommends "imaginative rehearsal" as a tool of deliberation.[87] For both of these reasons, then, it will be natural to view deliberative reflection as being at home in an individual's mind; and Dewey did regard reflection as an individual matter.[88] If we are to make good on a conception of democratic reasoning that really spans the continuum of end-means, however, we will need to conceive of an embodied form of collective reflection. Second, we will have to employ our imaginations, again, in an effort to conceive of a way of institutionalizing the stages of democratic deliberation about ends that creates pockets of specialized concern and expertise while at the same time remaining adequately open to democratically — that is, collectively — generated revision.

While these are by no means easy problems, the exciting thing is that the reformed Deweyan pragmatism I have sketched here poses them for us. These are problems that we must face if we are to arrive at an acceptable account of democratic deliberation. Therefore, the constructive pragmatism that takes seriously the end of truth but also insists on leaving the specification of ends, including truth, open to specification, reclaims the promise of Dewey's inspiring rhetoric about deliberative democracy — rhetoric that would, without this openness, ring hollow in technocratic halls.

---

86 *Practical Reasoning about Final Ends*, Chapter 8.

87 In *Dewey's Ethical Thought*, 185–89, Welchman argues that the plumbing of emotional responses is the principal role of imaginative rehearsal, which hence was intended to respond to Lippmann's charge that pragmatism made insufficient place for the emotions. She concludes, partly on this basis, that imaginative rehearsal is not the only method of deliberation that Dewey recognizes.

88 Cf. Honneth, "Between Proceduralism and Teleology," citing the 1932 *Ethics*, *LW* 7:163, 165f.

CANADIAN JOURNAL OF PHILOSOPHY
Supplementary Volume 24

A Pragmatist Theory of Convergence

JOSEPH HEATH
University of Toronto

One of the defining characteristics of pragmatism over the years has been its commitment to the primacy of practical over theoretical rationality. This has often been motivated by doubts about the adequacy of the "representationalist paradigm" that has dominated philosophy of mind and epistemology in the modern period. Thus, many pragmatists have sought to replace the notion of representation with one or another explanatory concept derived from the analysis of action or behaviour. But this strategy has encountered persistent difficulties, and precisely where one might expect. Without some primitive notion of representation, it is difficult to provide an account of the conceptual *content* of our beliefs, the standards of *correctness* that govern our practices of inference, or the expectation of *convergence* that informs scientific inquiry. These difficulties, which pertain to the analysis of meaning, justification, and truth respectively, have done a lot to keep pragmatism more a set of promissory notes than a coherent philosophical program.

Several recent contributions to the literature, however, suggest that these difficulties are becoming increasingly tractable. Robert Brandom has shown how a *compositional* theory of meaning can be developed from a set of primitive action-theoretic concepts, Michael Williams has developed a *dialogical* contextualist epistemology that explains warranted assertibility in terms of the practice of justification, and various "minimalist" theories of truth have shown that most of our everyday "truth-talk" can be redeemed without positing any substantive correspondence relations between mind and world.[1] While the details of any

---

1 Robert Brandom, *Making It Explicit* (Cambridge, MA: Harvard University Press,

of these theories may ultimately prove incorrect, they remain significant in that they have provided, for the first time, a blueprint for the development of a comprehensive pragmatist view.

One area in which pragmatist theories remain weak, however, is in the analysis of convergence. If the content of propositional attitudes and the justification conditions that govern their adoption are secured by our practices, then it is unclear why we expect to find agreement on theoretical or factual issues, but widespread disagreement over aesthetic or evaluative judgments. It is noteworthy that many minimalists who eliminate representation from their theories of truth turn around and reintroduce it when it comes time to explain the different levels of convergence exhibited by factual and non-factual discourse.[2] The line of explanation is certainly tempting — we can secure agreement about factual beliefs because these serve to represent actual states of affairs, in the physical world that we all share; we cannot secure agreement over desires or values because these attitudes are either not representational or else serve to represent private, affective states.

This is a line of thought that I intend to resist. In this paper, I would like to show that the difference in levels of convergence exhibited between beliefs and desires can be explained without reference to the representational nature of beliefs, but entirely through the pragmatic requirements of social interaction. I do so by examining some of the rather surprising results that have turned up in recent analyses of the epistemic conditions underlying game-theoretic equilibria. I argue that these findings — in particular, the discovery that strategically rational agents cannot "agree to disagree" on factual questions[3] — are not problematic modelling assumptions, as game theorists have been inclined to suppose. Rather, they show that the pragmatic requirements of so-

---

1994); Michael Williams, *Unnatural Doubts* (Oxford: Blackwell, 1991). On minimalism, see Paul Horwich, *Truth* (Oxford: Blackwell, 1990).

2 Especially Crispin Wright, *Truth and Objectivity* (Cambridge, MA: Harvard University Press, 1992).

3 See Robert J. Aumann, "Agreeing to Disagree," *Annals of Statistics* 4 (1976): 1236–39.

cial interaction impose a convergence constraint on the belief systems of all participants. The fact that no such agreement is necessary in the case of desires, in this view, explains our willingness to live with persistent disagreement in this domain.

The primary advantage of this analysis is that it is able to account for the fact that different discourses exhibit varying *degrees* of convergence. One of the weaknesses of the traditional representational account is that it divides our propositional attitudes sharply into two classes: those which should exhibit complete convergence, and those which should exhibit little or none. The problem is that a variety of rather dissimilar judgments get lumped together in the non-factual class, so questions of moral obligation, evaluative judgment, aesthetic sensibility, and sheer preference receive uniform treatment, despite the fact that their respective discourses exhibit significantly different levels of convergence. I will conclude by showing how these different types of judgment can be classified, from an action-theoretic point of view, and the levels of convergence of their associated discourses explained by the pragmatic requirements of social interaction. The most important consequence of this analysis is that it is able to show how the relatively high level of convergence that we expect in moral judgment can be explained, given the "non-factual" character of the associated discourse.

I

In order to motivate this discussion, I would first like to offer a brief summary of the problems with the story that is usually told about convergence. There are two components to this view. First, there is the claim that cognition is fundamentally representational; what it produces as output in some way reproduces or "mirrors" what it gets as input. Whether or not cognitive systems of this type are functioning correctly is to be assessed in terms of the fidelity of this process. Thus the ideal governing the operation of such systems is one of transparency. If the input is thought of as a bundle of information, cognition may produce a computational or notational transformation as output, but all of the information will be preserved. When this is done successfully, it will be possible to run the same process backwards, and reconstruct the original input from the copy made through cognition.[4]

In this view, it is helpful to distinguish between intentional states, which are merely *about* something, and cognitive states, which *represent* something. The latter will be a subset of the former. All by ourselves, we may be unable to tell which of our intentional states are genuinely cognitive.[5] However, social interaction affords us the opportunity to communicate our intentional states to one another, and so to compare and contrast. We find that while many of our intentional states are different, many are the same (or equivalent). The most obvious explanation is that, in cases where the output of our cognitive processes is the same, it is because the input was the same.

The second major component of the view concerns the explanation that is given of how we could each have received the same input. The most obvious hypothesis is that it all came from the same source. Thus it is reasonable to suppose that there is a single world, external to us all, that provides us with sensory information, etc. This is commonly expressed by the idea that a unified physical world provides the "best explanation" for the convergence that our cognitive states exhibit (as opposed to, e.g., a plurality of virtual environments synchronized to provide us all with identical sensations). In cases where our intentional states are not the same or equivalent, two explanations are available. There is the possibility that the states are cognitive, but that the input they process is private, i.e., has its source in the individual's own body. It is often thought that desires are intentional states of this type. In this view, they would be representations of private phenomenal states of affect or disposition. The alternative is that there are intentional states that are not representational at all, but perhaps constructive, such as works of imagination.

---

4 Some accommodation must be made for coarsening, which is considered permissible. Here I am treating input as "pre-processed," so that everything that comes in is intended to be preserved.

5 For instance, according to proponents of this view, we may not be aware that we are projecting subjective responses onto the environment. See J.L. Mackie, *Ethics: Inventing Right and Wrong* (London: Penguin, 1997), 42, where he calls this the "pathetic fallacy."

This line of reasoning has its merits. However, there are several respects in which it does not do the job it is called upon to perform. One of the characteristic features of our dealings with the external world is not just that we "happen" to converge in our beliefs, but that we "expect" to find such convergence. The expectation is not of the weak inductive variety ("I wouldn't be surprised if ..."), it is of the sanctionable normative variety ("There's something wrong with you unless ..."). When two people disagree in their beliefs about the physical world, we automatically suppose that one of them is mistaken. Crispin Wright articulates this idea by saying that discourse about the physical world exhibits what he calls "cognitive command." A discourse satisfies cognitive command if and only if it is *a priori* that differences of opinion arising within it can be satisfactorily explained only in terms of divergent input, unsuitable conditions, or malfunction.[6] It is the *a priori* status of this presumption that signals its normative force.

In the "best explanation" account of convergence outlined above, it is unclear where this normative force would come from. One might suppose that, having provided an explanation for the level of convergence exhibited by some of our cognitive states, it is then possible to anticipate that inquiries which seek to extend our knowledge of the physical world will also result in high levels of agreement. This might be what licenses our expectation of convergence in scientific inquiry, and our willingness to accept disagreement in many other non-scientific domains. But the standard objection to this line of reasoning is that the "unified" physical world switches from being an empirical hypothesis to a normative ideal when the transition is made from explaining convergence to licensing the expectation of convergence. The physical world posited to explain the similarity among our representations is one that transcends our recognitional capacities, which is why it can supply a norm for our expectations. But it is unclear how such an object could ever be posited on the basis of finite evidence — thus the standard objection to realism, viz., that it is metaphysical in the objectionable sense.[7]

-----

6 Wright, *Truth and Objectivity*, 92–93.

7 See Crispin Wright, "Introduction" to *Realism, Meaning and Truth*, 2nd. ed. (Oxford: Blackwell, 1993).

This problem is symptomatic of deeper difficulties. The idea that our beliefs happen to converge, and that our desires happen not to — leading us to seek an explanation for the difference — is a deeply unrealistic account of how our discursive practices operate. Sociological analyses of the practices of so-called "mundane reasoning" have shown that agents consistently *use* the assumption that beliefs must converge in order to construct their accounts of "what really happened" at a particular place and time. Melvin Pollner, for instance, has studied the way in which the line of questioning pursued by judges in traffic court is governed by the goal of constructing a coherent, "objective" account of events.[8] The definitive temporal sequence of events, for instance, is constructed subject to the constraint that incompatible events not occur simultaneously. Contradictory testimony from witnesses is interpreted as the result of error, or hidden motives, and so on. The idea that there is a single, correct story about what occurred is an assumption that is, on the one hand, completely unfalsifiable, but on the other hand, an essential inferential component of any narrative that might eventually be settled upon.

The conclusion of Pollner's research is that the level of convergence exhibited in our beliefs about the physical world is not something that we happen to discover, it is a *practical accomplishment*. Furthermore, it is a practical accomplishment that agents often use extraordinary ingenuity in order to achieve, developing complex and unlikely stories to account for divergence. This is not a new idea. Kant argued that the expectation of an unified, coherent, shared physical world was a regulative idea governing our cognitive activity. Such an idea could never come from either sensibility or understanding, and so it could not be the world, *qua* phenomenon, that explains the level of convergence exhibited by our systems of belief. What we need, as Kant recognized, is some story that explains where the normative expectation of convergence comes from.

In this respect, the fact that the expectation of convergence is a nonfalsifiable assumption acquires significance. The fact that people dis-

---

8 Melvin Pollner, *Mundane Reason* (Cambridge: Cambridge University Press, 1987).

agree about "what happened" can *always* be explained in terms of differences in perspective, error, improper motivation, and so on. The ideal of convergent beliefs says, in effect, that "all things being equal" agents exposed to the same stimulus will form the same beliefs. Whenever they fail to do so, this is simply proof that all things were not equal. Examples of how generously this principle can be applied abound. For instance, it has become something of joke among economists that, whenever they encounter an activity that, according to their models, should not occur (like most of the buying and selling on the stock market, or currency exchanges), they reply that "it must be some kind of asymmetric information."[9] The underlying point is a serious one. Whenever one encounters differences in belief (speculative trading implies that the buyer thinks the price will go up, while the seller thinks it will go down), it is always possible to make these beliefs consistent by supposing that agents are reasoning the same way, but using different information. Thus any superficial disagreement in belief can be explained as the product of an underlying agreement plus asymmetric information.

The important point is that these strategies are not specific to the case of beliefs about the physical world, but can be applied to any intentional state. Gary Becker, for instance, has argued influentially that just as agents' beliefs are convergent, so are their desires. He claimed that differences in manifest preference for particular market goods can be explained without positing differences in taste.[10] Instead, he suggested that agents have a uniform desire to consume the same "commodities," which they manufacture internally using market goods as inputs. In this view, each agent can be characterized by some production function, that takes market goods, along with the agent's own time and "consumption capital," as inputs. Agents all start out with the same basic tastes, but accumulate different levels of consumption capital. This makes them capable of converting goods into commodities at dif-

---

9 Eric Rasmusen, *Games and Information* (Cambridge, MA: Blackwell, 1989), 165.

10 Gary Becker, *Accounting for Tastes* (Cambridge, MA: Harvard University Press, 1996), 24.

ferent rates. For example, they acquire the capacity to convert good music into listening enjoyment through repeated exposure. Becker argues that a model of this type, combined with asymmetric information about the productive capacity of various market goods, is more than sufficient to explain any observed differences in demand for market goods.

What Becker claims, in effect, is that "all things being equal" people will have the same desires. In cases where they exhibit differences in their choices, it is because all things are not equal, but there exists some asymmetry in the distribution of consumption capital or information. The implication of this argument is that *discourse about what is desirable will satisfy Wright's cognitive command constraint*. And for those who think this obtains only because Becker makes unduly generous use of the *ceteris paribus* clauses, it should be noted that his framework does have considerable explanatory value, particularly for the analysis of advertising on consumption patterns. [11] Becker presents his uniformity-of-desire hypothesis as the "best explanation" of a variety of significant economic phenomena.

I am inclined to view Becker's position as a *reductio* of its own basic strategy. It shows that whether or not a particular discourse can be characterized as convergent is ultimately not an empirical question. Any discourse can be characterized as convergent at some level — there is a generic mechanism available for doing so. Surface disagreement can always be explained away by positing a deeper underlying agreement, whether it be in the case of beliefs or desires. Thus explanatory strategies that attempt to get at the underlying source of agreement or disagreement, like Becker's analysis of taste, or the representationalist analysis of cognition and the physical world, are guaranteed to succeed. For that reason, they are devoid of explanatory value.

In my view, this approach goes wrong when it attempts to posit deep structures in order to explain surface patterns of agreement and disagreement. The level of surface agreement in a given discourse should be explained, in my view, by surface features of that discourse.

---

11 Ibid., 203–24.

It should be understood as a direct result of the level of *discipline* imposed by that discourse upon its participants. The rules governing any discursive practice impose constraints on the level of convergence that it must exhibit, because these rules fix the criteria of warranted assertibility for that discourse, and so indirectly determine the intelligibility of statements made within it. High levels of convergence can be obtained by placing extremely narrow constraints on the "entry moves" available to participants.[12] In the case of formalized languages like mathematics, disagreement is excluded by making it impossible to have an asymmetric distribution of language entry moves. The only way to start out an argument is with an axiom, and an axiom is always available to everyone playing the game. On the other hand, discourse which describes the physical world may have entry rules that allow asymmetric opportunities to make claims. One person may "see it happen," another may not. These may result in disagreements, since the second agent may not accept the reliability of the first, and so on. Specialized subdiscourses like science attempt to minimize these asymmetries by, for instance, requiring that all experimental findings be reproducible. This has the effect of lowering the level of disagreement. Other discourses, such as the aesthetic, make a point of allowing entirely private experiences (such as the free play of the imagination harmonizing with the lawfulness of the understanding) to count as warranted entry moves.

The consequence of this view is that the level of convergence exhibited by a given discourse will be a product of the norms, or "proprieties," that govern it. To speak in a slightly misleading fashion: "society" has the discretion to require as much or as little agreement as it likes (although as the level of tolerable disagreement increases, the level of intelligibility begins to fray). The question that must then

---

12 "Language entry move" is an expression used by Wilfrid Sellars to designate an action through through which an agent comes to occupy a position in a language game that is not based on a transition from some other point in the game. See Sellars, "Some Reflections on Language Games," in his *Science, Perception and Reality* (New York: Routledge & Kegan Paul, 1963), 329. See also Brandom, *Making It Explicit*, 221–22.

be asked is why the different discursive practices that we participate in institutionalize different levels of convergence.

In my view, the traditional theory goes wrong in taking agreement, rather than disagreement, to be the *explanandum*. Within the representationalist paradigm, where agents are thought to formulate their ideas independently, each in her own head, agreement certainly does seem to be more mysterious than disagreement. The linguistic turn, however, suggests that agents formulate their thoughts using the public medium of language, whose appropriate use is pinned down by an underlying uniformity of linguistic practice. From this perspective, it is actually disagreement that starts to look mysterious. When Wittgenstein says, for instance, that he is justified in asserting "this is red" *because he speaks English*, it suggests that anyone who disagrees with the assertion is simply not using the words correctly.[13] For this reason, devices like first-person authority, which weaken the kind of discursive commitment that agents incur through their utterances, are important because they *permit disagreement*. The extent to which different discourses exhibit convergence is therefore determined by the extent to which they constrain the use of devices, such as first-person authority, that allow disagreements to develop and persist. And in my view, the extent to which discourses constrain the use of such devices is determined in turn by the pragmatic consequences that follow from "agreeing to disagree" in their domain. This thesis can be illustrated by considering some differences in the consequences that follow from disagreement about belief and disagreement about desire.

II

In order to motivate this position, I would like to divert the discussion briefly in order to articulate the more general pragmatist strategy that informs my response. Here I take Charles Sanders Peirce's analysis of how we come to "fix" our beliefs as paradigmatic. In the standard

---

13 Ludwig Wittgenstein, *Philosophical Investigations*, trans. G.E.M. Ancombe (Oxford: Blackwell, 1967), 117 [§381].

representationalist view, we form beliefs because the world in a certain sense imposes itself upon us. Our environment impinges upon our senses, causing us to form impressions of the world around us. Peirce's view constitutes a clever inversion of this picture. He claimed that belief formation is not a passive response to the world, but is an active process in which we pick out the information that we need in order to conduct our activities. Our system of beliefs is formed as a sedimentary by-product of our actions. In Peirce's view, we do not form any beliefs at all about innumerable features of our environment — because we do not need them. There is nothing in the world in general that compels us to have one or another conviction about which road leads to which town. But when we are trying to get to one of these towns, and encounter a fork in the road, we are forced to make a choice.[14] Pierce defines a belief as simply a policy that one is willing to act upon.

To modify Peirce's example slightly, I have noticed that of the people who live in my neighbourhood, those who own cars generally know which direction the various one-way streets run. People who don't own cars, but get around on foot, invariably have no idea. Of course, walking through the neighbourhood, it is as plain as day which direction the traffic flows. But pedestrians don't need to know this to get where they are going, and so simply have no beliefs about it. This feature of their environment is not *salient*, because it is not needed for any practical purpose.

Thus Peirce's answer to the question why we develop beliefs about the world is that we *need to for practical purposes*. I would like to propose a similar account of convergence. The reason that we work so hard to align our beliefs about the physical world is that we need to in order to successfully coordinate our actions, which is to say, for practical purposes. (And the reason that we do not develop convergent desires is that we can get along just fine without them.) Thus what I propose is something like an intersubjective generalization of the Peircean account of belief formation. My task is then to show why,

---

14 C.S. Peirce, *Collected Works of Charles Sanders Pierce*, vol. 5. (Cambridge, MA: Belknap, 1934), 359.

and in what sense, we need to have agreement in belief but not desire. The answer lies, I will argue, in the demanding epistemic requirements for fixing stable expectations in contexts of social interaction.

Both the Peircean point and my own can be formulated more precisely by situating them within a formal model of action. According to the usual characterization of practical rationality as utility maximization, any decision problem can be exhaustively represented using three components: actions, states, and outcomes. All three of these are events. The difference between them is that the action is an event that the agent controls, while the state is an event that is outside of his control. The outcome is then a third event that is produced through the causal interaction of the first two. This relationship can be represented by a function that maps actions and states onto outcomes: $f: A \times S \rightarrow O$.

When reasoning instrumentally, the agent is not interesting in performing any actions "for their own sake," but is instead interested in the outcomes that can be achieved. Thus she begins by ranking these outcomes from best to worst. This *preference ordering* is normally thought to be an expression of the relative desirability of these outcomes. However, the agent is unable to pick an outcome directly; she can only choose an action. And once an action is selected, the outcome that results is entirely a function of which state obtains (which is entirely outside the agent's control). This means that unless the agent has some knowledge, or at least some estimate, of which state will obtain, her preference ordering is completely useless as a guide to action. In order to reason back from outcomes to actions, the agent must assign some probability to the occurrence of the relevant states. Once this is done, she can select the action that produces the highest probability-weighted satisfaction of her desires, as expressed by her preference ordering over these outcomes.

Because instrumental reasoning depends upon the use of beliefs about states to project preferences over outcomes onto the set of actions, decision theorists draw a sharp distinction between certainty, risk, and uncertainty. When the agent is certain that a given state will obtain, her preference ordering over actions will directly mirror her preference ordering over outcomes. In cases where there is some risk, i.e., where she does not know with certainty which state will obtain but knows the relative likelihood of every state, then her preference ordering over actions will be a slightly refracted version of the ordering over outcomes. However, if she does not know *at all* which state will obtain, then her preference ordering over actions will simply be undefined. Decision theorists accommodate this by defining the beliefs that agents hold in decision-theoretic models to be subjective probabilities.[15] When it comes time to act, agents need to have some expectation about which state will obtain. Even if it is completely wrong, some belief is better than none, because it gives the agent some basis for action. Thus agents are said to *parameterize* their environment.

If one adopts Davidson's conception of decision theory, under which it is treated as an interpretive structure used to analyze action into the twin components of belief and desire, then the Peircean view of belief formation is an immediate consequence.[16] The impossibility of rational action under uncertainty guarantees that any action can be interpreted as the product of some determinate set of beliefs. And since the only evidence one ever has that an agent has a given belief is that she acts in a certain way, if one adopts a broadly anti-realist stance towards these beliefs then they become simply policies that agents act upon.

However, decision theory handles only those cases in which agents act in non-social environments. An important wrinkle develops when a second rational agent is introduced into the framework. The situation that is of interest arises in the context of what game theorists call "interdependent choice." This is a situation in which the outcome is determined *jointly* by the actions of two separate agents. It was mentioned earlier that both actions and states are events that combine to cause an outcome. Now what needs to be considered is a case in which the action of the first agent combines with the action of a second agent in order to produce an outcome. Taking A_1 as the set of actions available to the first agent and A_2 as the set available to the second, the set

---

15 Here I am following L.J. Savage, *The Foundation of Statistics* (New York: John Wiley & Sons, 1954).

16 Donald Davidson, "A New Basis for Decision Theory," *Theory and Decision* 18 (1985): 87–98.

of outcomes can then be given by $f: A_1 \times A_2 \rightarrow O$.[17] Recall that the only difference between an action and a state was that an action is an event under the agent's control, while a state is not. Thus the concept of a state is agent relative. In a situation of interdependent choice, the first agent's action is a state for the second, just as the second agent's action is a state for the first.

The question that arises is how agents are supposed to develop rational beliefs about the state that will prevail in such a context. In the decision-theoretic case, beliefs could be treated as exogenous to the choice problem, and so subjective probabilities would suffice. In a simple decision problem, the agent could solve the problem of assigning probabilities to states first, then move on to the problem of deciding what to do. But when agents are interacting with one another, each agent must solve both of these problems simultaneously. In order to decide what to do, the first agent must determine the probability of various states obtaining. But since these states are simply the second agent's actions, the first agent must determine what the second player intends to do. In order to figure this out, he must figure out what the second player's beliefs are. But since the second agent's beliefs about what state will obtain are equivalent to her beliefs about what the first agent will do, and since this is precisely what the first agent is still trying to decide, a regress of anticipations arises.

The objective of game-theoretic analysis is to find a way of working through this regress of anticipations in such a way as to allow a stable set of beliefs to emerge for all players. A game-theoretic "solution" is therefore an *equilibrium* of beliefs, and game theory is a general mechanism for determining beliefs about the relative probabilities of various states. For each player, *strategic reasoning* operates by working through the cycles of anticipation in such a way as to turn other players' actions (which have not yet been planned or performed) into events that will occur with specific probabilities. Once reduced in this way, each player's choice can then be handled as a simple decision problem.

---

17 Natural events can still be included, by simply treating nature as one more "player," the probability of whose moves are fixed in advance and common knowledge among the players.

However, it turns out that in order to get a stable equilibrium, it is not sufficient for agents simply to develop *some* system of beliefs. They must achieve what game theorists call "consistent alignment of beliefs" (CAB).[18] This requirement reflects two constraints: not only must each agent develop a set of expectations that is internally consistent, these expectations must also be "aligned," which means that each must ascribe to the other a set of intentions that corresponds to his own expectations and a set of expectations that correspond to his own intentions. Each agent must, in effect, believe that everyone has the same beliefs, and that these beliefs are correct. And in order to successfully coordinate upon an equilibrium, everyone must *in fact* have the same correct beliefs. Thus agents, in order to select a utility-maximizing course of action in contexts of social interaction, must presuppose that the belief sets of all players converge, and in order for these actions to actually produce the outcomes that they were intended to produce, the belief sets of all players must actually converge.

The more surprising consequence is that not only must players assign a convergent set of beliefs to one another about how each intends to play, but they must also assign the same set of beliefs to one another about the probability of every state of nature that might occur. This is one version of the so-called Harsanyi doctrine, which states that the prior probability of all relevant states of nature must be common knowledge among all players. Thus it will not be adequate for players to assign subjective probabilities to the natural states that form the parameters of the game; they must all assign the same probabilities, know that they have all assigned these probabilities, and so on. This assumption is often rendered implicit in game theory models by having "nature" represented as a pseudo-player who moves with fixed probability. This has the effect of treating nature's move as part of the equilibrium, and so slips the common prior assumption in under the CAB constraint. (Strictly speaking, this is not introduced as a necessity, but rather as a modelling assumption. However, I will argue below that the consequences of relaxing this con-

---

18 See Shaun P. Hargreaves Heap and Yanis Varoufakis, *Game Theory: A Critical Introduction* (London: Routledge, 1995), 52.

straint show it to be a pragmatic necessity on par with Peirce's requirement that we "fix" our beliefs.)

At a strictly intuitive level, the reason that players' beliefs must converge in this way is that players are only able to get to a stable set of expectations by "mirroring" each others' reasoning processes ("If I did this, then she'd think that, and then do this ..."). They cannot just assign subjective probabilities to the occurrence of each others' actions, because they must treat these actions as the product of a set of rational beliefs about the anticipated interaction. Thus they must develop beliefs about each others' beliefs, beliefs about each others' beliefs about each others' beliefs, and so on. This means that they must take an interest in the way that their own beliefs "fit" with the system of beliefs they are ascribing to others. It turns out that a system of beliefs determined in this way will only be internally consistent if it is possible to hit upon a set of expectations that would be self-enforcing, i.e., if everyone adopted them, then no one would have any reason to do anything that falsified them. This is what generates the CAB constraint. Suppose I start out by assigning some probability to another person's action. Once I have settled on this belief, I will then be able to determine my own best course of action. However, I must realize that if the intention I ascribe to the other player is correct, then she must also anticipate what I intend to do, since she is capable of reproducing the process of reasoning that led me to determine my own best response. I must therefore check to see whether the action that I expect her to perform will still be a best response for her, given her anticipation of my own intended action. If it is not, then the initial intention that I ascribed to her must be incorrect, because it would not be a best response given the inferences that she is able to draw from it.

The most minimal constraint on game-theoretic equilibria is therefore that the system of beliefs that underlie them not exhibit this defect. This is what the Nash solution concept captures: each player's strategy must be a best response to the strategies of the others.[19] In

---

19 For an overview, see Drew Fudenberg and Jean Tirole, *Game Theory* (Cambridge, MA: MIT Press), 11–14.

cases where we succeed in coordinating upon an equilibrium, this means that our beliefs will be the same. I do a_1 because I expect you to do a_2, you do a_2 because you expect me to do a_1 (and I expect you to do a_2 because I expect you to expect me to do a_1, you expect me to do a_1 because you expect me to expect you to do a_2, etc.) In cases where we fail to coordinate upon an equilibrium, we each believe that our beliefs are the same, but they will turn out not to be. But if either of us thought that there was any disagreement about what each expected the other to do, this would give us each a reason to change what we intended to do, and so the equilibrium would unravel.

This is already an interesting result. It suggests that in order to act successfully in social contexts, we need to come up with not just *a* set of beliefs about how others will act, but the *same* set of beliefs about how all of us will act. The fact that we also need to assume that we all assign the same probability to all natural events follows from a straightforward extension of the logic that generated the CAB constraint. We get to an equilibrium by mirroring each other's reasoning processes. If your choice of action is governed both by expectations about how I will act and by information about some state of nature, I need to know what your beliefs are about this state of nature in order to anticipate your move. You need to know what my beliefs are about your beliefs about this state of nature in order to anticipate my move, in order to plan your own, and so on. If we disagree about what the probability of this state is, we will be unable to mirror each others' reasoning in such a way as to produce any meaningful narrowing of the range of possible actions.

In order to get around this difficulty, game theorists eliminate disagreement about natural events by introducing asymmetric information states. Suppose we both want to go on a picnic, but not if it rains. If I think it is going to rain with a probability of 30 per cent, and you think it is going to rain with a probability of 70 per cent, then we have a problem. What should I suppose you will do: act on the basis of your expectation of what I will do, based on my expectation that it probably will not rain; or act on the basis of my expectation of what you will do, based on your expectation that it probably will rain? The solution suggested by John Harsanyi is to suppose that we both start out assigning the same prior probability to the chance of rain — say 30 per cent — but then allow you to acquire information that leads you to update your prior — say you look out the window and see clouds.[20] If you have no chance to signal me, then we work off the common prior in order to fix the equilibrium. If you can perform some action that I can observe after acquiring this information, then I will update my prior based upon what I see you do, and we will fix the equilibrium based on our jointly updated priors. Either way, we will act on the basis of an estimate of the probability of rain that is common knowledge, and so will not "agree to disagree."[21]

It should be noted that neither the CAB constraint nor the Harsanyi doctrine follow directly from the instrumental conception of rationality. They are additional assumptions, both of which many game theorists regard as problematic. However, game theorists persist in making them, because without them it is impossible to define a solution concept that places any meaningful constraints on the strategies the players may adopt.[22] This means that without CAB, rationality would massively underdetermine the choice of action in all but the most elementary of social interactions. In its defense, it is often pointed out that if players fail to achieve CAB, i.e., they make a mistake as to which equilibrium will be played, they will immediately adjust their belief systems in order to achieve it as soon as the error is discovered.

In any case, I would like to suggest that rather than being a problematic modelling assumption, the CAB constraint shows that convergence in empirical belief has an enormous pragmatic significance for social interaction. Just as we need to assign some probability to events in order to act in decision-theoretic contexts, we need to assign some potentially convergent system of beliefs to all persons in order to act

---

20 John Harsanyi, "Games with Incomplete Information Played by 'Bayesian' Players," 3 parts, *Management Science* 14 (1967–68) 159–82, 320–34, 486–502.

21 This is admittedly informal, but conveys the basic idea underlying Aumann's argument. For reflection on these issues, see Robert J. Aumann, "Correlated Equilibrium as an Expression of Bayesian Rationality," *Econometrica* 55 (1987): 1–18.

22 Aumann, "Correlated Equilibrium," 12–15.

in strategic contexts. Thus convergence in empirical beliefs is not a metaphysical necessity, but it is a pragmatic necessity insofar as we want to pursue projects that require instrumental reasoning in contexts of interdependent choice. If we fail to develop a set of convergent beliefs, the price we pay is that our actions will fail to achieve our desired outcomes (and often needlessly so). Thus in order to act successfully in strategic contexts, we must actually align our beliefs in such a way as to satisfy this reciprocally imputed system of consistent beliefs. We need agreement in order to carry out our plans, *even if these plans are formulated and pursued in an entirely individualistic manner.*

This analysis, in my view, provides a clue as to where the "regulative idea" that governs the notion of representation and cognitive command comes from. The requirement that we think of one another as working off a common prior, responding in the same way to the same information, is imposed by the structure of social interaction, as a practical postulate. It is necessary in order to construct the cognitive framework needed to interact socially. It is only by expecting our belief systems to converge, and expecting one another to expect our belief systems to converge, that we are able to develop even halfway determinate expectations about how each of us will behave. We are capable of relinquishing this assumption, but the cost will be a complete inability to act rationally in contexts of social interaction.

It is significant to note the difference between belief and desire in this context. There is no particular reason for agents to have a "consistent alignment of preferences." Preferences are in general not interdependent, i.e., it is seldom the case that what I prefer depends upon what you prefer *and* what you prefer depends upon what I prefer. As a result, there is usually no regress of preference, and so no need for consistent alignment in order to sort things out. Agents can therefore be in complete disagreement over which outcomes are better or worse without it providing any significant interference in their ability to plan a course of action. So even though we are capable of treating one another's preferences as merely the surface expression of an underlying set of identical tastes, as Becker has shown, there is no practical reason for us to do so. Failure to think of our preferences in these terms does not in any way compromise our ability to plan and execute instrumental actions.

III

I stated at the outset that one of the advantages of this approach is that it is able to explain the fact that certain discourses exhibit levels of convergence that are somewhere in the middle range between, say, mathematics and gastronomy. My primary concern in this remaining section will be to explain the level of convergence exhibited by moral discourse, which is, despite the tenor of much recent philosophical discussion, actually quite high.[23] In order to present this argument, I must introduce a few complications into the model of rational action outlined above.

One of the facts that I repeatedly glossed over in the previous section is that even though strategic reasoning requires that agents develop a system of internally consistent beliefs, very few interaction problems present agents with a single set of beliefs that could satisfy this constraint. This is the problem of multiple equilibria — there may be many sets of strategies that, if agents were to hit upon them, would induce a stable set of expectations. However, instrumental rationality alone does not provide any mechanism that would allow agents to hit upon the same set of beliefs. Having internal consistency and a common prior significantly reduces the number of equilibria, but it usually does not narrow it down to a single set. Game theorists have therefore supposed that strategic reasoning would need to be supplemented by some other mechanism that would favour one of these equilibria by making it "focal" or "salient."

This has led many rational choice theorists to argue that shared rules of conduct, i.e., social norms, play an important role in regulating social interaction, by focusing expectations on particular equilibria. Norms, in this sense, are rules that directly prescribe particular actions — they say "do x," not "if you want y, do x."[24] This non-teleological

---

23 Consider, for instance, the examples assembled by C.S. Lewis, *The Abolition of Man* (London: Oxford University Press, 1944), 41–48.

24 This is Jon Elster's formulation, in *The Cement of Society* (Cambridge: Cambridge University Press, 1989).

structure means that the reasons for action they provide are not out-come dependent, and so do not get caught up in the regress of anticipations that generates the indeterminacy of strategic reasoning. When such rules are common knowledge among agents, they are capable of providing secure expectations about the likely course of the interaction.

Many theorists who are overly impressed with the instrumental conception of rationality limit the role of norms to equilibrium selection, thereby supposing that they always play a role that is strictly complementary to standard instrumental reasoning. However, socio-theoretic considerations have led many theorists to claim that social action is "multidimensional," viz., that social norms provide reasons for action that can trump strategic considerations. I take moral rules to be social norms of this type. In this view, expressed for instance by Jon Elster, social norms act as deontic constraints that effectively limit the range of actions that are subject to instrumental deliberation.[25] Norms are thus able to provide a massive reduction in the complexity of social interaction, by directly motivating conformity to particular institutional patterns.

But regardless of whether one views social norms as subordinate or superordinate to instrumental deliberation, it is a consequence of this entire family of views that, given the indeterminacy of game-theo-retic reasoning, social interaction will require a considerable degree of agreement about a set of effective social norms. (Under either view, the norms must be common knowledge and accepted by all in order to function effectively.) This means that there will be strong pragmatic reasons for maintaining agreement on a set of rules of conduct, since the stability and predictability of social interaction will break down in their absence. To see the significance of such agreement, one need only consider the difference between encountering a stranger from within one's own culture and a stranger from a different culture. In the former case, the interaction is structured by a set of shared expectations that serve to dramatically reduce the number of relevant contingencies. This

---

25 See Elster, *The Cement of Society*, 97–151; see also Joseph Heath, "Foundationalism and Practical Reason," *Mind* 106 (1997): 451–74.

gives the overall interaction a *routine* character. A stranger from another culture, on the other hand, with whom one does not share expectations, presents a serious interaction problem, since one is suddenly left without most of resources that are normally drawn upon in the organization of interpersonal affairs. While a strict game-theoretic analysis is unable to capture the difference between these two cases, the introduction of social norms as a mechanism for focusing or fixing expectations is able to resolve the problem.

There is a long-standing tradition in sociological theory that considers what we normally call morality to be just a subset of these norms.[26] According to the view in which normative reasons for action are able to trump instrumental reasons, social norms have many of the characteristics normally thought to be specific to moral imperatives: they command categorically, their form is deontological, their content is both impersonal and generalizable, and above all, they impose constraints on the pursuit of individual advantage. Furthermore, it has often been noted that everyday social norms are sanctioned in exactly the same way as moral offences, and persistent violation often provokes moral outrage.[27] Also, conflicts that arise concerning the basic norms of, e.g., politeness and civility are routinely resolved through appeal to more abstract and explicitly moral principles.[28] If this equation is correct, then the pragmatist analysis developed here suggests that the pressures that lead to convergence in systems of empirical beliefs will also lead to convergence in the set of social norms that govern our interactions. Moral discourse can be expected to yeild a high level of agreement, because we cannot agree to disagree in this domain without seriously impairing our practical efficacy in contexts of social interaction.

---

26 See Emile Durkheim, *Moral Education*, trans. Everett K. Wilson and Herman Schnurer (New York: Free Press, 1961).

27 Harold Garfinkel, "Studies in the Routine Grounds of Everyday Activities," in his *Studies in Ethnomethodology* (Cambridge: Polity Press, 1984): 35–75.

28 See, e.g., Judith Martin, *Miss Manners Rescues Civilization* (New York: Crown, 1996), 29–63.

Naturally, there is a conventional element in the system of norms that is absent in the case of beliefs about the world. A norm that serves to focus expectations in a pure coordination problem, for instance, will be pragmatically successful as long as it prescribes *some* set of equilibrium strategies, regardless of *which* particular set it prescribes.[29] The same is not true of the common prior in belief systems. It is important for agents to have the same beliefs, but it is also important that things in the world turn out the way they were supposed to. Normatively prescribed expectations, on the other hand, are self-fulfilling, insofar as the adoption of a particular expectation provides each agent with a reason to behave in a way that conforms to the normative pattern. It is therefore important that agents share the same norm, but it does not particularly matter which norm they share. This means that the pragmatic usefulness of a norm extends only as far as the sphere of individuals for whom it can serve as a coordination mechanism, and that other individuals, within a different sphere of interaction, are able to get along just as well with an entirely different norm.

In large measure, it is this conventional element that explains the enormous cultural variation in the set of normatively prescribed social obligations that individuals uphold. However, it is highly significant to note that these large-scale cultural differences coincide to a significant degree with geographic and political boundaries that have traditionally limited the amount of social interaction that could occur between members of the different cultural groups. Once social interaction does become more common, either as the result of migration or through improvements in transport and communication, it tends to generate enormous pressure for the standardization of social practices (starting with the basic rules governing respect for persons, extending then to economic and political decision-making, language use, and fi-

---

29 This is captured by Kant's idea that moral reasoning is governed by the regulative idea of the kingdom of ends. The laws governing this realm have no substantive content, but are merely those that all could will in common. This is unlike the laws governing the physical realm, which are not only subject to the formal constraint that they be the same for all, but also have their substantive content fixed.

nally social and family routines). This built-in tendency towards convergence is a such a striking characteristic of polyethnic societies that national minority groups often seek to defend their cultural particularity by limiting the level of social interaction that can occur among cultural groups, primarily through developing autonomous institutions.[30]

This analysis suggests that we should expect high levels of convergence in the normative rules governing conduct among agents who interact on a sufficiently regular basis. On the other hand, individuals who interact infrequently, and so have no opportunity or need to develop institutions to regularize these exchanges, will often adopt a broadly instrumental stance towards one another. Hence the pressure towards convergence in the domain of norms will be low, but because they are interacting strategically, there will still be a powerful incentive to develop a system of shared beliefs. This explains why there is greater transcultural pressures towards agreement in empirical belief systems than there is in moral rules. But it is also something that we should expect to change, as the development of communication and transportation technology continues to remove the barriers that have traditionally limited the level of social interaction among members of different national and cultural groups.

It should be noted that, according to this view, increased social interaction will not generate any tendency to level out differences in the *values* to which agents adhere. (Here values are understood as culturally shared standards that agents employ in reflecting upon and revising their "first-order" desires.[31]) Evaluative judgments consist of a ranking of outcomes not according to personal preferences, but according to socially shared standards for ranking alternative states. Clearly, in the context of strategic interaction, agents' preferences and desires can vary to an arbitrary degree without generating any pragmatic difficulties. Similarly, in norm-governed interactions, the precise reason

30 Will Kymlicka, *Multicultural Citizenship* (Oxford: Clarendon Press, 1995).

31 See Charles Taylor, "What is Human Agency?" in *Human Agency and Language: Philosophical Papers 1* (Cambridge: Cambridge University Press, 1985).

for which agents conform to normatively prescribed expectations is not always pragmatically significant. So while shared values may be helpful in some ways, e.g., by simplifying the task of justifying certain social practices, the lack of shared values does not generate any pragmatic problems in the Peircean sense. Thus there is no reason to think that peoples' values will converge in the long run, but also no reason to think that this will impede their ability to achieve consensus on matters of moral principle.

IV

According to the view that I have been developing, the mistake that traditional accounts of convergence make is to think our empirical beliefs exhibit high levels of convergence because they are "about" the physical world. Aesthetic judgments are just as much "about" the world, but they leave much more room for persistent disagreement.[32] In order to understand the difference, it is important to look at the structure of the discourse in question, to see where the opportunities for disagreement arise. I suggested earlier that the rules governing language entry moves provide a mechanism that regulated the level of acceptable disagreement. Mathematics, even though it is not "about" the physical world at all, is able to minimize disagreement by stipulating that any entry move or inference that is available to one participant must be available to all others. This has the effect of eliminating, among other things, all first-person authority. Scientific discourse can be understood as a regimentation of "mundane" discourse about the world that also eliminates certain forms of first-person authority. If I claim to have seen one car swerve just before the accident, this assertion enjoys considerable *prima facie* warrant. If I claim to have seen cold fusion in a beaker, this assertion has no "scientific" warrant until it has been reproduced by others.

---

32 Even here there are very high levels of agreement (although the patterns of convergence vary according to class and status group; see Pierre Bourdieu, *Distinction*, trans. Richard Nice [Cambridge, MA: Harvard University Press, 1984]).

What this shows, in my view, is that we are capable of constructing language games that permit as much or as little convergence as we like. Rawls's "constructive" political philosophy, for instance, can be seen as a proposal for a regimented version of our everyday discourse about norms. The framework guarantees high levels of agreement about a basic institutional structure by imposing limits on the entry moves available to participants. This is captured by the notion of a "public use of reason," which eliminates the opportunity to make valid entry moves based on substantive value commitments — what Rawls calls "comprehensive doctrines." The requirement that any proposal for a conception of justice be freestanding guarantees a symmetric distribution of opportunities to make warranted entry moves, and so vastly increases the potential for convergence in outcome.

The pragmatic reason for developing a discourse of this type is perfectly explicit in Rawls's work.[33] The facts of cultural pluralism in modern societies make it harder to get to consensus on the basis of shared values, because no set of them are sufficiently widely shared. Our traditional forms of normative and political discourse permitted claims based on substantive value judgments, because these institutions arose in the context of culturally homogenous societies. So while there was always a latent potential for disagreement in the structure of our political discourse, it seldom surfaced because of an underlying consensus on questions of value. With the development of culturally plural societies, this latent potential began to be actualized, and so the "loophole" needed to be closed.

The pragmatist theory that I have outlined does not in any way explain the particular character of any one of these discourses. What it does is provide an action-theoretic analysis of the structural reasons why highly regimented discourses should be favoured in particular domains. We have a discourse about the physical world in which we try to limit disagreement, which provides us with the "official" beliefs that we use to coordinate social interactions. We also have a set of

---

33 John Rawls, *Political Liberalism* (New York: Columbia University Press, 1993), xxiv–xxvii.

procedures for fixing authoritative norms to govern social interaction (which include, e.g., basic principles of arbitration and bargaining). In both cases, there is no pragmatic alternative to having discourses of this type, since without some set of shared beliefs and norms, our capacity to engage in successful social interaction is dramatically impaired. Ultimately, the level of convergence exhibited by any particular discourse is determined by the level of inconvenience that would flow from having to agree to disagree in such a domain.

CANADIAN JOURNAL OF PHILOSOPHY
Supplementary Volume 24

Pragmatism and Change of View

ISAAC LEVI
Columbia University

Foundationalism in epistemology imposes two demands on the beliefs of intelligent inquirers: (1) that *current* beliefs be justified, and (2) that there be foundational premisses and principles of reasoning that are self-certifying on the basis of which the merits of other current beliefs and principles may be derived. Many anti-foundationalists give up (2) but not (1). They demand that current beliefs be justified by showing these beliefs to be integrated into a systematically satisfactory network of beliefs. Pragmatists belong among those who give up *both* (2) and (1).

Pragmatists do not think that the project of justifying current beliefs is implementable. In this respect, they are sceptics. Such scepticism does not imply that because agent X at time t cannot justify his current beliefs, he should cease having them. Scepticism about reasons does not imply scepticism with respect to belief. In "The Fixation of Belief" Peirce explicitly dismissed doxastic scepticism when he observed that merely writing down a question challenging some current assumption is not sufficient to create the sort of doubt that should occasion an inquiry. Real and living doubt that calls for inquiry arises only if the inquirer initially has no opinion concerning the issue under discussion or has acquired a good reason for ceasing to believe what he initially took for granted. If an inquirer is initially convinced about the answer to some question and has not been given good reason to doubt it, a mere Cartesian "paper doubt" cannot legitimately provoke inquiry.

I am convinced that I am now in front of my wordprocessor composing an essay. I readily concede that it is a logical possibility that I am dreaming. I concede that it is a logical possibility that I am a brain in a vat. But the doubts these logical possibilities raise are paper doubts.

It is clear that many earnest philosophers are and have been exercised by such matters. But not only do I not in fact doubt that I am now engaged in a writing activity before my wordprocessor; I deny that I *should* come to doubt that I am now so engaged. To the contrary, the burden is on the sceptic to show me why I should cease being certain about my current activity. I have no need for a coherentist justification any more than I am under an obligation to give a foundationalist justification of my belief that I am now using a wordprocessor.

This claim may be denied for reasons I shall now explain. I am committed to believe fully the logical consequences of my belief together with the remainder of my full beliefs. I lack the logical omniscience to believe the logical consequences of my beliefs. Whatever memory and computational capacity I have is compromised by passions that sometimes overtake my reason. Even so I am committed to improve my doxastic performance by learning to control my passions and receiving assistance in enhancing my computational capacity. When I claim on behalf of the classical pragmatists and myself that there is no need to justify current beliefs, I mean that there is no need to justify current doxastic commitments. However, current doxastic performance in fulfilling such commitments may be subject to criticism and efforts recommended to remedy deficiencies. These criticisms concern (1) the identification of the agent's doxastic commitments, (2) how well the agent is doing in fulfilling the commitments, and (3) what steps should be taken to improve performance. To the extent to which I fail to fulfil doxastic commitments such as my commitment to fully believing that I am writing on a wordprocessor in a Windows environment (which is a logical consequence of my fully believing that I am writing on my wordprocessor and my other beliefs, including the conviction that my wordprocessor is running in Windows 3.1), one may, indeed, say that my current beliefs are incoherent in a manner that ought to be repaired. In this sense, it may be suggested that current conviction is always subject to critical review, and for good reason — counter to what seems to have been Peirce's view.

It is, indeed, true that when I recognize incoherence in the sense of a failure to fulfil a doxastic commitment when required to do so, and can identify the means to remedy the failure, I am under an obligation as a rational agent to make the repairs. But the repairs to be made do not call for modifying my doxastic commitments. Nor do they require that I justify my having or retaining them. The recognized presence of incoherence calls for repair of my doxastic performance — i.e., my success and failure in efforts to fulfil my doxastic commitments. The sense in which the coherence of my current views is subject to critical review is the sense in which failure of coherence is failure of doxastic performance.

Failure to fulfil my current doxastic commitments does not call for critically examining the doxastic commitments themselves. There is no demand here for deriving the current full beliefs understood as doxastic commitments from some epistemically privileged foundation. Nor is there a demand for showing that the current doxastic commitments constitute a more satisfactory system than any alternative scheme. There is no need at all for justifying the current doxastic commitments in either a foundationalist or a coherentist sense.

Peirce, as I understand and admire him, was a fan of the principle of *doxastic inertia*, according to which there is no need to justify current beliefs, but only *changes* in belief. These changes of belief state may expand the current state by adding new information or contract the current state by removing information already present. Whether the change is an expansion or a contraction, its justification should be based on the inquirer's assumption that what is fully believed in the current state is true. The inquirer's current state of full belief is the standard by which she currently judges truth. The inquirer is committed to being perfectly free of doubt regarding the truth of any proposition that is a consequence of that state of full belief. In that sense, there is no serious possibility that it is false. The current state of full belief is the inquirer's *standard for serious possibility*.

If inquirer X is certain that the British had an election by May 1997, X judges it true that the British had the election, is free from all doubt on this score, and discounts as a serious possibility the logical possibility that it is false. X may be in doubt as to how many more seats the Tories have than the Liberal Democrats, and may examine the body of items he fully believes for evidence justifying a conjecture on that score — i.e., for justifying an expansion of his state of full belief in one way or another. He will not, in general, be opinionated on every issue. Still, X will be certain about the answer to some questions.

To be sure, X may be challenged to give up his conviction that the election took place. He may come to have good reason to cease being certain based on his current state of belief, according to which that conviction is true. But as long as X does not change that conviction, there is no serious possibility, according to X, that the conviction is false.

Conceding that X's full beliefs may be revised in the future admits that it is possible *for* X to be in states of full belief alternative to his current state. Even though it is not seriously possible *that h* according to X's current state of full belief, it may be possible *for* X to be in a potential state of full belief according to which it is possible *that h*.

Let us, then, stipulate that it is possible for X to entertain the serious possibility that *h* if and only if it is possible that *h* relative to one potential state of full belief in X's conceptual space (the set of potential states of full belief available to X). Given a suitable set of assumptions about the structure of X's conceptual space,[1] this stipulation is equivalent to judging it possible that *h* if and only if *h* is possible relative to the weakest or least informative state of full belief in X's conceptual space. This state is the state of maximal ignorance. Let us call *h logically possible* when this condition is met. Unless X is in a state of maximal ignorance, he is not rationally obliged to judge it seriously possible that *h* just because it is logically possible. In the current state of full belief, X may be perfectly free of doubt concerning the falsity of *h*. There is not, from his point of view, even an infinitesimal probability that *h* is true. Changes in full belief are changes in standards for serious possibility.[2]

---

1 I. Levi, *The Fixation of Belief and Its Undoing* (Cambridge: Cambridge University Press, 1991), Chapter 2.

2 In ibid., I require that the set of potential states of full belief be a Boolean algebra closed under meets and coins of arbitrary cardinality. I also suggested that it could be atomless, so that there would not be any maximally informative but consistent potential states of full belief. No potential belief state is a maximally consistent opinion about a possible world. To be sure, we may use the set of deductively closed theories or potential corpora in a suitably specified language *L* to represent a subset of the set of potential states of full belief. But when the set of potential states constitutes an atomless algebra, it is clear that the set of potential states (which is an atomic algebra) cannot represent all of the potential states. X's standard for serious possibility defines the space over which

Peirce's interest in justifying change in full belief was extended by Dewey to include justifying changes in other propositional attitudes and activities, such as the evaluation of options in practical and political deliberation and the creation of prized objects such as works of art. Peirce, James, and Dewey all shared a problematic focused on giving an account of problem-solving inquiry in which solutions to problems always involve justifying changes in point of view, appealing at the outset to the point of view initially endorsed as the provider of reasons for making the change. There are important differences between the three great American pragmatists. But a preoccupation with the clarification of problem-solving inquiry based on a generalization of the principle of doxastic inertia to attitudes other than full belief is common ground among them, and constitutes the insight of American pragmatism that I admire.

Pragmatists are not the only philosophers who have abandoned the project of justifying current beliefs as well as the quest for a foundation for belief. Quine suggests that we cease being obsessed by questions of justification altogether and seek instead to explain the acquisition of beliefs.[3] Charles Peirce vigorously chastised John Dewey for allegedly injecting considerations of natural history into the study of the logic and methodology of inquiry.[4] I write "allegedly" because Dewey seems to have disavowed the intention to embrace a natural-

---

conditional probability judgments are defined. In particular, if X judges that h is positively probable, X judges that h is seriously possible. Conversely, if X judges that h is seriously possible, X judges that h is either positively probable or carries an infinitesimal nonstandard probability. But X's judgments of positive probability (whether standard or infinitesimal) lack truth-values. Hence, so must X's judgments of serious possibility. The claim that it is possible *for* X to shift to a belief state according to which it is true that h does carry a truth-value. At least this is so as long as it is a claim about X's abilities and not his entitlements. X's judgment that it is seriously possible *that h* is not such a claim.

3 W.V. Quine, *Ontological Relativity and Other Essays* (New York: Columbia University Press, 1969).

4 Peirce, "Review of John Dewey's *Studies in Logical Theory,*" *The Nation* 19 (1904): 219–20.

ized epistemology of the sort that Quine envisaged. Dewey distanced himself from the attempt to replace the examination of criteria for the proper conduct of problem-solving inquiry by biological and psychological accounts of learning. He thought it important, however, to recognize the biological and social "matrices" of problem-solving inquiry; for the natural and social situations of inquiring agents help circumscribe the kinds of attitudes and abilities such inquirers may have. Even those who, like myself, think that the prescriptive norms of rationality that characterize the attitudes preclude a biological or social reduction of the attitudes should concede Dewey's point.[5] Unlike Quine, Dewey was interested in the proper conduct of inquiry just as much as he was in the natural history of inquiry. Dewey's *Logic* is devoted to sketching features of properly conducted inquiry. His interest is prescriptive and emphasizes focusing on the problems that created the occasion for inquiry.

Rorty, who seeks to locate Dewey in his personal pantheon of philosophical heroes along with Wittgenstein and Heidegger, ignores this central preoccupation of Dewey's philosophy. It is no doubt true that Dewey shares a hostility to foundationalism with Wittgenstein and Heidegger. But neither Wittgenstein nor Heidegger entertained the idea of writing a book like Dewey's *Logic: A Theory of Inquiry* that is devoted to sketching a conception of the common structure of properly conducted inquiries. Nor did these authors envisage extending Dewey's variant on Peirce's belief-doubt model of inquiry as presented in his *Logic* to moral inquiry or to the construction and criticism of works of art.

Dewey thought it important to appreciate that scientific methods of approaching problems could be extended to other areas of human experience. The tension between science and the humanities ought to

---

5 As Peirce himself does in a letter of 1905 to Dewey. Peirce states his concession and complaint against Dewey as follows: "What you [Dewey] had a right to say was that for certain logical problems the entire development of cognition and along with it that of its object become pertinent, and therefore should be taken into account. What you do say is that no inquiry for which this development is not pertinent should be permitted." (*Collected Papers of Charles Sanders Peirce* [Cambridge, MA: Belknap, 1966], 8.244.) As I understand Dewey's *Logic*, Dewey accepted Peirce's point.

be bridged by bringing scientific methods of problem-solving to bear on moral and political problems and in the creation of works of art. Such methods address conflicts between rival candidate solutions to problems in an experimental spirit that seeks to avoid begging the question in favour of one answer rather than another. Dewey's attitude presupposed that there are no obstacles to addressing such conflicts without begging the questions under dispute. In particular, one should not place roadblocks in the path of inquiry by presupposing that some conflicts confront incommensurable themes with one another, so that it is impossible to examine the rival views without begging the question. Rorty does not endorse this central teaching of Dewey's, but embraces instead the view that conflict in science is, as Kuhn suggests, often a conflict between incommensurable conjectures. Science resembles ethics because the conflict between incommensurables, in the final analysis, boils down to a conflict between values that cannot be resolved through inquiry. Rorty bridges the gap between the sciences and the humanities by suggesting that scientific inquiry, like moral reflection, constantly confronts conflicts between competing values that are irresolvable. Dewey claimed that moral conflict is an occasion for doubt concerning competing value commitments that should be an occasion for problem-solving inquiry, just as scientific inquiry aims to settle doubts concerning competing conjectures through inquiry. Thanks to Rorty, we have seen an alleged Renaissance of interest in pragmatism, and especially in the pragmatism of Dewey; but it seems to me that this revival has been achieved at the cost of suppressing salient features of Dewey's philosophy.

But historical accuracy is not my concern here any more than it seems to have been among many other contemporary admirers and critics of the pragmatists. I take myself to be a pragmatist even though I disagree with each of the classical pragmatists in some respect or other. My identification as a pragmatist is based on a preoccupation with the importance of understanding the main features of problem-solving inquiry and deliberation that I share in common with the classical pragmatists. This preoccupation is not central to the concerns of Lewis, Quine, Wittgenstein, Heidegger, or Rorty. Nor is the question of problem-solving inquiry to be confused with the investigation of forms of communication that sometimes do and sometimes do not promote such inquiry.

To recapitulate, what distinguishes the pragmatist perspective is that the current point of view needs no justification. Changing that point of view does. When one considers the aspect of an agent's point of view that constitutes the agent's state of full belief, this inertial principle becomes the principle of doxastic inertia, according to which the current state of full belief is the current standard for serious possibility. The status quo needs no justification. To the contrary, it is inappropriate to require inquirers to justify their current beliefs unless good reason can be offered to show that they should give them up.

Peirce, James, and Dewey all agreed that well-conducted inquiry aims to identify a strategy for legitimately relieving doubt and, hence, for justifying changes in view. They also agreed that such justification involves, in Dewey's phrase, an "adaptation of means to ends." The inquirer is to justify adding new items to her belief state because such expansion best promotes the goals the inquirer should be promoting.

The kind of justification that a pragmatist, therefore, requires for changing beliefs must have the form of an argument that purports to show that the change in question best promotes the aims of the inquiry among the available options. In this respect, pragmatism is quite earnestly practical.

One implication of this view is that pragmatists should take seriously the idea of applying principles of rational choice to evaluating changes in belief. Ironically, many students of Bayesian decision theory are interested in changes in view; but rarely do they take the idea of understanding such changes to be decisions. To the contrary, they seek to understand how changes in beliefs have an impact on how decisions are made rather than how changes in view are the outcome of deliberation.

As an example of the decision-theoretic orientation of the pragmatists, consider John Dewey's notion of warranted assertibility.[6] An inquiring agent X seeks to answer an as yet unsettled question. Dewey called the answer that X obtains or *asserts* at the conclusion of inquiry a "judgment." The conjectures that constitute potential solutions of the problem, as well as the settled background information, techniques, and methods taken as noncontroversial resources in the context of the

---

6 Dewey, *Logic: The Theory of Inquiry* (New York: Henry Holt, 1938), 120.

specific inquiry, are called "propositions." Judgments are "asserted," while propositions are "affirmed." When the inquiry is properly conducted with appropriate adaptation of means to ends, Dewey called the judgments that are asserted at the conclusion of the inquiry "warranted assertions." The warranted assertion obtained at the conclusion of one inquiry becomes a resource for another inquiry. It becomes an affirmed proposition.

Dewey understood the contrast between propositions and assertions or judgments as a distinction between resources or means for reaching a conclusion and solutions attempting to realize the goals of a problem. He thought that this way of drawing the distinction, one that emphasizes the idea that in inquiry means are adjusted to ends, is more useful than more familiar ways in which logicians and philosophers of language have used these notions. I do not mean to defend the particular categories used by Dewey to characterize the kinds of deliberation that go on in properly conducted inquiry. The important point is that he was thinking of inquiry aimed at fixing belief as a species of practical deliberation, and his distinction between affirming propositions and asserting judgments is a reflection of this emphasis on practical deliberation.

Russell interpreted Dewey as claiming that a belief is warranted "if, as a tool, it is useful in some activity, i.e., if it is a cause of satisfaction of desire."[7] On this view, the pragmatist sees the goals of inquiry as pursuing what works in promoting the practical, economic, moral, prudential, or aesthetic values of the inquirer. The classical pragmatists did not, however, reduce the goals of scientific inquiry to moral, political, economic, prudential, or aesthetic values. Peirce saw the aims of scientific inquiry to be relieving doubt in a manner that in the long run would promote a convergence on a true, complete story of the world. This view of what the aims of inquiry are or ought to be understands the scientific justification of changes of view as showing that certain changes promote cognitive goals distinct from moral, political, economic, prudential, or aesthetic ones.

---

7 Bertrand Russell, *Inquiry into Meaning and Truth* (London: Allen and Unwin, 1940), 322.

The pragmatists all insisted that scientific inquiry and, indeed, all inquiry that is concerned with change in belief resembles practical deliberation in taking into account the consequences of various choices for the goals of the given deliberation. With the (possible) exception of Dewey, they all claimed that a concern with the avoidance of error is a component of the goals of scientific inquiry.[8] Dewey was an unabashed instrumentalist regarding scientific theorizing. Nonetheless, in his *Logic* he sought to distinguish scientific inquiry from common-sense deliberation focused on practical issues by emphasizing that inquirers investigate theoretical structures for their own sake, even though these structures may have a bearing on more practical concerns. Like the other pragmatists, Dewey thought that inquirers adopted proximate goals in their inquiries that are distinctive of their disciplines. None of the classical pragmatists, including Dewey, took for granted that the goals of scientific inquiry are moral, aesthetic, political, economic, or other purely practical goals.

Given what we know, advocating goals for justifying changes in belief that are peculiarly cognitive is incompatible with endorsing some single, permanent, non-trivial standard of value. Dewey was a value pluralist who rejected appeals to maximizing overall welfare or ful-

---

8 There is a sense in which the aim of an inquiry is to reach a justified conclusion, or a justified change of view. But in examining the conditions for successful justification, pragmatists insist that a justified conclusion is optimal among the available solutions with respect to the goals or aims of the deliberation. For both Peirce and James, a concern to avoid error is a desideratum in fixing beliefs. The respect in which it is a desideratum constituent in the goal of efforts to fix beliefs makes reference to a goal which justifications aim to show is optimally implemented by the conclusions they justify. Peirce could concede that the aim of inquiry is to obtain a justified belief; but, in his messianic realist mood, this means obtaining a belief that relieves doubt in a way that promotes convergence of the opinions of the community on the true, complete story. James could concede that inquiry aims at justified belief as well, arguing that justification concerns the best way to seek truth and shun error. And Dewey could also hold that inquiry aims at justified belief (or coming to believe) while denying that truth is a desideratum of the aims that determine what constitutes a justified belief. See Dewey, "Propositions, Warranted Assertibility and Truth," *Journal of Philosophy* (1941), for an interesting elaboration of his view.

filling a network of obligations derived from practical reason as standards of value that should control how we ought to conduct our lives and how we ought to think. Only a self-indulgent wishful thinker could claim that that evidence shows that promoting convergence of opinion in the infinite long run on the true, complete story of the world will promote the net of pleasure over pain or the general welfare or is a requirement of practical reason.

Cognitive goals are values that are in competition with moral, aesthetic, economic, political, etc., goals. Inquirers can be torn between their commitments to engage in inquiry, seeking to promote cognitive goals, various political or moral objectives, and pecuniary interest.

As Dewey above all insisted, we pursue many different and sometimes competing goals and values that themselves cannot be assessed according to the principle of utility or a coherent network of categorical imperatives. Value pluralism, for Dewey as for Berlin and Williams, is evidenced by the presence of moral conflicts. For Dewey, such conflicts provoke inquiries aimed at removing the doubts about values that they generate.

Thus, the thesis that justification of change of belief succeeds when it shows that one way of changing beliefs best promotes the goals of the inquiry is quite consonant with the goals being special cognitive goals rather than moral, political, economic, aesthetic, or practical ones. It does not preclude rational agents from pursuing other objectives as well, as long as these objectives do not come into conflict with the special cognitive goals of inquiry. When they do conflict, there is good reason for reflection on how to resolve the conflict. Often the cognitive goals will be favoured; but sometimes they may not be.

Peirce was quite clear about this. He recognized that agents could seek to relieve doubts in ways that have little to do with cognitive values. In particular, inquirers might seek to relieve their doubts by methods that display no regard for the facts of the matter. In "The Fixation of Belief," he felt obliged to argue for using methods that do seek to get at the truth. He revealed, thereby, that he understood that agents are often conflicted as to the goals of fixing belief and that there is a point to deliberation aimed at resolving such conflict.

According to Peirce, an inquirer should seek to remove doubt via methods that have an established track record as reliable means for finding true answers to questions. If the methods currently in use do not prove satisfactory, they may have to be modified. But Peirce insisted that adjusting the methods for fixing belief in the face of recalcitrant experience will eventually lead to correct non-trivial answers to questions. The sense in which scientific method is a fixed method is the sense in which it is any method that is adopted that, in the context, is judged to afford high expectation of yielding true answers to questions. To the extent that a method ceases to promise such success, it ceases to be scientific. For Peirce, what is fixed, strictly speaking, is the goal of finding correct answers to questions. It is the pursuit of that goal that Peirce took to be the "logical method" of science that ought to be "loved and reverenced" as a bride. He did not assume that the methods that would be means for pursuing that goal are fixed and immune to revision any more than he thought that the beliefs that would be fixed by using such methods would be fixed for all time. Peirce would have disapproved of "method" in that sense just as much as Feyerabend did. He recognized that pursuing this goal in an earnest fashion can occasion sacrifice of other goals. Justification of belief in scientific inquiry resembles justification of other kinds of decisions in that it invokes principles of rational decision-making. But the justification is not practical in the sense in which Russell alleged it was, for the substantive values it promotes are autonomous cognitive goals.

For Peirce and for James, if not for Dewey, relieving doubt in ways that will yield true beliefs was a central component of the cognitive goals of scientific inquiry. How did the pragmatists conceive of truth?

Peirce did not equate truth with what the inquirer believes. At the turn of the century as in the 1870s, Peirce did speak of the inevitability of finding the truth via the scientific method. But whether he wrote that "the opinion which is fated to be ultimately agreed to by all who investigate, is what we mean by truth" as he did in 1878, or "science is foredestined to reach the truth of every problem with as unerring an infallibility as the instincts of animals do their work" as he did after 1900, there are clear indications that he could not equate truth with what the community of inquirers would believe in the limit.

By the turn of the century Peirce explicitly acknowledged a distinction between convergence in relative frequencies with absolute certainty and with moral certainty. If a fair coin were tossed infinitely many times, it might land heads up every time even though it is morally certain not to according to what we now call the strong law of large numbers. Moreover, Peirce was prepared to argue that it is morally certain that random sampling from a given population in accordance with techniques for estimating the constitution of the population (e.g., the proportions of individuals in the population exhibiting various traits in a predesignated list) will converge on a correct answer. Convergence of this kind appears to have been central to Peirce's claim that induction will secure convergence given that abduction and deduction have been properly carried out. But all he claimed for this convergence is that it is "foredestined to reach the truth of every problem with as unerring an infallibility *as the instincts of animals do their work.*" I take it the instincts of animals are no better than morally infallible.

Thus, by the turn of the century Peirce was explicitly conceding that the consensus obtained via induction might in the limit contain error. The convergence to the truth he envisaged was a convergence to the truth that is morally but not absolutely certain to occur — i.e., not with probability 1.[9]

I do not know whether Peirce took this view in 1878. But the various formulations of his so-called definition of truth after the turn of the century cannot plausibly be regarded as synonymy-securing definitions. (Cheryl Misak correctly makes this point for different reasons.)[10] And it is also clear that whatever his earlier view had been, this emendation did not seem to alter his understanding of truth or make a difference to his view of the importance of truth. Peirce often said that the convergence to the truth is something that inquirers aim and hope for. For him, convergence on the truth is a goal of inquiry, and the methods of inquiry are to be assessed in terms of how well they promote that goal. If the goal is realized either for a single question or *per impossibile* on all conceivable issues, what inquirers will then agree on will be true. The *moral* certainty that a certain method of inquiry will find the answer to a given question in the long run may very well recommend the use of the method to us even though there is no *absolute* guarantee that the truth will be found.

---

9 Peirce, *Collected Papers* 7.214.

10 Misak, *Truth and the End of Inquiry* (Oxford: Clarendon Press, 1991), 36.

No matter what problem a scientific inquirer investigates, he does not place roadblocks in the path of inquiry by supposing that the true answer to that question is inaccessible to inquiry. The "hope" in science is that there are no "incognizables," and scientific inquirers act on that hope. If the community of inquirers investigating their special problems were to persist into the infinite long run, the hope is that they would come up with the true, complete story of the world. Each inquirer pursuing his or her particular puzzles contributes to this ultimate goal of inquiry.

I myself do not sympathize with Peirce's vision of the aims of inquiry. Nor, so it appears, did John Dewey.[11] The great American pragmatists shared a common commitment to the belief-doubt model of inquiry according to which the target of philosophical reflection when it comes to belief should be justified change. But Peirce and Dewey did not see eye to eye concerning the relevance of truth to the proper conduct of inquiry. In general, pragmatists did not share a common view of truth as a goal of inquiry.

To be sure, the belief-doubt model of inquiry presupposes a distinction between what agent X at time t takes for granted as settled, free of doubt, and certainly true and what might be true and might be false. According to the pragmatist view, not only is the object of X's full belief or doubt truth-valued, but so is X's attitude of full belief. Moreover, according to X at time t, X's full belief at t that h is true and certainly so. According to X at t, there is no serious possibility that h is false. In these respects, it seems to me that whether they explicitly said so or not, all of the pragmatists thought that belief is directed to the truth.

Truth as conceived by the pragmatists is not equivalent to what X or anyone else believes. According to X at t, everything X believes at t is true. This does not imply, however, that X at t is fully opinionated, so that if it is true that h, X at t believes that h.

---

11 Dewey did endorse Peirce's early formula of truth as "the opinion which is fated to be ultimately agreed to by all who investigate" as the best definition of truth "from the logical standpoint" (*Logic*, 345, note 6). But there is no evidence that he thought the aim of inquiry was to find the truth so conceived.

Nor is truth understood to be what X at t asserts with warrant or was warranted in asserting at the end of previous inquiries. For one thing, some of X's beliefs at t might not have been the outcome of well-conducted inquiry. X might fully believe that h without having obtained the conviction as a result of previous inquiry, and might have no good reason to cease believing that h. From X's point of view, it is true that h even though X has no warrant for asserting that h.

Furthermore, if X is in suspense concerning h, X may lack a warrant for asserting either h or $\sim h$. Yet, according to X at t exactly one of these is true.

Pragmatists do not claim that the truth conditions for h are given by spelling out necessary and sufficient conditions for making a warranted assertion that h. Relative to X's state of full belief K at t (and the problem X is addressing at that time), X might judge that he would be justified or warranted in expanding K by adding h. But pragmatists can coherently claim (and Peirce surely did claim) that h might be true even though X lacks a warrant for asserting that h and, hence, is not justified in coming to full belief that h. Moreover, when X has a warrant for expanding K by adding h, his warrant is grounded in the information contained in K — X's state of full belief at t prior to the expansion. When in state K, X is committed not only to judging that he is justified in expanding K by adding h, but that it is nonetheless seriously possible that expansion by adding h leads to error.

Dewey protested Russell's allegation that his view "substitutes 'warranted assertibility' for 'truth',"[12] but admitted that, under certain conditions, he has no objection to Russell's allegation. What could those "certain conditions" be?

To say that h is a warranted assertion at the conclusion of an inquiry is to say that when K is X's state of full belief prior to adopting an answer or solution to the problem under study, X is warranted, given the relevant features of the problem, in expanding K by adding h. That is to say, X is justified in shifting to belief state K^+_h. Keep in mind, however, that judging the truth of h is not evaluating a potential change in belief state. In relating truth to warranted assertibility, which is a feature of a

---

12 Dewey, "Propositions, Warranted Assertibility and Truth," 265.

change of state of full belief, we may evaluate the matter prospectively from the belief state K or retrospectively from the belief state K^+_h.

Let us first consider the prospective point of view. X is committed already to judging every sentence in K to be true. By hypothesis, neither h nor ~h is in K. Both sentences are possibly false and possibly true in the sense of serious possibility relative to which risks are assessed in practical deliberations. We are supposing that h is a warranted assertion. That is to say, given the problem under consideration, X is justified in expanding K by adding h. It is obvious that the truth of h cannot be equated with the warranted assertibility of h. From X's vantage point in K, K is warranted in expanding by adding h even though it is a serious possibility that h is false.

Consider, then, the retrospective point of view when X is in the expanded state of full belief K^+_h. There are two cases to consider:

> *Case 1:* h is in K, so that $K^+_h = K$ and K is not the product of justifiably expanding some previous state by adding h. Indeed, h may have initially gained entry into X's convictions without any justification whatsoever. However, X has no good reason to remove h; for we are supposing that dubious pedigree is not a good reason for removal. In this case, h is not warrantedly assertible as far as X is concerned. Yet, X is committed to judging that h is true.

> *Case 2:* Neither h nor ~h is in K, so that K^+_h is a non-degenerate expansion of K. Moreover, it is warranted in the sense that X can judge that he was justified in expanding K by adding h given what X had previously believed and the problem being addressed. From X's retrospective point of view, moreover, h is true (something X did not take for granted initially). From this retrospective point of view, therefore, h is true if and only if K was warrantedly expandable by adding h.

Thus, Dewey accepts Russell's claim that he substitutes warranted assertibility for truth for case 2 of the retrospective perspective. X may judge that h is true if and only if X was warranted in the previous inquiry in expanding K by adding h. From Dewey's point of view, the substitution is unacceptable in the other cases. Dewey's complaint about Russell's allegation was that the equation of warranted assertibility with truth is a highly context-dependent affair — a point to which Russell is totally insensitive.

The contrast between the insensitivity to context displayed in the semantical views of Russell and the sensitivity of Dewey's ideas to context is also found in a comparison of the views of Frege with those of Peirce.

Peirce advanced an "unpsychologistic" view of logic in his theory of extension and intension or breadth and depth as early as 1865.[13] According to Peirce's theory, a symbol carries both intension and extension relative to the information available to the inquirer. In an appropriate state of ignorance, agent X will regard "man" and "risible man" as carrying distinct intensions and regard the issue of the identity of their extensions as unsettled. If X finds out that there are no non-risible men, X acquires new information according to which the extensions and intensions of both symbols are identical.

Consider then Frege's classic morning star/evening star example. We are invited to suppose for the sake of the argument that the morning star is identical with the evening star. That is to say, we are invited to consider a state of full belief where this identity is taken to be free of doubt. Frege assumed without argument that *in that setting* there will be a difference between the information carried by "the morning star = the morning star" and "the morning star = the evening star." "The morning star = the evening star" is supposed to carry new information. "The morning star = the morning star" does not.

According to Peirce's view, Frege's assumption is false. Neither sentence expresses an addition to the information already available according to X's state of full belief. According to Peirce, there would be no difference in the connotation of "the morning star" and of "the evening star." And there is no difference in the denotations of these terms as X judges them to be.

Frege committed the fallacy of supposing that *from the inquirer's point of view* "the morning star = the evening star" carries new information whereas "the morning star = the morning star" does not. Relative to

---

13 See Peirce, Harvard Lectures of 1865, Lectures X and XI, W1: 272–302. Also in the Lowell Lectures of 1866, W1: 358–504 and "Upon Logical Comprehension and Extension," W2: 70–86.

the body of information hypothesized, neither sentence carries new information. Frege's "puzzle" does not even get off the ground.

To be sure, if X were to come to doubt the identity of the morning star and the evening star, he would cease believing that identity statement. The senses of "the morning star" and the "evening star" would no longer be the same. And X would be in a state of suspense as to whether their references are the same. Yet, he would continue to believe that the morning star is identical to the morning star. So relative to X's state of information prior to coming to doubt, X can recognize a distinction between the two identity claims with respect to vulnerability to being given up. Giving up the belief expressed by "the morning star = the morning star" incurs a greater loss of informational value than giving up the belief expressed by "the morning star = the evening star." It is possible coherently to give up belief that the latter is true without coming to doubt the very existence of the morning star and of the evening star. That is not so in giving up "the morning star = the morning star." But this difference in comparing the losses of valuable information incurred by ceasing to believe these sentences is not a difference in the new information carried by the two identity statements in the given state of information.

Perhaps, the difference between the two statements is a difference in X's degree of certainty. But if both statements are consequences of X's state of information at a given time, X is committed to judging each one of them to be true. X is committed to ruling out the logical possibility that either one of them is false as what I call a serious possibility. There is no serious doubt that both are true. This does not mean merely that the difference between the degree of certainty or subjective probability assigned these two sentences and maximum certainty is negligible. It means rather that there is no such difference — not even an infinitesimal one. X fully believes of each of these statements that it is true.[14]

---

14 A distinction between degrees of certainty or probability and degrees of vulnerability to being given up is explicitly advanced in Levi, *The Enterprise of Knowledge* (Cambridge, MA: MIT Press, 1980), Chapters 1–3 and in earlier publications in the 1970s.

It may be objected that without something like a context-independent notion of sense and of reference, the possibility of communication collapses. Suppose X is convinced that the morning star is identical with the evening star and Y is in suspense. Peirce's view suggests that for X, the senses of "the morning star" and the "evening star" are the same and X judges the two terms to have a common reference. Y assigns different senses to these terms and judges the references differently (that is to say, regards both their identity and difference to be possible). How can X and Y communicate on the topic of the morning star? There is no common meaning to use in communication.

Not so! Although X and Y have different beliefs, they share many beliefs, and so they both believe. Consider the state of full belief or information they share in common. Relative to that state, as in Y's state, the referential identity of the terms is in doubt and the senses are different. Even though X is not in doubt, he can discourse and communicate with Y without begging any questions concerning issues under dispute by interpreting Y's expressions of his views relative to this common doctrine. But if Z disagrees with X in some other way, X may interpret these terms in communicating with Z relative to his shared assumptions with Z. There is no need to invoke a fixed context-insensitive sense or reference for the purpose of communication. Peirce, I believe, would have responded as early as 1865 in this fashion to Frege's puzzle and to the worry about communication it occasions. In any case, I endorse this view.

To be sure, X and Y might agree that they share many beliefs in common but differ concerning what these beliefs are. As a result, they might misconstrue each other, as agents often do. Even so, they manage to understand each other well enough to engage successfully in joint inquiries.

Not only could Peirce take this position, so could James and Dewey. This common ground is reflected in their consensus that an inquirer can and does make judgments of truth, that from the inquirer's point of view these judgments are true beyond doubt and yet might be amended in future inquiry, and that from the inquirer's point of view truth is not equated with what is judged true from that point of view.

For pragmatists, the controversial issues about truth concern truth as a goal or constituent of the goals of inquiry.

Peirce claimed that scientific inquirers seek the true, complete story of the world as the aim of inquiry. Whatever this might mean in precise detail, it does suggest that when an inquirer contemplates changing her state of information or full belief, she should ask how that change will affect the prospects of approaching the true complete story in the long run.

Such an inquirer needs to reckon the risk of importing error into her state of full belief not only at the state she changes to, but at states subsequent to that insofar as such errors will be retained in the final story (if there be such). In making such a reckoning, the inquirer should operate on the assumption that everything she currently believes is true. Or so I have been saying in concert with the classical pragmatists.

The upshot is that if X gives up anything currently fully believed, he incurs a risk that he will not restore it at any point and will thereby undermine the effort to converge on the true, complete story. Peirce's messianic realism leads to the surprising result that one should never remove a conviction already endorsed. This is surprising, of course, because Peirce not only thinks that one needs a good reason to give up current beliefs, but also holds that inquirers will, in general, confront such good reasons. The messianic realism embedded in Peirce's conception of the value of truth clashes with this corrigibilism.

Corrigibilism conflicts with any view of the aims of inquiry that recommends that the risk of importing error at some stage after the next stage, and as judged from the current point of view, should *ceteris paribus* be minimized. It does not matter whether we abandon worries about the risk of error at the end of days, during X's lifetime, or any time after he comes to doubt that the morning star is identical with the evening star. Not only does the inquirer lose information by such a contraction, but she incurs a risk of error in doing so. It is difficult to see how someone concerned to avoid error in the long run could defend giving anything up.

At one time,[15] I thought that Peirce was alert to this difficulty. I am no longer sure. But the difficulty is present in his thought all the same. Any inquirer X who is certain that everything in his current state of

---

15 See my *The Enterprise of Knowledge*.

full belief is true and who judges that sometime in the future he might abandon some thesis about whose truth he is currently certain must assign positive probability to the prospect that at future stages in his career he will import error that will remain in his belief state. The only way X can be fully convinced that inquiry will "progress" towards the true, complete story is by guaranteeing that nothing currently judged to be true is ever abandoned. If he conducts inquiries in any way that incurs a risk that some currently believed extra-logical truths will be abandoned, he incurs a risk of frustrating progress towards the truth. But it makes no sense whatsoever for X to deliberately give up information he values and at the same time incur a positive risk of error he cares to avoid. Such an inquirer purchases the worst of all possibilities.

Advocates of progress towards the truth might suggest that inquirers should never be certain that the current doctrine is free of falsehood. One argument for this view claims that the past record of inquiry argues for the presence of error in the current state of belief. Perhaps, the past record testifies to a secular trend in favour of removing error from that record and, hence, in favour of progress.

Keep in mind that the judgment that the past record of inquiry is strewn with error (as well as truth) is predicated on the assumption that the *current* perspective is error free. For if the current perspect is not error free, on what basis do we judge the past record to be strewn with error? How can we judge that the current doctrine contains error by appealing to the premise contained in the current doctrine that false beliefs appear in past inquiry? What principle of selectivity entitles us to judge this element of the current doctrine true and insist that the rest contains error? Surely we ought to respect the total (relevant) evidence requirement. Here the total evidence is constituted by the current doctrine.

According to the belief-doubt model, a state of full belief serves as a standard for distinguishing what is possibly true from what is not possibly true. An inquirer in doubt with respect to h endorses a standard where the logical possibility both that h is true and that h is false are not ruled out as serious possibilities. Inquiry is motivated by an interest in removing such doubts.

Strictly speaking, those who wish to allow the possibility of error in the current doctrine are not construing that doctrine as the standard for serious possibility. Perhaps the standard for serious possibility is taken to be the set of logical truths, or perhaps logical, mathematical, and other conceptual truths. The current doctrine could then be possibly false. But in that case it is unclear to me why anyone should undertake inquiries to improve the current doctrine, as apologists for progressive science do. Accepting some conjecture in the current doctrine does not relieve doubt. The inquirer, after all, acknowledges that the conjecture is but a conjecture, and hence might be false. Even if the conjecture is judged highly probable, doubt has not been removed, and will not be removed unless information is added to the standard for serious possibility. Changing the current doctrine will not help settle anything — even for the time being. Those who insist that X should allow for the serious possibility that his current doctrine is false cannot be committed to the belief-doubt model. Epistemologists of this persuasion ought to explain why anyone should wish to inquire.

Sceptics might be prepared to bite the bullet and insist that there is no point to inquiry seeking to remove doubts. Epistemic salvation is found in resting in a permanent state of suspense. For me, such *ataraxia* is a form of suicide.

Scepticism supplemented by the view that agents should make assessments of personal probability will not help. Even if agents make probability judgments (as I suppose they do), making such judgments does not remove doubt. It is no incentive to inquiry that one might change one's credal probabilities.

These considerations suggest that if we are to retain Peircean corrigibilism according to which states of belief are sometimes legitimately altered, his messianic realism or its variants have to be abandoned. There are two options. We can deny that avoidance of error is a desideratum in inquiry. Alternatively, we can urge a form of *secular realism* according to which inquirers should be concerned to avoid error as judged by the current doctrine only for changes of the current doctrine and not for any subsequent changes. I have opted for secular realism in my work.

John Dewey, as I understand him, shared my scepticism about the prospects of progress towards the true, complete story. In contrast to the view I have taken, however, Dewey seems to have ignored avoidance of error as a desideratum in inquiry altogether. Rorty has made indifference to avoidance of error a cornerstone of his brand of pragmatism.

Such indifference is excessive. A concern to avoid error is an important ingredient in accounts of why it makes sense in inquiry to avoid relieving doubt to the maximum by contradicting ourselves or at least to the maximum that consistency will allow by becoming maximally opinionated. We temper the urge to settle our doubts completely by the reflection that in so doing we increase the risk of error incurred. Unless we care about avoiding falsity in efforts to relieve our doubts, we may reasonably contemplate contradicting ourselves as optimal because doing so relieves doubt maximally. And if, for some reason or other, contradicting oneself is ruled out of consideration, seeking relief from doubt without regard to whether we avoid error would recommend becoming maximally opinionated. Secular realists who are concerned to avoid error in the next change of belief but no further are able to recognize the best move at the next stage as involving a best trade-off between risk of error (at the next change) and the information gained. Considerations of such trade-offs will rarely license maximal opinionation.

For this reason, Dewey's (and Rorty's) indifference to the concern to avoid error (i.e., to importing false belief) ought to be rejected. Even so, Dewey's indifference seems to be related to a project of his that is as compelling as it is problematic — the characterization of inquiry aimed at resolving conflicts in value commitments.

States of full belief can plausibly be said to be truth-valued. James and Dewey would have agreed with Peirce that belief is directed at the truth in the sense that believing that h is judging that the belief that h is true. The bone of contention between the classical pragmatists concerned the question whether avoidance of error is a desideratum of individual inquiries according to the belief-doubt model.

Dewey, however, wished to extend the belief-doubt model so that it applied to other non-truth-valued propositional attitudes — in particular, to attitudes of valuing. Dewey understood rightly that there is room for some sort of distinction between settled value judgments and commitments and issues that are unsettled and, in that sense, subject to question or doubt. But the contrast between belief and doubt in this setting seems somewhat problematic. Even if one insists on speaking of value judgments as beliefs, it is doubtful whether one can consider such beliefs as uncertain in the sense that they are probably true or probably false. And if that is problematic, so is the notion of their being truth-valued altogether.[16]

I do not propose to examine this matter more closely here. I do want, however, to emphasize its significance. If value judgments lack truth-values, then inquiries concerned to settle unsettled questions of value cannot be inquiries where there is a concern to avoid error as well as to relieve doubt. Either students of the belief-doubt model must acknowledge that in one kind of inquiry avoidance of error does matter whereas in another it does not, or, if this looks like an untenable dualism, the concern to avoid error should be downgraded as a desideratum in all types of inquiry. Whether or not Dewey thought in these terms, it is clear that it followed the latter strategy.

My own inclination is to follow the former approach and accept the dualism. Changing states of full belief should, I think, take into account the question of error. Changing value commitments may not incur risk of error. The difference is an important but by no means an

---

16 Crispin Wright, in *Truth and Objectivity* (Cambridge, MA: Harvard University Press, 1992), seems to have overlooked the difficulty of comparing judgments like "x is better than y" and "y is better than x" with respect to how probable it is that they are true or false. Suppose I judged each of these sentences equally likely to be true. Should I then judge x and y equally good? If so, I cannot be *in suspense as to the truth* of the first two evaluations. I am convinced concerning the third. Indeed, there is no way that I can coherently assign probabilities to the first two alternatives and remain in suspense between them. But in that case, how can I suspend judgment concerning the truth of these alternatives at all? Perhaps I can be in some sort of suspense between them, but not with respect to truth-value. If this is so, these alternatives cannot be alleged to carry truth-values. Similar arguments apply to show that judgments of probability and judgments of serious possibility cannot be said to carry truth-values. See my *The Enterprise of Knowledge* and *Decisions and Revisions* (Cambridge: Cambridge University Press, 1984), Chapter 11, for somewhat more elaborate arguments as to why judgments of serious possibility, probability, and judgments of value cannot be treated as truth-value-bearing judgments of truth or falsity. It seems to me that Wright has left out of account certain "platitudes" that impose serious constraints on the attitudes that can be truth-value bearing and the way linguistic expressions of them are to be understood.

unprecedented one. There are other attitudes that lack truth-values besides value judgments. Judgments of (credal) probability and judgments of serious possibility do so as well; and these judgments are subject to revision in ways where risk of error cannot be the immediate issue.

But now several important questions need to be answered: In what sense, if any, may we suspend judgment concerning values, probabilities, and the like? Dewey clearly thought we could be in doubt as to what we ought to do; but can we say that a person in doubt as to what is to be done may entertain conjectures on this score, no more than one of which is true? If judgments of probability or of value are truth-valued, it seems plausible to suppose that probabilities can be assigned to such conjectures when in a state of doubt that express the inquirer's judgment of the risk of error to be incurred in removing doubt. If such probabilities cannot be assigned coherently, suspension of judgment cannot be between rival truth-value-bearing hypotheses.

In inquiries where truth-value-bearing beliefs are altered, the concern to avoid error checks our headlong dash to relieve our doubts. But in inquiries concerned to change value judgments, probability judgments, or other propositional attitudes where risking error when removing doubt proves to be an incoherent idea, what kinds of consideration can check the tendency to opinionation? Answering this question seems to me to be crucial to carrying out Dewey's ambitious philosophical project in a manner that respects the key ideas of the belief-doubt model of inquiry. I myself hope that some form of this program can be brought to a satisfactory conclusion. Although I have some fragmentary ideas related to the problem, I lack a comprehensive approach as to how to carry it off.

CANADIAN JOURNAL OF PHILOSOPHY
Supplementary Volume 24

Doubt: Affective States and the Regulation of Inquiry*

CHRISTOPHER HOOKWAY
University of Sheffield

Pragmatists challenge a sharp separation of issues of theoretical and practical rationality. This can encourage a sort of anti-realism: our classifications and theories are shaped by our interests and practical concerns. However, it need not do this. A more fundamental theme is that cognition is itself an activity, the attempt to solve problems and discover truths effectively and responsibly. Evidence has to be collected, experiments have to be devised and carried out, dialogues must be engaged in with fellow inquirers, decisions must be made about when we have scrutinized our opinions enough to trust our results. Even if our goals are "purely cognitive," the attempt to achieve them through inquiry and deliberation is an activity. The normative standards that guide its conduct, like those governing any activity, will include standards of practical rationality. Indeed, we might suggest that a belief is *justified* so long as it is the product of responsible, well-executed inquiry.

It is uncontroversial that our affective states have a role in practical rationality. We assess the rationality of desires and goals, and we can examine the role of emotions and attitudes in planning our conduct

* Earlier versions of this paper were read at the University of Bradford and at Bolton Institute of Higher Education I am very grateful for the valuable comments and criticisms I received on each of those occasions. I have also been helped by comments and suggestions from Tobies Grimaltos.

and carrying out our plans. Emotions can serve both as an aid to practical rationality and as an impediment to it. The classical pragmatists claimed that it also has a role in theoretical or cognitive rationality. For Peirce, one of the defining features of scientific inquiry is the fact that it is guided by a distinctive desire. And, as I have argued elsewhere, both Peirce and James insisted that distinctive sentiments were required for us to be able to reason well and trust our inductive strategies.[1] I believe that contemporary epistemology has suffered through its failure to take seriously the role of affective factors in cognition,[2] and this paper forms part of an attempt to remedy this lack.

My concern is with the role of states of *doubt*, of finding things puzzling or problematic. After introducing the issue and explaining its importance (Section I), I take note of some puzzling and influential claims on this topic made by C.S. Peirce in some of his most famous writings (Section II). After discussing what is puzzling about his claims, in the remainder of the paper I pursue three topics. First, I argue that theoretical rationality requires a distinctive kind of self-trust, which must include trust in our affective responses to propositions, inferences, and inquiries. Second, I argue that this can be used to explain why our instinctive feelings of doubt (or lack of doubt) possess a defeasible authority over philosophical challenges and arguments. Finally, I raise some issues about how we should think about the cognitive dimension of emotions. If the claims made here are correct, then the Peircean views are much less puzzling than initially appears.

I Doubt

To *doubt* a proposition is to take an evaluative stance towards it. In ordinary English, this may involve thinking that it is probably false: if I doubt that the mechanic has finished servicing my car, then I tenta-

---

1 "Mimicking Foundationalism: On Sentiments and Self-control," *European Journal of Philosophy* 1 (1993): 156–74.

2 For an interesting exception to this, see Catherine Elgin's *Considered Judgment* (Princeton, NJ: Princeton University Press, 1996), Chapter 5.

tively anticipate that he has not. But, especially in philosophy, it also covers cases where we find that the available evidence is insufficient to warrant either acceptance or rejection of a proposition — or hold that it is unclear whether the evidence is sufficient for that purpose. Of course, evaluations using this concept have been central to epistemology for two thousand years: standard sceptical arguments suggest a mismatch between our practice of doubting propositions and the evaluative standards which, we accept, we should employ. Reflection upon the structure of our system of beliefs is supposed to suggest that there are many things we do not naturally doubt, or we find it impossible to doubt, that in fact merit the evaluative stance which doubt involves. Much post-Cartesian epistemology has agreed that deep sceptical doubts should be used to raise the fundamental philosophical problems about knowledge. If I cannot rule out the possibility that my disembodied brain is suspended in a vat of chemicals, and stimulated by powerful scientists to experience a wholly illusory external world, then I ought to abandon my everyday beliefs about my surroundings and initiate inquiries into just how reliable my senses are.

As a matter of fact, of course, we do not *feel* such doubts. While acknowledging them as philosophical "oughts," we retain our everyday confidence in our beliefs about the world. Like some other philosophers influenced by the common-sense tradition, Peirce and the other pragmatists tend to dismiss these philosophical anxieties as "unreal," "unnatural," "paper doubts"; we should not doubt in philosophy what we do not doubt in our hearts. An issue is thus raised about whether the fact that we do not feel any doubt about our everyday beliefs should be assigned any philosophical weight. Does the fact that I feel certain of the existence of the external world have any legitimate authority over the considered philosophical judgment that this is a matter that intellectual responsibility *requires* me to doubt? Is there any way of sustaining the view that our natural dispositions to doubt and certainty possess any sort of intellectual authority?

These cases are superficially similar to many others where we (reasonably) judge that we ought to doubt propositions which our actions and motivations show that we rely upon in practice, and which we have no inclination to make objects of serious inquiry. Our failure to doubt *these* things is taken as a sign of irrationality. Examples might include the trust one continues to give to a close friend when presented with evidence that seems to establish that she has been unfaithful, or the readiness with which one hangs on to pet theories in the face of evidence that (one acknowledges) ought to be disturbing. If someone were to use the fact that our behaviour shows we do not really doubt these things as grounds for denying that there is anything wrong with our refusal to take the counter-evidence seriously in practice, we would respond that our failure to doubt these propositions is an epistemic failing. It does not show that we *ought* not to doubt them. Our failure to doubt these propositions "in our hearts" may reveal the weakness of our epistemic characters rather than the superior epistemological authority of our "hearts." If weight is to be attached to the fact that we do not take sceptical doubts seriously, then it is necessary to explain how they differ from the irrational failure to adjust one's beliefs to the evidence that we have just described. Why isn't our refusal to take sceptical "doubts" seriously similarly a mark of irrationality?

Sometimes Peirce defends his strategy by pointing out that doubts normally require "a reason": we need grounds for doubting propositions that we currently accept. He appears to think that the Cartesian method of doubt calls for ungrounded, unreasoned doubts: we are to doubt things simply by deciding to do so. However, this cannot be quite right. The first Meditation is full of reasons for questioning the legitimacy of currently held opinions. One might argue that the reasons offered by sceptical challenges are of the wrong kind: doubts are improperly entered or raised.[3] However, there is little sign of Peirce arguing in this fashion in the passages under discussion. While it is incumbent upon someone who rejects the significance of these familiar sceptical challenges to try to *explain* what is wrong with them, the *prima facie* authority of our instinctive refusal to doubt need not be based upon the details of such an explanation.

We need not rule out the possibility that it will turn out that this *is* "irrationality," or perhaps a way of coping with our desperate epistemological position. No adequate explanation of what is wrong with

---

3 See, for example, Stanley Cavell, *The Claim of Reason* (Oxford: Oxford University Press, 1979) and Michael Williams, *Unnatural Doubts* (Oxford: Blackwell, 1991), passim.

the challenges may be forthcoming. Any authority claimed for our in-stinctive dispositions to doubt and inquire may thus be defeasible. The question we have to consider concerns how they can possess even a defeasible authority. The position sketched below allows for the pos-sibility that we are rational to trust our instinctive feelings of doubts and rationality. Such trust is defeasible; we can envisage circumstances in which we would be forced to give it up. But in general, we have more reason to trust our instinctive judgments of rationality than we do the products of distinctively philosophical reasoning.[4] This, I shall suggest, is a pervasive theme in pragmatist epistemology, and repre-sents an important epistemological insight.

II Doubt and Belief

In "The Fixation of Belief," Peirce adopted a simple picture of "inquiry": our stable corpus of settled beliefs is shaken by a "surprising experi-ence" which gives rise to doubt about some of the propositions that were previously believed (W3:247ff).[5] These doubts motivate us to the activity of inquiry which is an attempt to eliminate the doubt, to re-place it by a new settled belief concerning the propositions in ques-tion. I believe that my car has been serviced, but on reaching the garage

---

4 If this is correct, then it suggests that there are rational limits to how reflective
   we should be in assessing our beliefs and inquiries; rational reflection is often
   fundamentally shallow. Mapping the limits of responsible or rational reflection
   was the main concern of my "Cognitive Virtues and Epistemic Evaluations,"
   International Journal of Philosophical Studies 2 (1994): 211–27. I discuss the topic
   further in Part 2 of *Scepticism* (London: Routledge, 1990) and in "Naturalised
   Epistemology and Epistemic Evaluation," *Inquiry* 37 (1994): 465–85.

5 References to Peirce's work employ two sources: they take the following standard forms. *Writings of Charles S. Peirce: A Chronological Edition* (Volumes 2 and 3),
   ed. M. Fisch et al. (Bloomington, IN: Indiana University Press, 1984–86) is re-
   ferred to in the text as "W" followed by volume and page. References to *Collected Papers of Charles Sanders Peirce*, ed. C. Hartshorne, P. Weiss, and A. Burks
   (Cambridge: Harvard University Press, 1931–58) identify volume and numbered
   paragraph.

I see the doors are locked and there is no sign of the car awaiting collection outside. Had the service been completed, I would have expected it to be outside, so a question is raised: perhaps the mechanics did not finish it after all. The unexpected experience presents me with a *problem*: the experience does not cohere with previously settled beliefs. Inquiry is an attempt to solve that problem, to remove the incoherence in my beliefs and expectations. Whether a "surprising experience" is the only thing that can present me with a problem may be questioned. But let us grant that it provides one possible source of problems which inquiries can try to solve.

Peirce's positive account of doubt exploited the view that propositional attitudes such as doubt and belief are to be distinguished by reference to their causal roles in shaping behaviour and cognition. There are two important differences between belief and doubt. Beliefs guide our desires and shape our actions: "The feeling of belief is a more or less sure indication of there being established in our nature some habit which will determine our actions" (W3:247). If I believe that the mechanic has completed the service, I shall head for the garage to collect my car. When I am in a state of doubt concerning a proposition, I will lack this sort of guidance in how to act. Doubt, in contrast, has a different positive effect: it is "an uneasy and unsettled state from which we struggle to free ourselves and pass into a state of belief" (ibid.). Thus both belief and doubt produce actions, but where beliefs prompt actions which would promote our goals if the belief were true, doubt prompts inquiry designed to eliminate the doubt.[6]

The second difference is that the effect of belief upon action is conditional. I shall only act upon my belief if I already possess a *desire* whose satisfaction requires use of my car as well as a body of appropriate background beliefs about my distance from the garage, the route to the taken to get there, and so on. Rather than make us act immedi-

---

6 Characterizing the kind of role in shaping actions which beliefs possess and doubts lack is not easy If my doubt that the car is ready for collection leads me to take the bus or train when I head for town, then that state can shape actions other than inquiries into the proposition doubted. I shall not pursue this issue here.

ately, a belief "puts us into such a condition that we shall behave in such a way when the occasion arises" (W3:247). The motivational force of doubt, we learn, is not conditional: it immediately stimulates us to action until it has been destroyed. So while the motivational force of a belief depends upon the presence of a desire, doubt is apparently intrinsically motivating. No independent desire to eliminate the doubt is required for us to be motivated to carry out the appropriate inquiry.

At first sight, this is extremely implausible, and it will be useful to work out exactly why this is. Peirce's account of doubt gives it two apparently distinct roles. First, it is an epistemic notion, an acknowledgement that the evidence available, or the results of our deliberations, requires us to suspend judgment on the matter in hand. A reason for doubt is something suggesting that we should abandon a settled belief or continue to suspend judgment on the matter. But second, it essentially involves possession of reasons for action; a reason for doubting some proposition is a reason for inquiring into its truth-value. The availability of this "reason to inquire" does not, it appears, require the cooperation of a desire to have a settled opinion concerning this truth value. Peirce treats doubt as a unified psychological state which embodies an epistemic evaluation and provides a reason for action. Well-entrenched Humean prejudices about reasons for action encourage the suspicion that Peirce has misidentified a complex hybrid state as a unitary one, and that this is the source of his claim that doubts motivate actions unconditionally. The state of doubt that he describes, the state of finding something doubtful or problematic, is composed of the epistemic state of finding that the evidence warrants suspension of judgment concerning the truth value of the proposition together with the *desire* not to be agnostic about it.

Another observation supports the same view. We can partially characterize someone's cognitive position at a particular time by listing their differing attitudes towards different propositions. Ignoring complexities introduced when we allow that beliefs may differ in strength, we might divide propositions into four classes:

1. Those that the agents accepts or believes
2. Those that the agent rejects or disbelieves
3. Those about which the agent is (calmly) agnostic
4. Those concerning which the agent is in a state of *doubt*: whether to believe or disbelieve them presents the agent with a problem

Calm agnosticism and active doubt both involve suspension of judgment concerning the truth of the proposition in question. But the agent is motivated to resolve this indeterminacy in the case of doubts, while agnosticism can be calm and undisturbing. Agnosticism need provide no immediate reason for carrying out an inquiry while, according to Peirce and other pragmatists, doubt does provide such a reason. It seems plausible that suspension of judgment on the proposition is a component of each. In the fourth class, this suspension of judgment is accompanied by a desire which is absent in the third. Once again, the idea of a unified state which is both an epistemic evaluation and the source of a reason for action seems problematic. Doubt appears to be a hybrid state composed of a state of agnosticism and a desire:

A is in a state of doubt concerning whether *p* if and only if

(1) *A* is agnostic concerning whether *p*

(2) *A* desires to have a firm opinion concerning whether *p*.

Peirce's original suggestion that doubt was a distinctive kind of mental state with a characteristic functional role in motivating inquiry is weakened. Suspension of belief and the desire to inquire appear to be distinct existences.

It is not yet clear whether the failure of Peirce's claims about doubt would undermine the uses made of the notion of "real doubt" in the discussions alluded to above. The following section will begin to look at the role that real doubts may have in our practice of inquiry and epistemic evaluation. We shall begin by looking at some claims of Peirce's and then move on to a defence of a view which is related to his. On this basis, in later sections of the paper, reasons will be given for rejecting the arguments just offered for the view that doubt should be seen as a hybrid or compound state which is composed of distinct states of suspension of judgment and desire.

III Doubt and the Regulation of Inquiry

What, then, is the role of states of doubt in carrying out inquiries? Our earlier discussion suggested that they are required for us to be motivated to carry out inquiries, providing the initial *push* required to ensure that we take problems seriously and try to solve them. However, this claim can be questioned.

Suppose that my philosophical reflections persuade me that I ought to doubt the existence of the external world. I judge that I have a reason to begin an inquiry which tries to answer the question "Is there an external world?" Although I feel no doubt that the external world exists, I may judge that this should be given no weight. Natural selection may have provided us with drives that prevent our efforts to reproduce being obstructed by the effects of reading too much philosophy. If I judge that I ought to investigate whether there is an external world and find it difficult to take such an inquiry seriously, it is not at all obvious that my reflective judgment should defer to my unreflective habits of doubt and investigation. Furthermore, it seems that we *can* inquire into the matter, even if no motivation is provided by a real doubt. I can ask the question "Is there an external world?" And I can reflect upon the strategies I might follow in order to answer it. It would be hard to deny that a sequence of actions designed to find the correct answer to a question that I have a formulated counts as an inquiry. So the claim that without real doubt there is no inquiry seems to be straightforwardly false.

In "Fixation of Belief" Peirce considers those philosophers who "have imagined that to start an inquiry it was only necessary to utter a question whether orally or by setting it down on paper":

> But the mere putting of a proposition into the interrogative form does not stimulate the mind to any struggle after belief. There must be a real and living doubt, and without this all discussion is idle ... When doubt ceases, mental action on the subject comes to an end; and, if it did go on, it would be without a purpose. Except that of self-criticism. (W3:248)[7]

Two different complaints are suggested by this passage. The first, considered above, is that without "living doubt," there is no deliberation or inquiry. Unless there is real doubt, "mental action on the subject comes to an end." The passage then appears to retreat from this bold claim: any apparent inquiry that did occur would be idle or without purpose. Perhaps idle or purposeless cognitive activity is not inquiry properly so called. The philosopher described in the previous para-

---

7 The final sentence was added to this 1877 passage in 1903 (*Collected Papers* 5.376).

graph may believe she is carrying out an inquiry when she is not, in fact, doing so.

Here is one way to set the issue up. Having enunciated the question "Is it the case that *p*?", someone can engage in an activity which he understands as an attempt to inquire into whether *p*. It is hard to see how the lack of a real doubt prevents this being the case. For the lack of real doubt to render this attempt "idle," we need an explanation of how the lack of a doubt has implications for the way in which the activity is conducted. Since inquiry is an activity that can be subject to rational self-control, can be subject to norms, we would need to tell a story about how the real doubt can have a role in the normative regulation of the inquiry. In the absence of a real doubt, the activity will not be controlled in the way that an inquiry should be. Doubt is not necessary only as a *stimulus* to real inquiry; it has a continuing role in monitoring the inquiry, in taking responsibility for how successful it is.

There is support for the claim that this idea is present in Peirce's discussion, although that is not essential to the claims I want to make here. In "Some Consequences of Four Incapacities" (1868) Peirce objects to the method of doubt:

> We cannot begin with complete doubt. We must begin with all the prejudices which we actually have when we enter upon the study of philosophy. These prejudices are not to be dispelled by a maxim, for they are things that it does not occur to us can be questioned. Hence this initial scepticism will be mere self-deception, and not real doubt; and no one who follows the Cartesian method will ever be satisfied until he has formally recovered all those beliefs which in form he has given up. (W2:212)

The suggestion here appears to be that unless we *really doubt* a proposition, our residual attachment to it will interfere with our deliberations. Part of the point is that we are not open to the truth: we will accept only one upshot to our inquiry, so we are not entering into it in the true scientific spirit. Also present is the suggestion that the belief will shape our inquiries in ways that we are unlikely to notice and unable to control. Unless real doubt is present, the inquiry will not be properly sensitive to norms of epistemic rationality. Can we make sense of this possibility?

The position to be sketched in the remaining sections of this paper explores how doubt may have an ineliminable role in the regulation and organization of responsible rational inquiry. Unless we are guided *inter alia* by our doubts, we will not be able to solve problems and answer questions effectively.

IV Habits and Evaluations

A pragmatist approach to mind, action, and cognition attaches importance to the fact that we possess batteries of habits which contribute to the shape of our character and whose action helps to determine the will. As well as habits that contribute to posture and gait, and as well as those which comprise practical skills such as the ability to ride a bicycle or dance a waltz, we possess cognitive habits. These include what Peirce called our *logica utens*, habits of inference, inquiry, and argument. My habits of inductive reasoning, my standards of plausibility and implausibility, my judgments of what stands in need of defence and what goes without saying, reflect and determine patterns in my systems of beliefs and my cognitive practice. Although we might be able to describe these patterns by formulating general principles or rules which they reflect, it is an important part of the phenomenology of deliberation and inquiry that we need not be reflectively aware of any such principles when we are guided by these habits. Their operation is not mediated through reflection upon the standards that they embody, and, in many cases, we are incapable of such reflection. The importance of this point for understanding practical rationality has long been acknowledged. It is part of the contribution of pragmatist logicians to emphasize that the same is true of theoretical or epistemic rationality.

This observation has immediate relevance to the matter we have been discussing. First, these are largely habits of *evaluation*: they guide us in recognizing when an inference is a good one, when evidence is sufficient for belief in some proposition, when hypotheses are so implausible that we need not take steps to eliminate them before accepting a rival, and so on. We are guided by habits of evaluation, and often we cannot explain or sometimes even describe the standards which guide our evaluations. Our sense that we are inquiring responsibly and effectively calls for confidence in our instinctive and habitual cognitive skills; it calls for a distinctive kind of "self-trust." We must be confident that trusting our *logica utens*, our habits of reasoning and evaluation, will guide us towards the truth. Our judgments track values that have positive logical (or practical) merit. We can have confidence in our judgments, taking responsibility for how well our inquiries are conducted, only if we assign a presumptive authority to these habitual evaluations, even if we cannot reflectively explain what this authority consists in. On pain of a crippling form of scepticism, we cannot reasonably hope to replace all such habitual evaluation by explicit acknowledgement of rules and formal standards. This is evident from the fact that (habitual) judgment is always involved in the application of explicit formal rules to complex real cases. In general: confidence in our ability to inquire responsibly requires a degree of trust in our habits of cognitive evaluation.

Of course, it is compatible with this that such habits of evaluation are flawed. Much irrationality depends upon flaws in our epistemic character: we are naturally and habitually disposed to accept attractive conclusions on the basis of inadequate evidence or to be unreasonably cautious. Our standards of reasoning (including habitual ones) guide us in identifying circumstances in which we would be irresponsible to trust our intuitive standards of reasoning. It is compatible with this that rationality is possible only if we assign our intuitive or instinctive standards a *prima facie* or presumptive plausibility. Responsible reasoning requires confidence or self-trust.[8]

Included among these cognitive habits and instincts is our capacity to find beliefs or propositions *doubtful*. When evidence conflicts with an established belief, our habitual *logica utens* leads us to judge whether it is sufficient to unsettle that belief. When inquiry into a matter calls for information where we are currently agnostic, habits of inquiry can contribute to making that matter problematic: the question emerges

---

8 The epistemic importance of the idea of self-trust has recently been emphasized by Keith Lehrer in *Self-Trust: A Study of Reason, Knowledge and Autonomy* (Oxford: Oxford University Press, 1997).

as one which we are motivated to answer. Hence if cognitive rationality and epistemic responsibility require a presumptive, but defeasible, trust in our cognitive habits, then it requires such a confidence in our capacity to judge when something is open to doubt.

We should emphasize one consequence of these observations. An important distinction can be drawn between:

1. Those norms and patterns of evaluation which guide us in the conduct of activities including those of inquiry and investigations

2. Those norms and standards of evaluation which we believe are guiding us in these activities

Cartesian epistemology requires that reflection and introspection can ensure that these coincide. If we are responsible, we are guided only by norms that we can reflectively formulate and endorse. The style of pragmatist epistemology that we are concerned with here rejects this Cartesian view. If our practice conflicts with those abstract normative standards which, we believe, we *ought* to be guided by, there is a defeasible presumption in favour of the norms implicit in our practice. We question our habitual standards only if we have evidence that they have led us into error or we can explain what is wrong with them. If we abandon this presumption, responsible, confident reasoning and inquiry is not possible. Although this does not establish that the presumption is *true*, it does establish that it would be irrational and self-defeating to reject it while continuing to hold that we can participate in responsible ratiocination. Self-trust is a necessary condition for responsible rationality.[9]

---

9 I shall not discuss in detail exactly why the sort of self-trust described here is rational. At least two strategies suggest themselves, both familiar from pragmatist writings. First: it could be defended as a regulative presumption. If it is not warranted, then responsible rationality would be impossible, so it is rational to proceed on the *hope* that it is warranted. Second: appeal could be made to the fact that it is "natural" and, indeed, unavoidable much of the time. If my behaviour shows that I endorse it, then, in the absence of a positive reason for doubting it, I am warranted in relying upon it.

V Doubts and Anxieties

How could states such as doubt have a role in organizing and regulating inquiries? When I judge that something ought to be done — for example, that I ought to check whether it rained in New York yesterday — my judgment has two features that call for philosophical explanation. First, it has a *normative* character: we need to understand how the judgment is related to, or grounded in, defensible epistemic ideals. Irrationality often involves being guided by such judgments when their normative status is questionable. The sort of self-trust we considered in the previous section involves trusting that our habitual and unreflective judgments about how we ought to conduct our inquiries reflect adequate epistemic norms. Second, it has the power to guide or motivate inquiries and deliberations. We have a tendency to act as our "ought" judgments decree. Such questions arise whether the norms concern how we should act or whether they govern our cognitive activities and functions.

What form does this "motivation" take when the evaluations we make take the form of doubting some proposition? One answer to this question is familiar and straightforward: having judged that its status is problematic, we are motivated to the sorts of actions and activities that serve as components of inquiries. Since inquiry is an activity, epistemic norms produce actions just as practical norms do. But there is another answer too. Our evaluations "spread" to other propositions, beliefs, and inferences that are suitably related to the object of our initial evaluation. When I believe a proposition, I am defeasibly committed to approving of any proposition which follows from it; when I approve of a form of inference, I am committed to accepting the results of its employment; when I doubt a proposition, I am committed to reassessing my endorsement of beliefs and inferences which depend upon it. Epistemic evaluations bring with them a network of commitments; we are committed to related evaluations of other beliefs, inferences, doubts, and inquiries. We can carry out inquiries guided by the habits of epistemic evaluation described in the last section only if we can be confident that our evaluations will spread through our beliefs and regulate our inquiries in accordance with this network of normative commitments. One way in which we might argue that inquiry in the absence of real doubt will be idle, or will be improperly regulated, would involve suggesting that our normative commitments would not then be reflected in the ways in which our epistemic evaluations spread through our whole corpus of beliefs and inferences. There will be no basis for a crucial kind of self-trust or confidence; we can no longer trust our habits of doubt, belief, and inference.

Once we reject the Cartesian ideal that we have reliable access to the normative standards that guide our inquiries and deliberations, we will best understand our ability to keep track of our epistemic commitments by acknowledging that we trust our cognitive habits to ensure that our evaluations spread through our system of beliefs in an appropriate way. If our evaluations do not engage with these habits, then we may begin to doubt that we can track appropriate epistemic norms as we deliberate and conduct our inquiries. And, the suggestion will be, inquiries that are focused on "unreal doubts" will be guided by evaluations which do not engage with our habits of evaluation in the right way.

An illustration of some of these points may be helpful. Suppose that I intend to carry out a task cooperatively with a friend. Information emerges which may cast doubt upon the friend's reliability or trustworthiness. But this new evidence is not decisive: it points towards the unreliability of the friend, but whether it should be sufficient to sway my opinion is a matter for judgment. Now compare two cases. I may genuinely come to doubt my friend's reliability: I take the evidence to be sufficient to raise a genuine doubt. Alternatively, I may judge that the evidence *ought* to shake my confidence, that it warrants a doubt which I do not, as a matter of fact, feel. In the latter case, my view about the friend's unreliability will affect my plans and other opinions only if I explicitly recall my judgment about how I ought to have responded. In the former case, the active real doubt will ensure that I am doubtful about beliefs and proposals which depend upon the friend's reliability without my needing to recall the judgment that I earlier made. I can trust my habits of cognitive evaluation, confident that (in most cases and in normal circumstances) new doubts will emerge when required by the initial doubt. Real doubts can regulate inquiries in ways that formally acknowledged but "unreal" or "unfelt" doubts do not.

In the last paragraph I spoke of unreal doubts as "unfelt." This introduces a further important theme in pragmatist epistemology. If habitual assessments are going to provide evaluations of our cognitive position which spread through our beliefs and inferences, helping us to honour our evaluative commitments, then it is important that evaluative states such as doubt have a strong affective flavour. Our doubts evaluate our cognitive situation rather as our emotions evaluate ourselves and our surroundings. The idea that sentiments and emotions have an ineliminable role in epistemic rationality was defended by both Peirce and William James, and I shall not discuss their views on the matter here.[10] Instead I shall simply try to make the idea plausible.

We can do so by considering an analogy. We might suppose that when I come to doubt a proposition, I become *anxious* about any tendency to accept it that I still possess; I shall also become anxious about any other beliefs I hold which may depend upon it. Suppose, then, that we think of doubt as a particular kind of anxiety. We can then understand doubt better by looking at more familiar cases of anxiety. It is an emotional response which normally involves the belief that I am in a position that involves a danger or risk of some harmful outcome. It also involves dispositions or inclinations to behave in distinctive ways, to focus on distinctive features of my situation to the exclusion of others, and to have thoughts and questions of particular kinds occur to me. We are familiar with how excessive anxiety can be incapacitating, undermining our ability to make sound judgments about how we should act. But it is also plausible that someone who never felt anxiety would be likely to fail to take necessary precautions and, in consequence, to embark on foolhardy projects. The successful regulation of actions may require, or at least be promoted by, the possession of an appropriate tendency to feel anxiety when one's situation presents a sufficient degree of risk or danger. By making me sensitive to risks and dangers, unreflectively alert to possible hazards, anxiety may enable me to act spontaneously and effectively and pre-

---

10 I have done so elsewhere: see "Mimicking Foundationalism" and "Sentiment and Self-control," in *The Rule of Reason: The Philosophy of Charles Sanders Peirce*, ed. Jacqueline Brunning and Paul Forster (Toronto: Toronto University Press, 1997), 201–22. Also relevant is "Cognitive Virtues and Epistemic Evaluations," *International Journal of Philosophical Studies* 2 (1994): 211–27.

vent me carelessly exposing myself to unnecessary risks. The emotional state provides a tool for collecting relevant information and planning actions in the light of it: we might even say that it is the form taken by my cognitive awareness of the riskiness of my position. It embodies my evaluative stance towards my situation. While we can explain my actions only by alluding to my desire to avoid the dangers in question, it would be a mistake sharply to distinguish my cognitive search for information about risks and dangers from my motivating anxieties.

Think of an experienced hiker, someone with a deep understanding of the local terrain, of the chances and effects of changes in the weather, of her own strengths and weaknesses, and so on. This knowledge can be manifested in judgments about, for example, when weather conditions make a particular route too risky. It is natural to think of this as involving more than just a body of propositional knowledge. It involves a complex kind of skill which may be manifested in the walker's ability to feel anxiety or feel secure in different circumstances: she will listen to the judgments of her heart, trusting her habits of judgment and her ability instinctively to *read* the weather and the terrain. When she trusts her judgments on such matters, she is, in a sense, using her own cognitive habits as a reliable instrument for judging the riskiness of the situation; she accepts the testimony of her own affective nature. When she feels alarmed or anxious, she is likely to seek an alternative route; when she feels secure in her position, she will not investigate the possibility of an alternative.

The way this case has been described might be misleading. It can appear to contrast an excessively intellectualist picture of deliberation with the suggestion that we should proceed in a somewhat zomboid manner, trusting our instincts and totally dispensing with reflection and careful thought about the position. My intention is, rather, to emphasize that inquiry and deliberation involve a complex interplay of intellectual reflection and trusting acquiescence in habitual judgments and sentimental responses. Finding a situation to be risky or dangerous is an assessment or evaluation of it. The situation has features which are likely to threaten my security or the success of my actions. Second, once I am anxious about my situation I will be motivated to avoid risks, to find alternative actions if possible, to take care not to expose myself unnecessarily to danger. This motivation is immediate or unconditional: my evaluation does not merely inform me that *if* I wish to avoid danger or risk, I should avoid acting in these circumstances. Through sensing the danger in my circumstances, I am *already* motivated to take precautions and avoiding acting if possible. I can decide that I should act in spite of feeling the anxiety: the reasons I possess are defeasible. And I can recognize that my evaluations should be ignored because they are irrational; they reflect a character that is *too* timid, too ready to be incapacitated by slight dangers. In spite of this, in general, my anxiety will be an assessment of the situation which does not need to be supplemented by the desire to avoid danger to affect my dispositions to action and to colour my deliberations.

The third point, relevant to the assessment of the hybrid view, is that these habitual and sentimental evaluations of our position can have a *content* which is not simply the content of some *belief* that the person has. Consider someone who is irrationally afraid of frogs.[11] He can simultaneously judge intellectually that frogs present us with no danger at all and affectively represent them as alarming or threatening. The affective representation tends to influence his behaviour, which he must fight against. He should not listen to the testimony of the heart; his self-trust should be qualified. Such examples illustrate that we should not view the cognitive aspect of anxiety as a simple combination of a belief and an attitude towards it. Our agent does not really possess the belief in question, and the content only influences his planning and deliberation through its emotional representation. In that case, it is plausible that even where belief and emotion are not in conflict, so that we trust the latter to guide our deliberations and our actions, the primary representation can be the emotional one. We believe the path to be dangerous *because* we trust our affective representation of it as risky, *because* we find ourselves motivated to avoid it or to take special care. I don't form a calm assessment of the degree of danger that I face, and then feel anxiety or not according to how desires and emotions interfere with this calm assessment. I normally *trust* my immediate emotional responses to arrive at a sensitive and reliable assessment

---

11 This example is discussed by Catherine Elgin in *Considered Judgment*, Chapter 5; see esp. 146–47.

of the degree of danger. My assessment of the situation is most directly expressed in the ways in which I am motivated to respond to it.

As we saw, feelings of anxiety and judgments about degree of risk can fail to be in harmony. I can judge that there is no danger, while anxieties shape my deliberations, causing me to expend much effort on considering possible dangers. And the calm confidence with which I deal with a situation can undermine my judgment that it is risky or alarming. We may explain away such cases: my feeling are neurotic and should be ignored. But there is a genuine possibility that, in some cases at least, affective responses are more trustworthy than reflective considered ones. This is because they can reveal a habitual sensitivity to subtle features of the situation which are not formally acknowledged by calm reflection. Habitual evaluative practices can reflect extensive experience and an acute sensitivity to the fine details of our environment. In such cases, we do better to trust the ways in which our affective natures shape our deliberations, taking seriously the questions that are pressed upon us.

As we noted above, Peirce's remarks about doubt suggest that it involves a kind of anxiety about any inquiry that relies upon a doubted proposition. Just as anxiety immediately motivates us to avoid danger or mitigate its effects, so doubt motivates us to remove the uncertainty that attaches to the proposition. And just as anxiety reflects the operation of "standards" of evaluation which are not explicitly formulated or reflectively applied, so are our doubts informed by our habitual and unreflective standards for assessing evidence. Once we take account of the fact that decisions about whether to accept or reject propositions must be made in the light of the totality of other information we possess, it is easy to see that they involve the manifestation of judgment, and not just the mechanical application of rules in the light of limited bodies of relevant evidence. Just as we can trust our affective responses to the dangers of the hillside, so we can trust our habitual or instinctive judgments about the acceptability of propositions. Such judgments can guide both our decision that some proposition should be made an object of investigation and our subsequent reflection that it has passed sufficient tests and can now be firmly accepted. And just as our awareness of danger may receive its primary manifestation in an affective representation, in an immediate motivation to avoid the danger or eliminate it, so our awareness that a propo-

sition is poorly supported may receive its primary manifestation in a
state of doubt or of epistemic anxiety. Possessing such affective pres-
entations may be as essential to the successful pursuit of truth as a
well-attuned sense of danger is to survival in the hills.

A plausible account of cognitive evaluation will thus incorporate
both conscious application of principles and habitual evaluations. It
must allow for the fact that we often criticize or lose trust in our evaluative habits: critical self-trust or confidence is the attitude towards our
cognitive habits that seems appropriate. The conclusion of this section
is that we can make sense of some of the distinctive features of pragmatist ideas about doubt through acknowledging that many of our
evaluative standards are habitual and manifested through our affective responses to our beliefs and inquiries.

VI Conclusion: Doubt and Agnosticism

At the end of Section II, we considered the suggestion that doubt is a
sort of hybrid state compromised of a state of suspension of judgment
and a desire: I am in a state of doubt concerning whether p if and only
if I am agnostic about whether p and I desire to have an opinion on
the matter. Agnosticism or suspension of belief provides a common
core to states of real doubt and calm agnosticism; these states differ
solely in that the former also contains a desire for information. This
view appeared to be plausible, yet it was at odds with Peirce's claim
that doubt was a distinct kind of psychological state characterized by
the fact that it provided an immediate, unconditional motivation to
inquiry. Although it is possible that we could combine the claim that
states of real doubt have an important role in the regulation of belief
and inquiry with the hybrid view of doubt, I shall now suggest that
this is not the best strategy to adopt. Agnosticism is not a unitary psychological state constituting the common core to complex states such
as doubt and calm agnosticism.

A common view of how information is stored in our minds employs a distinction between different kinds of beliefs. Some beliefs are
explicitly psychologically real: I believe that my computer is black because I have explicitly registered that piece of information. There are
other propositions which I believe only because the information they

express is readily available to me: when asked whether I have a prime number of siblings, I can answer immediately although this involves an inference from more fundamental beliefs. In another case, I may believe that I am in a dangerous situation where this consists in my trusting a largely affective response to my position. In each case, I possess a piece of information, and it can guide my actions and deliberations in analogous and intelligible ways. The psychological reality of the beliefs is quite different.

Consider two cases where I rapidly descend into the valley because the weather is becoming dangerous. In each case, it is true that I believe that the situation is becoming dangerous; and in each case I desire to avoid danger. The first case is one in which the belief and desire are "distinct existences." Perhaps I have accepted the testimony of a radio weatherman that it will soon become foggy, and I have formed a general policy of avoiding exposure to fog on high ground. The second is a case in which I trust my judgment of the changing conditions, listening to my heart's reasons. My belief that the weather is dangerous reflects trust in my anxious reaction, in my urge to leave the hilltops as soon as I can. In that case, although I possess both belief and desire, they are not distinct existences; were the desire absent, I would lack the belief.

A related point was made by Thomas Nagel.[12] That someone is in pain itself provides a reason for helping them; it does not need to be accompanied by an *independent* desire to contribute to the alleviation of suffering. Perhaps we could not recognize something as a *person* who was *in pain* unless we possessed dispositions to sympathize, feel concern, and offer help when we could. Possession of the concept of pain commits us (defeasibly) to a sympathetic concern for those we identify as subjects of pain. It does not follow from this that we do *not* desire to help those whose pain we acknowledge. It is sufficient that the recognition of the pain and the desire are not independent: we have a defeasible inclination to help this person in virtue of having recognized that she is in pain. I would have reason to help her if and only if I believed she was in pain and I desired to alleviate the suffering of

13 Nagel, *The Possibility of Altruism* (Oxford: Oxford University Press, 1970).

people in pain. But it would be wrong to suppose that this reason could be factored into the recognition that the person is in pain and a separate and contingent sympathetic desire.

A related distinction may be drawn among propositions that we are agnostic about. There are at least three possibilities. Some propositions may be consciously acknowledged to be unsettled: I *may* have a file of propositions concerning which, I am aware, I suspend judgment. In other cases, the vast majority, my agnosticism may consist in the fact that the proposition is "stored" nowhere at all. In such cases, it may be difficult to tell whether I am agnostic about the matter, or whether I possess information which, in the circumstances, I cannot recall. There may be no effective way of establishing whether I am agnostic about it. A third possibility is relevant here. I may have a relatively stable belief which is rarely manifested in action. When evidence comes in that challenges it, then the question whether that is sufficient to warrant agnosticism may not be settled until the belief becomes relevant to a further inquiry. I am agnostic if, were I to need to rely on this information, I would enter a state of active doubt. It is only in this situation that the habitual criteria of evidential assessment become operative and can make a judgment on the sufficiency of the disturbing evidence. It is not settled whether I am agnostic about the proposition until it is fixed whether we should be motivated to inquire into the matter. We trust our affective dispositions to doubt to determine whether we are agnostic about the proposition or not. In such cases, we are agnostic about the proposition *in virtue of the fact that we are disposed to doubt it*. If that is right, then we cannot view the state of agnosticism as a psychological constituent of the doubt.

If this is right, then the hybrid view becomes implausible. We can agree that calm agnosticism and real doubt both involve suspension of judgment. The hybrid view goes beyond this in claiming that this suspension of judgment is a unitary kind of psychological state which forms a psychological constituent of each. This further view now seems implausible. In some cases, I suspend judgment in a proposition *in virtue of* doubting it; in other cases, I suspend judgment in virtue of the fact that neither it, nor its negation, is stored accessibly in my mind. There may be other kinds of suspension of judgment too. But the idea of real doubt as a distinctive cognitive state, with a fundamental role in regulating inquiries, can be retained.

It does not follow from this that Cartesian worries are of no philosophical significance. I am not arguing that these observations refute scepticism. It is conceivable that the habitual patterns of evaluation we have been discussing are impediments rather than aids to the responsible search for the truth. A weaker conclusion does follow, however: rationality requires a defeasible confidence or trust in our habits of inquiry and evaluation.[13] When philosophical models of rationality cast doubt upon our habits of reasoning and inquiry, our confidence in our habits can warrant us in (at least) hoping that this is to be explained through inadequacies in our philosophical models.

---

13 This then gives rise to the philosophical task of arriving at an explanation of our cognitive habits and goals that vindicates this presumption of their adequacy If we fail in this task, then scepticism may be unavoidable. Much of Peirce's work can be read as an attempt to carry out this task.

CANADIAN JOURNAL OF PHILOSOPHY
Supplementary Volume 24

Pragmatism and Moral Knowledge*

DAVID BAKHURST
Queen's University at Kingston

I

In the last twenty years there has been a dramatic revival of interest in the idea that there can be genuine moral knowledge. The non-cognitivist assumptions that dominated so much twentieth-century ethical theory no longer seem the obvious truths they once did to so many thinkers. It is now common to hear the claim that moral values are genuine constituents of the furniture of the world — or at least of its upholstery — and that moral deliberation and judgment legitimately aspire to truth. Morality, it is frequently argued, is a realm of discovery rather than invention, and moral reasoning, and the play of moral imagination, must be constrained by how the moral facts stand.[1]

Such "realist" or "cognitivist" views in ethics take many forms.[1] This essay considers whether a pragmatist account of moral knowledge

---

* I am grateful to Christine Sypnowich for her comments on an earlier draft.

1 Margaret Little elegantly describes varieties of moral realism on the contemporary scene in her two-part review of the literature in *Philosophical Books* 35 (1994): 145–53 and 225–33. Little organizes her discussion around the "deep and fascinating divide" between the blend of realism and naturalism advanced by American philosophers such as Richard Boyd, David Brink, and Peter Railton, with its roots in naturalistic epistemology and the philosophy of science, and the moral cognitivism that originated in Britain in the work of John McDowell, David Wiggins, Jonathan Dancy, Sabina Lovibond, and others, which Little describes as a form of non-naturalism. Representative readings from both camps, and their common non-cognitivist opponents, are collected in Geoffrey Sayre-McCord, ed., *Essays on Moral Realism* (Ithaca, NY: Cornell University Press, 1988).

might fruitfully be developed.[2] My project will recommend itself only to those who believe that pragmatist insights serve to support relatively robust conceptions of truth and justification. Those who see pragmatism as deconstructing all philosophical accounts of truth, and

---

David McNaughton's *Moral Vision* (Oxford: Basil Blackwell, 1988), is an excellent introduction to the British variety.

It is important to be wary of the labels often attached to positions in this debate. Some of the British group, for example, are in fact reluctant to describe themselves as "moral realists," preferring the term "cognitivism" (though in my view this also has unfortunate associations) (see, e.g., Wiggins's *Needs, Values, Truth* [Oxford: Basil Blackwell, 1987], 330–31, 335 n. 19, and his "Moral Cognitivism, Moral Relativism and Motivating Moral Beliefs," *Proceedings of the Aristotelian Society* 91 (1990–91): Section 3). In addition, their position can be seen as a form of non-naturalism only if the term "naturalism" is reserved for positions committed to deploying exclusively natural-scientific forms of explanation. The British writers, inspired as they are by Aristotle and Wittgenstein, are best seen as pressing for a broader conception of the natural, which would encompass our moral sensibilities (and indeed our other conceptual capacities) as aspects of our nature, even though these cannot be rendered transparent by the explanatory resources of natural science. This is an explicit theme in the recent writings of John McDowell, who urges that we extend our concept of nature to encompass the "second nature" human beings acquire through enculturation (see his *Mind and World* [Cambridge, MA: Harvard University Press, 1994] and "Two Sorts of Naturalism" in *Virtues and Reasons. Philippa Foot and Moral Theory*, eds. Rosalind Hursthouse, Gavin Lawrence, and Warren Quinn [Oxford: Clarendon Press, 1995], 149–79).

Note also that Little does not discuss communitarians like Alasdair MacIntyre and Charles Taylor, whose historicist accounts of moral knowledge have affinities with the British school. There are also figures, such as Michael Smith (see, e.g., *The Moral Problem* [Oxford: Blackwell, 1994]), who do not fit neatly into either camp.

2 Precedents are to be found in Cheryl Misak's "Pragmatism, Empiricism and Morality," in Sabina Lovibond and S.G. Williams, eds., *Essays for David Wiggins. Identity, Truth and Value* (Oxford: Basil Blackwell, 1996), 201–18, and in recent writings of Hilary Putnam's (see, e.g., the essays in Part 2 of *Realism with a Human Face* (Cambridge, MA: Harvard University Press, 1990). David Wiggins cautiously deploys Peircian insights in developing his moral cognitivism; see "Truth as Predicated of Moral Judgments" and "Postscript" (Part 3) in *Needs, Values, Truth*, 139–84 and 329–50. Pragmatist themes also inform the view of

---

revealing the parochial or ethnocentric character of the justification of belief, will find my approach misguided. I will not attempt to refute such views, except by endeavouring to reveal the depth and attractiveness of a cognitivist approach.

II

Let us begin by reflecting on the suggestion, made by Cheryl Misak, that a broadly Peircian conception of truth be applied to moral judgment.[3] On this view, a belief is true if it would permanently withstand sustained, far-reaching critical inquiry. A true belief is one which will survive any trials inquiry could subject it to. Rorty is right that to call a judgment (or belief, claim, sentence, etc.) "true" is to pay it a compliment. But what is crucial is that some compliments are warranted, others not. We are right to commend a judgment as true if we believe that the reasons that support it would not be undermined no matter how far we were to inquire into the matter.

It seems natural to extend this account to moral judgment. When we deliberate about some moral problem, we aspire to arrive at a judgment supported by grounds that will withstand scrutiny. Why deny that such judgments can be genuinely true? One reason, at the heart of many forms of non-cognitivism, appeals to a sharp distinction between facts and values. It is argued that while empirical judgments about matters of everyday or scientific fact are answerable to experience, moral judgments are ultimately expressions of value, which are

---

moral knowledge developed in Charles Larmore's *The Morals of Modernity* (Cambridge: Cambridge University Press, 1996) (see, e.g., 59). Of the classical pragmatists, John Dewey was most preoccupied with ethical issues, and his voluminous (and sadly neglected) writings, though hard to square with much that passes for moral realism, contain many insights that might inform contemporary debates about the scope and limits of moral cognitivism, and its relation to naturalism.

3 Misak develops this idea in "Pragmatism, Empiricism and Morality" and in her forthcoming *Moral Deliberation: Truth, Conflict, and Modesty* (London: Routledge). I am indebted to her for allowing me to read the latter work in manuscript.

not objects of rational assessment or inquiry at all. Misak responds to this familiar objection by endorsing a radical form of epistemological holism. Quine, in pragmatist spirit, famously attacked the analytic-synthetic distinction and concluded that all beliefs face the tribunal of experience. Let us follow Putnam's recommendation and endorse another lesson of classical pragmatism. We must reject the fact-value distinction as well and grant that judgments in both classes (insofar as we can distinguish them) represent beliefs. So long as we work with a suitably broad notion of experience — so that experience includes anything which in impinging upon us can provide reasons for us to revise our judgments — we can assert, hardly outlandishly, that judgments about whether some object or action is desirable are accountable to experience and can and should be the outcome of reflective inquiry.

The framework of epistemic holism suits the post-foundationalist spirit of most contemporary moral realism. It involves a thoroughgoing fallibilism in which no component in our system of beliefs is immune from revision under pressure from recalcitrant experience, and it acknowledges that there is no vantage point beyond that system from which to improve it. Its guiding metaphor is Neurath's boat. We must work from within our conceptions, adjusting the beliefs challenged by experience in light of other beliefs in which we retain confidence. This picture, applied to moral realism, has the effect of ridding the latter of any whiff of dogmatism or authoritarianism. Someone who endorses such a holism must recognize that, although a true belief is one which would stand the trials of inquiry come what may, nothing guarantees that any particular belief will not be undermined by subsequent experience.

One significant difference between such a pragmatist position and many contemporary forms of moral realism is that the former will likely aspire to have immediate consequences for moral practice. Although moral realists often hold that the adoption of their preferred variety of realism would not leave our "first-order" moral views untouched, they rarely make this the subject of sustained discussion. The pragmatist, in contrast, can be expected to ask, as soon as content is given to the notion of moral inquiry, whether our practices of moral deliberation and debate are in good order and how circumstances might be changed better to facilitate sustained and rigorous inquiry. We might (as Misak hopes to) deploy the Peircian framework in support of left-wing liberal democracy on the grounds that free and open critical debate between exponents of contrasting ethical standpoints, in an atmosphere of tolerance, is essential to serious inquiry. And some moral views — relativism and nihilism, for instance — might be rejected for, as Peirce puts it, blocking "the way of inquiry."[4] Indeed, such a charge might be levelled against the very non-cognitivist assumption which we earlier considered as a challenge to cognitivism: the denial that our attitudes and desires are open to rational criticism. However these arguments might go, we should expect a pragmatist account of moral knowledge not to feign neutrality with respect to first-order moral positions (as so much meta-ethical writing does), but to inherit the activist spirit characteristic of the pragmatist tradition.

III

It might be thought odd to press pragmatism into the service of moral realism, since pragmatism is commonly associated with views antithetical to any kind of realism. For example, pragmatists are famous for stressing the intimate relation between theory and practice, which they usually explicate by endorsing a criterion of significance which ties the meaning of propositions to their consequences for experience. Such an approach clearly has affinities with verificationism, a stance not usually associated with realism.

Yet despite this association, the pragmatist's criterion of significance need not prove an obstacle to a sane form of realism. Pragmatists typically invoke their criterion of significance to play a negative role: to rule out as unsound hypotheses whose truth would make no recognizable difference to experience. This is incompatible with extreme forms of "metaphysical" realism that represent reality as a transcendent "in itself," inaccessible directly to experience, but it need not conflict with the basic realist idea that judgment is accountable to a reality which has the character it does, for the most part, independently of

---

4 C.S. Peirce, *Collected Papers* (Cambridge, MA: Harvard University Press, 1931), 1.135.

our beliefs about it. The criterion makes difficulties for sensible forms of realism only when combined with an austere conception of experience of a kind associated with classical empiricism or logical positivism. If we suppose that thought constructs a picture of the world out of such slender experiential materials, it is hardly surprising that we can find no rational warrant for belief in much that we naturally take to be constitutive of the world independent of thought. Some form of idealism seems inevitable. But the deliverances of experience need not be conceptualized so austerely. Our conception of experience should not be dictated by philosophy (or rather, by what philosophers suppose that science reveals experience to be), but should be gleaned from reflection, with as much sensitivity as possible, on experience as it manifests itself to us. This is a lesson heeded by many within the pragmatist tradition, Peirce included, and when suitably finessed, it allows us to countenance the idea that sense experience affords us access to a reality that is in many respects determinate independently of thought.

Another potential obstacle to realism lies in pragmatists' tendencies, when explaining the idea that true beliefs are those that survive the trials of inquiry, to collapse the concept of truth into that of agreement. Peirce himself writes that "the opinion which is fated to be ultimately agreed to by all who investigate is what we mean by the truth, and the object represented in this opinion is the real."[5] Here it seems that, "at the end of inquiry," human agreement determines truth. But such a conclusion surely does violence to the idea that our beliefs are accountable to a reality that is as it is independent of how we take it to be.

Some pragmatists respond that to suppose that reality might remain opaque to us when inquiry has been taken as far as possible is to work with a transcendent concept of the real, typical of classical "correspondentist" theories of truth, according to which reality and our beliefs about it might never be in harmony. Once we jettison metaphysical realism, it is argued, the identification of truth and agreement at the end of inquiry is benign. However, if we can draw a distinction between the

---

5 Peirce, "How to Make Our Ideas Clear," in C. Kloesal, ed., *Writings of Charles S. Peirce. A Chronological Edition*, vol.3 (1872–78) (Bloomington, IN: Indiana University Press, 1986), 273.

truth and beliefs presently justified by inquiry by our best lights, as our fallibilism requires us to, can we not make sense of the idea that the truth might elude us however bright our lights were? Much mischief is done here by the concept of "the end of inquiry," and cognate idealizations. It *seems* innocuous to say that if inquiry is pursued to the limit, belief and truth cannot fail to coincide. But the claim is innocuous only so long as we suppose that, at the end of inquiry, agreement does not determine truth, but inquiry rests because inquirers have converged upon the truth about reality as it is independent of agreement. On the latter reading, however, the notions of truth and reality are deployed to elucidate the idea of "the end of inquiry" and not vice versa.

The pragmatist is best advised to give up talk of the end of inquiry (except perhaps in formulating certain regulative ideals of investigation) and claim only that true beliefs are those that would survive critical scrutiny however far inquiry were to be pursued. We aspire to beliefs that will continue to command assent when challenged by experience. There is no reason why such a position should compromise a natural realism. Indeed, Peirce himself argued that at the basis of the scientific method of inquiry lies the hypothesis that "there are real things, whose characters are entirely independent of our opinions about them."[6] Moreover, he argued that there are no grounds to doubt this hypothesis. Indeed, the hypothesis is a presupposition of inquiry, since whenever we seek to decide between conflicting propositions, we concede "that there is some *one* thing to which a proposition should conform."[7] It is also supported by the outcome of inquiry, which is, of course, a conception of the world as existing for the most part in resolute independence from human belief. In light of all this, one might even invite the pragmatist to say that true beliefs are fit to survive the trials of inquiry *because* they get reality right, so long as this is said without philosophical pretension (for the "because" can pull no weight in a substantive philosophical theory of the relation between mind and world).

---

6 Peirce, "The Fixation of Belief," in Peirce, *op. cit.*, 254.

7 Ibid.

IV

If pragmatist insights need not compromise a sensible form of realism, and if the pragmatist's holistic epistemology can be extended to encompass value judgments, then the way is open for her to embrace some kind of moral cognitivism or realism. Why should we suppose, however, that moral judgment is best illuminated by a realist treatment? Many cognitivists maintain that a presumption of realism is contained in the very nature of our moral thought and talk. Michael Smith, for example, asserts that

> we seem to think moral questions have correct answers; that the correct answers are made correct by objective moral facts; that moral facts are wholly determined by circumstances; and that, by engaging in moral conversation and argument, we can discover what these objective moral facts determined by the circumstances are.[8]

We ought, cognitivists often argue, to take appearances at face value in the absence of compelling philosophical reasons to do otherwise.

At first sight, Smith's claim looks incredible. Surely many members of Western cultures have beliefs about morality which are broadly subjectivist or relativist in kind.[9] We might wonder whether Smith has taught Ethics 101 recently. The cognitivist's point, however, is not that people endorse realist views of morality, but that the presumption of realism is implicit in the character of moral experience and deliberation. When we are impressed that a certain action is, or would be, wrong we appear to register a fact of the matter obtaining independently of our will. When we agonize over which course of action is, or would be, morally appropriate we seem to be searching for the truth of the matter. Thus, regardless of what people might say about the

---

8 Smith, *The Moral Problem* (Oxford: Blackwell), 6.

9 This has been a constant lament of communitarian political philosophy. See, e.g., Charles Taylor, *The Malaise of Modernity* (Toronto: Anansi, 1991), republished as *The Ethics of Authenticity* (Cambridge, MA: Harvard University Press, 1991).

nature of morality, reflection upon the phenomenology of moral experience reveals an implicit commitment to realism.

It might be suggested, however, that phenomenology is a poor guide in this context. It is, after all, a central fact about human existence that human beings create numerous practices and institutions which appear, to participants sufficiently absorbed in them, to provide objective, even categorical, reasons for action that issue from the existence of values that are in some sense objective. Yet when these institutions are viewed from the appropriate critical distance, the appearance of objectivity and categoricity evaporates. The requirements of etiquette, to use an example of Philippa Foot's,[10] can appear to have objective standing to those who fail to see that the institution emerged to further various human ends and concerns (or, we might say, to fulfil a certain social function), and that the values it appears to disclose, and the requirements it places us under, are reflections of those ends and concerns and entirely conditional upon our commitment to them.

Sport provides yet more gross examples.[11] Immersed in a game of soccer, a player can feel as if the rules bind his actions categorically. More than this, one can become so passionately absorbed in a game like soccer that one comes to adopt a kind of Platonism about the rules, so that when debating whether certain rules might be changed to enhance the game (about, say, whether the goals should be enlarged to promote more scoring), it feels as if one is seeking to discover some objective fact about what, as it were, the essence of the game requires. When Bill Shankley, the late manager of Liverpool Football Club, remarked, with a kind of perverse irony, that "football is not a matter of life and death, it's more important," he brought out the fact that it is possible to become so involved in some activity (even a simple pastime) that we lose sight of the fact that it is entirely a human creation and we are bound by its precepts only by our own choice or commitment.

---

10 See her "Morality as a System of Hypothetical Imperatives," in her *Virtues and Vices* (Oxford: Oxford University Press, 1978), 157–73.

11 A more subtle example is Marx's analysis of our perception of economic forces and relations, though its complexity precludes its discussion here.

When it comes to institutions or practices like etiquette and soccer, a little reflection by participants suffices to dispel the appearance that they are responding to brutely objective values and categorical reasons. Reflection destroys objectivity (to adopt a maxim of Bernard Williams's). Should we not see morality as similarly an institution or practice? Of course, the critic of cognitivism might argue, moral Platonism is much more resilient to reflection than the rules and strategies of soccer. The realist presumptions of moral experience are not dispelled by the mere suggestion that objective values might not exist. But this resilience is easily explained. Centuries of religious belief, for instance, have entrenched the thought that in morality we are accountable to something beyond ourselves, to a moral order not of our making. But this belief survives the collapse of religion only as a fetish. The insight of non-cognitivism, shared of course with existentialism, is that the moral order issues from us. No doubt non-cognitivists originally developed this insight poorly, by either celebrating a crass subjectivism (emotivism) or trying to concoct moral objectivity out of such arthritic philosophical devices as universalizability (prescriptivism). But now there are more subtle non-cognitivists on the scene (such as Blackburn, Gibbard, and Williams). Moreover, the critic continues, one would think that the pragmatist would want to join their ranks. For, notwithstanding the attractions of epistemic holism, the pragmatist, with her naturalistic sensibilities and her stress on the practical, should surely be drawn to a vision of morality as a human institution, a creation of human agency that draws its rationale from the promotion of human interests rather than the quest to discover the contours of a moral reality supposedly existing independently of human commitments and desires.

How should the pragmatist reply? The challenge deploys the concept of an institution in the following way. Institutions are said to be human creations or inventions, which are informed by human interests and exist to fulfil certain functions or serve certain ends or purposes (though these interests, purposes, etc., may be only obscurely understood by participants in the institutions themselves). The challenge assumes that once we grant that morality is an institution, as the pragmatist will want to, then this in itself undermines the idea that there are objective values and correspondingly categorical moral reasons. But, even given that the loose notion of an institution can be tightened up, the argument is far too quick. Why not suppose that by participating in an institution such as morality, agents develop skills which enable them to discern objects and courses of action which are genuinely of value and that the recognition of such values can furnish them with reasons for action that are categorical in the sense of being unconditional upon any desires they happen to have? After all, the pragmatist might continue, our paradigm of cognitive inquiry, natural science, is equally a human institution. It is a contingent fact of human history that scientific practices of inquiry emerged and established themselves. Those practices are certainly informed by human interests and purposes (our interest in the prediction of events and technological control of nature), and, as Putnam has stressed, the scientific theories which emerge reflect certain fundamental epistemic values. None of this impugns the truth of those theories or shows that the world they describe is a mere construct. Scientific theories are artifacts, but that does not mean that the world they describe is one. By the same token, the institution of morality may be an artifact, but it does not follow that it creates the values apparently discerned by moral agents. We can see the institution, not as constructing the good, but as enabling or empowering agents to perceive it.

I think the pragmatist should agree that to argue for cognitivism by invoking the phenomenology of moral experience is not very effective, even as a dialectical ploy. We need to explain the possibility of moral experience as it presents itself to us by developing a plausible metaphysics of value to complement our holistic epistemology. However, our choice is not, as the challenge implies, either (1) to acknowledge the anthropocentricity of our moral practices by portraying morality as an institution premised on human interests and purposes, and thereby denying that morality is really a domain of inquiry; or (2) to embrace a kind of moral Platonism and concede that moral reality somehow has its shape independent of our appetitive nature. These unattractive options are not exclusive. We should aspire to capture both the anthropocentricity of morality and its objectivity.

In this project, the pragmatist can take her lead from the insightful discussion by David Wiggins in his "A Sensible Subjectivism?"[12] Here

---

12 Wiggins, *Needs, Values, Truth*, 185-214; see esp. Sections 8–10.

Wiggins engages in speculative anthropology to suggest how a practice of evaluation that has its roots in primitive subjective responses to aspects of the world can naturally grow into a genuinely cognitive mode of inquiry. Wiggins imagines a human community that has evolved to a stage at which some objects regularly evoke certain evaluative responses (e.g., some objects please, delight, or amuse, etc., others disgust, shock, or dismay, etc.). Objects come to be grouped together in virtue of the responses they evoke (objects are classed as pleasing or delightful or amusing, etc., disgusting or shocking or dismaying, etc.). In such a situation, the properties of being amusing, delightful, or disgusting, etc., will not be explicable without appeal to the corresponding responses, and the responses will come to be characterized by appeal to the kind of properties that provoke them (e.g., the reaction of disgust is understood as that elicited by something disgusting). When the reason for a subject's response (e.g., of disgust) is not evident, she will explain her response by appeal to some property or properties of the object to which she reacted in disgust (e.g., it's slimy). It now becomes possible to point to such properties to cultivate a person's responses, and a dialectic can begin in which individuals refine their responses by coming more finely to differentiate between properties and, in turn, their finer-grained responses encourage yet finer differentiations between properties. (We see this kind of process in the development of aesthetic sensibilities; e.g., when we learn to listen to a kind of music, such as jazz, or to appreciate foods or wines.) This dialectic of refinement presupposes that subjects see the presence of certain properties, not just as explaining co-related responses, but as *justifying* them. And now it becomes possible to argue about whether certain responses are really appropriate to their objects and about whether objects really merit the responses we feel are appropriate to them. We can ponder the correct extension of, e.g., the predicate "is disgusting," and its correctness can be conceived as defined by features of the world, insofar as they appropriately evoke in us certain responses, and not just by the arbitrary play of human subjectivity. Once critical reflection on such issues ensues, our activities of evaluation have come to constitute a genuinely cognitive mode of inquiry aimed at establishing enduring beliefs about matters of value.

Wiggins takes pains to underline that predicates like "is disgusting," "is amusing," "is appalling," etc., will be irresolvably anthropocentric. It will not be possible to specify, in purely natural terms, some common feature(s) that disgusting (or amusing or appalling) objects share. What these objects share is that they are such as to merit certain responses, and no-one incapable of appreciating those responses could grasp their common character and learn to deploy the predicates in question. Our activities of evaluation will thus be intelligible only "from within." Furthermore, the standards of correctness which govern those activities — standards by which we assess what constitutes good judgment in matters of evaluation — are immanent within them. They cannot be authenticated from some external vantage point. Moreover, in hard cases the standards and their application will likely be the site of lively and enduring controversy. One seeks to vindicate one's amusement by arguing that the object which provoked it really was funny. But, Wiggins argues, whether something is funny will often be essentially contestable. The contestability will concern both what it takes for something to be funny and whether any particular object has what it takes. All we can do is reflect critically, and we can only reflect within the terms established by our activities themselves. Nevertheless, we can see the process of the emergence of evaluative practices, as Wiggins describes it, as one which opens up stretches of reality to participants, enabling them to discriminate and reflect upon evaluative properties of objects which are genuine features of the world, despite their thorough anthropocentricity. Moreover, it will be natural to see the recognition of the presence of such properties as engaging the will, as providing agents with reasons for action.[13] If our activities of moral evaluation are the result of a process of evolution such as Wiggins describes, we can see how morality can be objective and anthropocentric, cognitive and practical.

How, then, should the cognitivist mark the difference between the practice of morality and other practices? The cognitivist should not deny that human institutions and practices are in fact aimed at the

---

13 Note that we should expect the pragmatist, with her stress on the practical character of belief, to be drawn to internalism in the theory of motivation — to the idea that an agent's cognitive states can themselves be sufficient to provide reasons for action.

recognition and pursuit of objective values. Good manners are a good, as are the skill, heroism, exhilaration, etc., which are exhibited on the soccer field. Someone who fails to acknowledge such goods is missing something. The goods in turn provide reasons to submit ourselves to the discipline required to engage in the institution or practice, to bind ourselves, for example, by requirements of etiquette or the rules of soccer and the sensibilities necessary for appreciating the game (perhaps only as a spectator). But in these cases the recognition of the objective goods at issue is neither as significant, nor as compelling, as in the case of morality. This is so for two reasons. First, we feel that the goods in question (or goods analogous to them) can be pursued, perhaps more successfully, by other means. There is no necessary relation between the pursuit of goods of this kind and submission to the discipline of the practice or institution in question. Second, we feel that to disregard or neglect the goods at issue is not catastrophic, either because this can be compensated by the recognition and pursuit of other goods, or because the neglect is inconsequential.

Consider etiquette. We have reasons to be courteous and polite that are indeed categorical in the sense of weighing with us unconditionally upon the presence of desires. These reasons issue from the value of good manners. We might very well deny, however, that manners are best served by cultivating the kind of formal system of rules and observances associated with the term "etiquette." Spontaneous courtesy and politeness is perhaps enough. So we might argue that the practice of etiquette should be dissolved and its good intentions absorbed into morality. In any case, rudeness is a vice which, at least in many cases, does not matter that much. Ill-mannered people can be redeemed by their other qualities (in a way, perhaps, that cruel or unjust people cannot).

In the case of soccer, or any sport, it can be argued that the sport is not the unique means of pursuing the goods in question (even though the goods will manifest themselves in a distinctive way in the context of the particular sport). Indeed, the goods may be better pursued some other way (perhaps because their standing is diminished through their juxtaposition in the sport in question with less desirable qualities — competitiveness, spectacle, violence, etc.). Thus, even if there are excellent reasons to appreciate athleticism, camaraderie, and excitement, one need not care about soccer in particular. And in any case, the goods the sport embodies are not essential ingredients of a meaningful or worthwhile life. Indeed, their recognition might be precluded by the acknowledgment of other genuine goods. These are goods that recommend themselves to agents whose lives have played out in such a way that they find meaning in this practice, and such goods need have no call on people whose lives are differently structured.

Matters stand otherwise with morality. We cannot see requirements disclosed by the practice of moral inquiry as optional, as reasons that can be disregarded if they conflict with our legitimate desires, projects, or commitments. An agent who recognizes that it is his moral duty to help someone in some situation, or to refrain from treating someone cruelly, cannot *decide* whether to care about these reasons if they conflict with his ends. However, this feature of the "inescapability" of moral requirements needs careful handling. The dictates of morality are not unavoidable because it is (necessarily) irrational to disregard them; the agent who ignores her moral reasons is not in the same boat as someone who recognizes that they have overwhelming epistemic reasons to believe p, but who somehow contrives to believe not-p. Rather, the inescapability of moral reasons derives, simply, from the character and significance of the moral properties from which they result. If one fully appreciates the significance of such properties as cruelty, courage, justice, etc., as they manifest themselves in moral cases, one will see that they often (though perhaps not always) generate reasons for action that are compelling. If someone fails to see why such reasons are compelling, she can only be directed to attend more carefully to the significance of the morally relevant features at work in the case at issue. Her failing is a failing of sensitivity or (as McDowell puts it) of humanity — a failure to see enough to care or to care enough to see. Thus the special force of moral requirements is something that can only impress itself upon those who participate in the practice of moral inquiry and participate with sufficient imagination and sensitivity. There is no formal or foundational reason why moral demands are inescapable.

But does this not imply that moral reasons weigh only with those who chose to engage in the practice of morality, and hence that moral reasons are ultimately conditional upon a desire so to participate? We should consider, however, what it would mean to reject morality. On the present account, one might reject morality on the grounds that the goods the institution seeks to promote are best realized some other way. However, in contrast to etiquette, it is difficult to see the practice of moral assessment as something that might be replaced by, or absorbed into, some other practice. This is because our contemporary secular vision of morality defines its fundamental concerns so broadly — pertaining to matters of human well-being, the character of meaningful and worthwhile lives, the legitimate forms of social organization, the limits of appropriate treatment, etc. — that we are inclined to view any reasonable attempt to address these concerns as a contribution to moral inquiry. Thus, when philosophical critics of morality (such as Marx, Nietzsche, or Foucault) attack the institution, we are prone to see them as exposing existing mores or social institutions as fraudulent in the name of some alternative moral vision.[14] They urge us to rethink our moral concepts rather than abandon them. (Of course, we might regard their alternatives as immoral; we just do not see them as amoral, as really beyond good and evil).

From within morality it is hard to imagine moral concerns losing their significance for us, while our lives continue to have some recognizable worth and meaning. It does not follow, of course, that circumstances may not cause an agent to lose faith in the moral life, to embrace Mephistophelian scepticism, as James calls it,[15] or even to devote herself to the promotion of evil. Such stances are pathological, but hardly incoherent. It might also be true that the only way to cause someone so disillusioned or perverted to engage again in moral behaviour would be to engender in them a desire to do so which derived its force independently of their perceptions of moral situations. This would not show, however, that the motivation of a normal moral agent is premised upon anything other than a clear-sighted, and fully cognitive, appreciation of what morality requires. Such an agent needs no reason

---

14 See, for example, Charles Taylor's "Foucault on Freedom and Truth," in his *Philosophy and the Human Sciences. Philosophical Papers II* (Cambridge: Cambridge University Press, 1985), 152–84.

15 William James, *The Will to Believe and Other Essays in Popular Philosophy* (New York: Longman, Green and Co., 1897), 23.

to be moral over and above the reasons revealed by moral inquiry itself. It is in this fact, and in the character of those reasons themselves, that the distinctiveness of the moral resides.

V

Let us grant that the pragmatist-cognitivist can successfully portray the institution of morality as a genuine domain of inquiry. We must now say something about the specific character of moral inquiry itself. Pragmatists typically work with a model of inquiry drawn from science. The aim of inquiry is to formulate general principles and laws that allow us to explain and predict phenomena. Inquiry proceeds through the interplay of theory and data derived from experience, broadly conceived. This model, however, has only limited application to the moral domain. It appears most appropriate when we consider inquiry into the moral adequacy of public institutions; i.e., reflection upon the form that the basic structure of society should take and the character of a just constitution. John Rawls's influential work on the principles of justice can be taken to illustrate the model. Rawls proceeds by deploying our moral intuitions about justice to formulate procedures for establishing principles of justice which are in turn scrutinized in light of experience (i.e., our moral intuitions, and the deliverances of reflection and thought experiment). We are to modify the principles and/or our interpretation of experience until we attain "reflective equilibrium."

It would be misleading, however, to assimilate the whole of moral reasoning and deliberation to this mode of inquiry. When seeking to formulate and justify principles of the Rawlsian type, we feel ourselves engaged in a collective process, public in orientation, in which we are accountable in our reasoning to all those the principles will bind. In such a context, it is not grotesque to see ourselves as guided by Peircian ideals of the end of inquiry. We aspire to principles which will survive critical scrutiny to comprise part of a stable and enduring picture of the just society. Much moral reasoning, however, is unlike this.

Suppose I am confronted with a dilemma. I have a friend, severely depressed after the death of his wife, who comes to me frequently to discuss his predicament. I feel that these discussions do not help overcome the depression, but rather only cause him to become ever more dependent on his state of depression itself, which has come to serve as an excuse for not rebuilding his life. Do I continue to humour my friend, or do I give him the truth as I see it, endangering our friendship and possibly precipitating a crisis which might worsen his state of mind rather than improve it? Moreover, *how* should I do what I decide needs to be done? When confronted with a case of this kind, my principal concern is to act on the best reasons available in a way which is wholly appropriate to the situation. When I reflect on the matter, I need not see my reflections as contributions to some public or communal process of moral inquiry, aimed at establishing an adequate theory of moral reality. Indeed, it might distort my judgment if I saw my deliberations in that way. I recognize that the decision I make must be accountable to others, in the sense that it must be supported by the best reasons available, but I need not care whether others actually appreciate those reasons. I am likely to care that my friend understand my reasons, and it is important that my decision be intelligible as an expression of values which I endorse as partly constitutive of my identity. The decision has to make narrative sense, as it were, in the story of my life, and I will be concerned that those who know me appreciate this. But beyond this I do not see my decision as public. It is, if not private, then personal; I do not see it as a contribution to a communal project.

It is also unclear whether moral judgment in such cases is best understood as the outcome of the application of principles and whether, therefore, moral inquiry of this kind should be seen as devoted to the formulation and testing of moral rules. As Jonathan Dancy has argued, moral principles are grossly overrated as devices for the justification of moral decisions.[16] It is obvious that a moral principle like "Lying is wrong" must be qualified if it is not to be refuted by those many cases in which it is appropriate to lie. Yet to build the exceptions into the principle, even if this were possible, would make it unwieldy. Moreover, it is hard to see how we could think of the qualified principle as determining whether a case was one in which lying would be wrong,

---

16 See Dancy, "Ethical Particularism and Morally Relevant Properties," *Mind* 92 (1983): 530–47; and *Moral Reasons* (Oxford: Blackwell, 1993).

since every new case would test the principle: in every new case we would have to decide whether this was an exception so far unincorporated into the principle. It is thus tempting to follow W.D. Ross and argue that moral principles should be seen as stating only *prima facie* obligations. The principle that lying is *prima facie* wrong tells us that any action which is a lie is the worse for it and that an action whose only morally relevant characteristic is that it is a lie would be wrong. In most moral cases of genuine complexity, there will be more than one *prima facie* principle that applies to the case (an action may be *prima facie* wrong for being a lie while *prima facie* right for being kind). But the rightness or wrongness of the action overall is not, Ross himself grants, determined by principle. We must exercise judgment in deciding which of the action's morally relevant considerations is most significant. The principles fall short of determining right and wrong.

Thus it seems that moral principles are of limited value in moral decision-making in hard cases. In such cases we must simply attend carefully to the specifics of the case to determine which among its properties are morally relevant and how they are so in this particular circumstance. We look for an informed and defensible judgment about the morally salient features of the case, and such a judgment will, in turn, likely furnish us with reasons for action. Dancy follows John McDowell in arguing that moral judgment and deliberation involve, not the application of rules to cases, but the exercise of sensibility, which might perhaps best be seen as akin to a perceptual capacity.[17] Such a

---

17 Charles Larmore (*Morals of Modernity*, 108–11) criticizes the perceptual model of moral knowledge, which he finds in McDowell's moral writings of the 1980s, on the grounds that it cannot account for the normative dimension of moral knowledge. Although Larmore grants that we can see that an action is bad, he holds that we cannot be said to see that some action ought to be done. Values are perceptible, reasons not. The argument rests on the principle that only what is the case is a possible object of perception; we cannot perceive what was, what will be, what might have been, or what ought to be. However, those who invoke the perceptual model typically hold (1) that the properties of an action (e.g., its cruelty) from which an agent's reasons for action result are genuinely perceived, and (2) that the agent's recognition that the presence of these properties constitutes reason for some action is not the result of inference, but is immediately apprehended. The agent *apprehends* that the action should not be

sensibility resists codification into principles. It cannot be inculcated through the teaching of rules, but must rather be acquired through a process of enculturation in which the agent is attuned to certain properties and comes to appreciate their significance. In short, the development of moral sensibility is a matter of the acquisition and cultivation of a *taste*.

This might seem too intuitionistic a position for any pragmatist to swallow. We should observe, however, that Dewey follows his telling critique of emotivism by arguing that the formation of taste is "the chief matter wherever values enter in, whether intellectual, esthetic or moral." He asserts that the judgments which follow from the exercise of taste must be seen, not as spontaneous intuitions, but "funded products of much thoughtful experience," and continues:

> Expertness of taste is at once the result and the reward of constant exercise of thinking. Instead of there being no disputing about tastes, they are the one thing worth disputing about, if by "dispute" is signified discussion involving reflective inquiry. Taste, if we use the word in its best sense, is the outcome of experience brought cumulatively to bear on the intelligent appreciation of the real worth of likings and enjoyments. There is nothing in which a person so completely reveals himself as in the things which he judges enjoyable and desirable. Such judgments are the sole alternative to the domination of belief by impulse, chance, blind habit and self-interest. The formation of a cultivated and effectively operative good judgment or taste with respect to what is esthetically admirable, intellectually acceptable and morally approvable is the supreme task set to human beings by the incidents of experience.[18]

---

done, because *he sees that it is cruel.* Thus, to speak of perceiving reasons does not imply a curious perceptual access to some (better) possible world. It is just a matter of apprehending what ought to be done in virtue of the perception of morally relevant features of the situation. (I also see no reason to hold, as Larmore does, that McDowell has now dropped a perceptual model of moral knowledge. In his recent writings, McDowell argues that perception involves the exercise of conceptual capacities [rather than the reception of a preconceptualized "given"] and, when veridical, issues in an awareness of how things are. Perception can put us in contact with the facts, and the deliverances of perception are essentially objects of critical reflection. This account seems tailor-made for a perceptual model of moral knowledge.)

18 John Dewey, *The Quest for Certainty*, in *John Dewey: The Later Works*, vol. 4, ed. Jo Ann Boydston (Carbondale, IL: Southern Illinois University Press, 1985), 209.

It seems clear that Dewey does not oppose matters of taste to matters of fact. On the contrary, the cultivation of taste is a prerequisite of moral inquiry, of reasoned debate about the morally relevant features of actions and how those features give us reason to act.

I have argued that the pragmatist must acknowledge the difference between two contrasting modes of moral inquiry. But mere recognition is not enough. Much work needs to be done to enrich our understanding of both. For example, radical ethical particularists, such as Jonathan Dancy, argue that principles play no substantive role in moral inquiry. This is because the moral relevance of some property in some situation is argued to be determined holistically: the property has the relevance it has in virtue of its relation to other properties of the case. It is thus said to be impossible to predict the relevance that the property will have when differently situated. On such a view, moral inquiry is often presented as if it is a matter of agents proceeding from case to case with their eyes open and their sensibilities alert. In so far as their judgments are informed by principles, these can only be rules of thumb which specify properties that are often morally relevant. This picture, however, seems to leave out various dimensions of moral consciousness that seem, in one way or another, to inform the moral inquiry of mature agents. For instance, we expect moral agents to be *committed*, to set themselves in favour of certain kinds of action and against others. Although such commitments are mutable in the face of experience, they figure as crucial constituents of identity. Agents seek to live meaningful and worthwhile lives which express a coherent moral personality. The natural form of the expression of such commitments, a form in which they can be recognized as imposing a discipline upon the expression of moral agency, is in the form of principles. It is thus hard to see how Dancy's austere form of particularism affords the resources to articulate the nature of an enduring, integral moral personality. The pragmatist's task is to find a role within the structure of moral enquiry for principles understood as neither explaining nor determining rightness or wrongness, but as the vehicles of commitment.[19]

---

19 The trick is to find a way for the principle "Cruel acts are wrong" to be true while accommodating the particularist's insights that (1) some cruel acts are right, and (2) cruelty is not always morally relevant in the same way (the moral

The pragmatist is also beholden to say something about the relation of the two modes of moral inquiry. They have rarely been kept in the same frame, since philosophers tend to be interested in one or the other. Yet it is clear that they should be woven into a single picture. The questions "How should I live?" and "What should I do, here, now?" demand different strategies of inquiry from the question "By what principles of justice should we live?," and we should not necessarily expect a smooth transition from answers to the former to answers to the latter, and vice versa. Nevertheless, to recognize a distinction between moral inquiry into public, political issues and personal moral issues is not necessarily to demarcate the public and the political, on the one hand, and the private and the personal, on the other, as separate moral realms. Questions of justice can intrude deeply into personal matters, and our theory of justice must, as Rawls admits, harmonize with moral intuitions that are rooted in personal moral convictions. Moreover, questions of the good are not best sidelined in political discussion, for it is hard to see how questions of right could be anything other than questions of what is required of us (or what discipline we must submit ourselves to) if we are to realize certain goods. It is to be hoped that by exploring the distinction between different modes of moral inquiry, the pragmatist can cast new light on these old issues.

VI

In this paper, I have sought to defend the idea that the pragmatist can advance a form of moral cognitivism by extending a broadly Peircian account of truth to encompass moral judgment. I have argued that the

---

relevance of cruelty so depends on its relation to other properties in particular cases that there may be times when the cruelty of an action is morally irrelevant, or even where the action is the better for being cruel). Perhaps the answer is to exploit an analogy with propositions like "Dogs are four-legged animals" (or "The cat is a carnivore") which are neither defeated by counterexample nor function as *prima facie* judgments. Such judgments express what might be called conceptual norms and play a crucial role in organizing the epistemic landscape. To see moral principles as vehicles of commitment is to recognize that they play a similar role to these conceptual norms.

pragmatist is well placed (1) to endorse an account of the genealogy of morality that admits both the anthropocentricity and the objectivity of moral values, and (2) to develop a textured appreciation of the specific character of moral inquiry. I have suggested that the latter requires acknowledging and exploring the contrast between moral inquiry as it is conducted into public, political issues, on the one hand, and personal moral concerns, on the other.

I turn finally to one further obstacle that might be thought to stand in the way of a pragmatist version of moral cognitivism. On a broadly Peircian account, genuine inquiry — that is, inquiry aimed at truth — brings about a gradual convergence in belief among inquirers. This link between inquiry and convergence persists even if the pragmatist sensibly resists the temptation to collapse the concept of truth into that of agreement under ideal circumstances of inquiry. For if inquiry is directed at uncovering reasons for belief that will withstand critical scrutiny, it is to be expected that, where good reasons to believe are revealed, unprejudiced inquirers will come to recognize their force. Thus, since convergence is (as Wiggins puts it) a "mark of truth," we should conclude that we are not in a domain of inquiry at all where investigation and debate do not contain the promise of convergence. This is either because there are frequently no rational grounds to choose between reasons in favour of some judgment and those against it, or because the reasons offered for some judgment legitimately derive their force from subjective preferences of the judger that are not objects of critical scrutiny (i.e., where "*A* suits my fancy" is acknowledged as a perfectly good reason for doing *A*).[20]

These considerations provoke the familiar non-cognitivist claim that there is widespread and massive disagreement on moral matters and little expectation that this disagreement will lessen over time. Indeed, even some who profess to be moral cognitivists admit that it is a striking feature of modernity that the more that reasonable people debate conceptions of the good, the less they agree: critical reflection tends to diversity, rather than unanimity, of opinion.[21] Hence the increasing rec-

---

20 See Wiggins, "Truth as Predicated of Moral Judgments," 139–84.

21 This is an important theme in Larmore's *The Morals of Modernity*.

ognition of the need for a purely "political" form of liberalism designed to secure consensus about principles of justice while remaining neutral with respect to all reasonably comprehensive conceptions of the good. Thus (and contra the closing remarks of Section V above), unless conceptions of the good are sidelined in political debate about justice, we will sink our political culture in irresolvable discord and animosity. Yet if this is the case, pragmatist views of truth are surely impossible to reconcile with moral cognitivism.

The nature and scope of moral disagreement, and its significance for moral inquiry, warrant a detailed and sustained treatment. There are, however, three basic points that might be made in response to the non-cognitivist. First, we must be careful not to exaggerate the extent of moral disagreement in contrast to disagreement on other matters. It will not do, for example, to hold up a physics textbook as evidence of unshakable agreement on matters of fact, while contrasting, say, the moral views of a Christian fundamentalist from the southern United States with a left-wing European humanities professor. The fundamentalist and the humanitarian will certainly have contrasting moral views, but they will also have very different "factual" beliefs about the natural world. Their factual disagreements should not undermine our confidence that there can be genuine inquiry into matters of fact, and the same goes for their moral differences. Furthermore, we must recognize that, behind the genuine and often radical disagreements that divide us on moral matters, there is a background of significant agreement. Almost everyone will agree that it is wrong to kill human beings (without *very* good cause) or to enslave them, that human beings are worthy of respect and should not be used merely as a means to the well-being of others. There is also significant agreement about basic human needs, and so on, and widespread consensus, even among representatives of very different cultures, about the kinds of considerations that are relevant in moral argument, about the scope and limits of moral responsibility and about the character of excuses. Of course, despite this agreement there is a great deal of immorality in the world, but probably no more than there is stupidity about matters of fact.

Does the course of modernity suggest a lessening of such agreement? Not at all. Modernity does bring a recognition that there is a plurality of ways to live a meaningful and morally worthwhile life, and that these ways of life may be incommensurable with one another in the sense that living according to one vision of the good may preclude living according to others. But such incommensurability does not rule out a person's recognizing, from within one moral way of life, the validity of alternative ways now closed to him or her. We cannot expect convergence upon a single vision of the good, analogous to the "one true picture" of the world (though perhaps we should not expect to arrive at the latter either), but recognition of the authenticity of alternative compelling visions of the good is agreement enough.

Second, the existence of moral disagreement only undermines cognitivism insofar as it suggests that our moral practices are unconstrained by the existence of moral facts. The cognitivist can argue, however, that a great deal of moral disagreement is entirely compatible with the truth of moral realism. Although our democratic sensibilities incline us to deny that there is moral expertise — the good is equally open to everyone able and willing to reflect and sympathize — it remains the case that moral judgment is difficult, both because it often rests on the exercise of sensibilities that cannot be cultivated by learning routines or procedures, and because our moral vision is so easily distorted by prejudice, self-interest, and desire. In light of this, and the fact that there can be a legitimate plurality of morally valid ways of living, it is hardly surprising that moral opinions exhibit significant diversity.

Third, the pragmatist does not in any case need to assert that a convergence of moral views is to be anticipated. The cognitivist requires the promise of convergence to be real, but she does not need a real convergence. What is crucial is that moral reflection and debate should aim at securing agreement among interlocutors, agreement premised upon the mutual recognition of compelling reasons for judgment. (Of course, this aim would be futile were agreement on particular issues never reached, but it is not undermined if a wholesale convergence of views is out of the question.) In addition, it should be the case that where agreement is reached, the best explanation of agreement in some judgment that p makes reference to, among other things, the fact that p. If moral discourse can take and sustain this form, we should grant that moral inquiry is possible.

It follows from this that the possibility of moral inquiry is ultimately a contingent matter. There are good reasons to hold that some widespread moral beliefs, such as the belief that slavery is wrong, are indeed premised upon the mutual recognition of good reasons, and that the wrongness of slavery forms part of the best explanation of why people came to believe that it is wrong. Yet appearances may be deceptive: the consensus may have another source. There can be no philosophical guarantee that cognitivism is true; all the philosopher can do is eliminate bad reasons to believe that it must be false. Its truth rests on whether genuine moral inquiry can be sustained. The issue turns on practice, not metaphysics, a conclusion any pragmatist will welcome. As such, moral cognitivism is, as Wiggins has remarked, a form of "speculative optimism."[22] The point of this paper has been to show that pragmatists, when sensitized to the distinctive character of morality in all its complexity, have reason to be optimists about the quest for moral truth, and about the betterment that will issue from the successful pursuit of that quest.

---

22 David Wiggins, "Moral Cognitivism, Moral Relativism and Motivating Moral Beliefs," *Proceedings of the Aristotelian Society* (1990–91), 79.

CANADIAN JOURNAL OF PHILOSOPHY
Supplementary Volume 24

Democratic Deliberations, Equality of Influence, and Pragmatism

JUDITH BAKER
York University

Democracy is committed to procedures of decision-making which express the values of both political equality and truth. One current program, that of strong or deliberative democracy, explicitly defends institutions which reflect the dual commitments to truth and equality. Like many other political theorists, however, deliberative democrats do not address the issue of a minority group which always loses the vote. The presumption is that free and equal deliberation by agents who think in terms of the common good is sufficient for political equality. I will argue, however, that the proposed deliberative procedures do not preclude persistent failure for a minority, and that this problem should lead us to acknowledge that power relations can underpin decision-making arrangements even within the ideal framework of deliberative democracy. Political equality and effective political equality seem to come apart.

In order to come closer to the idea of effective political equality, this paper will look at the notion of equality of influence. It may seem tautological, and so redundant, to argue that political egalitarians and particularly deliberative democrats need to recognize equality of influence. This notion, understood in terms of equal access to collective decisions and outcomes, seems central to the ideal of citizens' participation in political decisions. But difficulties emerge, and the ideal is contested, because "equal access" does not do enough work. If access to collective decision-making is understood in terms of formal rules and procedures which assure equal voting weight, influence drops out. If equal access means "equal access to political influence," we worry that equality of influence will be measured in terms of successful outcomes. But if my influence is equal to that of other citizens just insofar as my capacity to lead others to vote as I do is the same as everyone else's, we are concerned that little room will be left for powers of reason and deliberation. Our commitment to equality here seems to conflict with that to truth. This paper will thus re-examine the ideal of equality of influence. It will maintain that effective political equality for members of racial and ethnic minorities requires equality of influence, and that this must issue in successful legislative decisions.

It is at this point that one might hope for help from the pragmatist/cognitivist perspective. A more generous understanding of inquiry and truth could avoid conflict between the demands of equality and truth. The pragmatist might offer a home for equality of influence within an enlarged view of deliberation or, alternatively, we might no longer need to fight for or worry about whether equality of influence is an ideal. This paper indeed finds within pragmatism a greater accommodation of special measures. These are the institutional procedures which may be needed to secure equal play within deliberation to members of disadvantaged groups. I will, however, argue that pragmatism, of the cognitivist-Peircian variety, does not itself prompt or justify measures sufficient for political equality. We must look to liberal democracy's independent commitment to autonomy to secure equality of influence.

I

Equality of influence for persistent ethnic or racial minorities might well be thought to start with measures that ensure group representation. The need to have all points of view present for an adequate discussion of issues has been persuasively argued by a number of writers, including Iris Young, Anne Phillips, and Melissa Williams. I will assume for this discussion that measures are accepted which allow for group representation and focus on the reform of legislative procedures, whose fairness with respect to marginalized groups has been questioned.

Particular legislative reforms serve here, however, only as examples. What must first be argued is that proposals respond to a genuine unfairness, and that they are themselves not anti-democratic or anti-egalitarian. I will argue in general support of such reforms, but the opposition to them is very persuasive.

Lani Guinier has put forth a strong argument that majority rule (winner-take-all) is legitimate only given four assumptions, including, prominently, a fluidity of the group constituting the majority.[1] This leads to a kind of reciprocity: members of any given minority can count on being themselves in the majority and have an interest in "going along" with the majority. Equally important, the majority members know they may themselves be a minority at some time. Under such conditions minority members can be expected to trust the majority to take into account their interests as well. This assumption, and, it is argued, the consequent legitimacy of a majority rule winner-take-all procedure, is vitiated by a persistent minority of a (relatively) homogeneous racial or ethnic group.

But Guinier's analysis seems to lose its plausibility if we imagine a Rousseauian legislature where each vote represents an individual opinion on a matter of common concern including, where appropriate, an opinion on the proper balance to be maintained among the various individual and minority interests. As Jeremy Waldron has argued, "Nothing tyrannical happens to me merely by virtue of the fact that my opinion is not acted on. Provided that the opinion that is acted upon takes my interests, along with everyone else's, properly into account, the fact that the opinion is not mine is not in itself a threat to my freedom or well-being."[2]

What is crucial is the model of deliberation and deliberators. Guinier's critique can seem redundant if one considers legislators on the model of deliberative democracy, who not only (rationally) deliberate in terms of the public good but impartially consider all views, as presented by their proponents. Indeed, it is the explicit claim of Bernard Manin that his deliberative ideal can justify majority rule.

---

1 Guinier, "No Two Seats: The Elusive Quest for Political Equality," *Virginia Law Review* 77, 8 (1991): 1413–1514.

2 Waldron, "Rights and Majorities: Rousseau Revisited," *NOMOS* 32, *Majorities and Minorities*, ed. John Chapman and Alan Wertheimer (New York: New York University Press, 1990), 64.

> We can now see the justification for the majority principle ... Because it comes at the close of a deliberative process in which everyone was able to take part, choose among several solutions, and remain free to approve or refuse the conclusions developed from the argument, the result carries legitimacy. The decision results from a process in which the minority point of view was also taken into consideration. Although the decision does not conform to all points of view, it is the result of the confrontation between them.[3]

The idea that one is not disenfranchised just because one's opinion is not acted on seems to apply to groups as well as individuals. For the fact that a racial group or historically disadvantaged group continues in a minority doesn't show that either the winning vote was incorrect or their interests were not properly weighed. Moreover, one cannot appeal to a notion of equality of influence which is reducible to equality of outcomes, for this would undermine the power of rationality and of political will in deliberation. Yet a persistent minority vote of groups who are unequal socially is not only suspect, casting doubt on the instantiation of the deliberative ideal, but seems to be in itself a source of illegitimacy which conflicts with the, or a, basis of democratic government. Although a justifiable form of equal influence cannot be thought reducible to equal success of outcomes, it is important to acknowledge the connection between political equality and success. If a conceptual link is to be convincingly drawn, full weight must first be given to the reasons offered by the contrary view.

I am very sympathetic to the stance of deliberative democrats, and convinced of the fundamental idea, that our legislative decisions will be more just to the extent that institutions for decision-making facilitate deliberation in terms of the public good rather than negotiations based on competing interests. Marginalized minority groups as well as the disadvantaged generally can be expected to fare better. In particular, marginalized groups can do better insofar as they are present to argue for their positions. For it is a central thesis of deliberative democracy that discussion and political deliberation can change initial preferences and interests. To find public arguments that are convinc-

---

3 Manin, "A Sketch of a Theory of Political Deliberation," *Political Theory* 15, 3 (1987): 359.

ing one must seek reasons whose appeal is general; it is thought that this will force one to be clearer about others' preferences as well as one's own. The reflection this requires, as well as openness to the perspectives of others, is expected to be able to transform initial views.

I am nonetheless bothered by what I think is an idealized and inadequate idea of rationality, or rational deliberation, which underlies some of the claims for deliberative democracy. This purified notion of reasoning is dominant in the work of political theorists, if not all pervasive. In light of the purposes of this paper, which wishes to understand how such a picture of reason affects positions on equality of influence, the essays on political equality by Ronald Dworkin are illuminating. Dworkin puts forth a very convincing analysis of why we should not value equality of influence: quite simply put, he argues that only the truth should count. His appeal to the truth should, however, lead us to re-examine the ways in which we listen to others. Our responses to those with whom we engage in decision-making are inadequately characterized in the terms he offers, for his division of political power into impact and influence leaves out an important dimension of giving due weight to our partners. Here is Dworkin's distinction:

> The intuitive difference is this: someone's impact in politics is the difference he can make, just on his own, by voting for or choosing one decision rather than another. Someone's influence, on the other hand, is the difference he can make not just on his own but also by leading or inducing others to believe or vote or choose as he does.[4]

He argues that when the sources of unequal influence are regarded as illegitimate, so too is unequal influence. This judgment is exemplified in the case of the wealth of a Rockefeller; we object to the influence of the rich because we think the injustice of their economic position allows them to perpetuate in the political arena what are unfair advantages. Dworkin wants to emphasize that no ideal of equal influence is at work in this case. A person thinks it is unjust that some people have as much money as a Rockefeller because that violates the distributive

---

4 Dworkin, "What is Equality? Part 4: Political Equality," *University of San Francisco Law Review* 22 (1987): 9.

principles of equality, and finds that this injustice allows them to multiply their unfair advantages. People who think inequality of influence in itself is illegitimate, however, must recognize the consequences of their view: for they would disallow that difference of influence which results from some individuals being more politically motivated or trained or charismatic, or having lived lives of conspicuous achievement or virtue. As so presented, equality of influence would dismantle both politics and deliberation. For, without abandoning our own judgment, we rightly trust the complex normative assessments of some people more than others. Our reasonable, rational, assessments of positions and arguments often depend upon our judging the rational abilities of those who present them. Moreover, we cannot have genuine deliberation, be open to the views of others, without making room for the differential skills of presentation, those which are most evident in politics. Here is Dworkin's strongest conclusion:

> People who accept equality of influence as a political constraint cannot treat their political lives as moral agency because that constraint corrupts the cardinal premise of moral conviction: that only truth counts. Political campaigning under some self-imposed limit of influence would not be moral agency but only a pointless minuet of deference.[5]

It is patently obvious, I think, that we should not want equality of influence, at least on Dworkin's understanding. Despite his arguments, however, I believe that there is something wrong with unequal influence that Dworkin's analysis does not reveal. We object to more than the perpetuating or multiplying of advantages which come from a position we regard as independently unjust.

What is wrong with Dworkin's understanding of influence? At first sight, one might think that the claim that nothing is wrong with unequal influence commits him to the view that there is in principle nothing wrong if someone has *no* influence. But Dworkin acknowledges that access to influence is required, and sufficient leverage to see to the success of some of one's proposals. The word "influence" seems

---

5 Ibid., 17.

pre-empted, yet I want to suggest that Dworkin's distinction of impact and influence leaves out a kind of effect or action on others, a form of influence, which we rightly think should be equally distributed. That other influence is the standing or claim another person has to our response, to our moving towards the other's view in order to find something mutually acceptable. It would not alter Dworkin's argument if this influence could be analyzed or adequately understood in terms of listening, of confronting another's views and arguments; but the reductive analysis fails.

Equally listening to all others presumes both an isolation and a certain passivity of reasoning. Moreover, to suppose the equal responsiveness due to others can be expressed by listening equally to the arguments of all in our deliberations is to assume that what justifies one's attention and an attempt at accommodation within deliberations is that other people may be right, and oneself wrong. Other people, on this view, are sources of truth.

This point needs to be clearly stated as well as defended. Of course, people are not merely voices of truth. There is a moral demand that one respond to the needs of others and, within contested boundaries, to their projects. On the Kantian view, this is based on the idea that each individual sets her own ends and as a result is to be treated with equal respect. The question is whether the demand placed on one is exhausted by those conditions acknowledged as part of the starting assumption of this paper: one is obliged to consider the projects and needs of others in deliberating in terms of the common good, to provide room for individuals to articulate them for themselves, and to be epistemically humble. These obligations are recognized by Millian liberalism, the program of deliberative democracy, and pragmatist enquiry, all of which regard others as sources of truth, as fellow inquirers. This justifies listening to their opinions as well as to their needs or desires.

Despite the difficulties in meeting these requirements, more may be required. If individuals are self-originating sources of ends, their equal standing is expressed in the attention I give to their projects, which include causes, the establishment of what they value, and a community which is just on their conception, as well as the satisfaction of needs and ambitions. They have a claim to my attention and to some influence on me, to the determination of decisions. This influence is not equivalent to the pull of independent truth; at least I will argue that it is not, and that the moral influence of others can be seen to have a direct or pointed political expression in justified demands for more meaningful participation in political deliberation and greater success in legislatures.

Dworkin recognizes one objectionable sort of unequal influence. When the sources of unequal influence are regarded as illegitimate, so too is unequal influence. So riches and bias should not, but do, make a difference in how many others go along with what an individual proposes. It seems obvious that reason's affect on others, and the unequal power it may confer to one who reasons well, is to be desired. It can be argued, however, that an illegitimate form of unequal participation and so unequal influence can be a function of the rational behaviour of deliberators if they have quite divergent views and ends. Unequal participation in legislation can be a feature of the deliberation of people who are not necessarily biased nor exclusively determined by self-interests. It is not, however, just that unequal influence can result *even if* everyone is behaving rationally. Rather, as a result of rational strategies of deliberation, members of minority groups will not have the same access to influence as members of the majority, at least if closure is short of consensus. Whether the procedure is envisaged as coming to an agreement about what should be done or as arriving at a joint intention, people committed to deliberation will look for common ground, for principles they and others share or can accept. An individual proceeds in stages, needs to look at the diverging positions in turn. A realistic model of reaching agreement is to be found in Henry Richardson's analysis of decision-making: people arrive at joint intentions by a series of steps, including informal sub-agreements between a growing number of partners, providing the kind of infrastructure that permits final joint intentions.[6]

An individual cannot hope to find agreement with everyone, and need not. As an experienced deliberator in a given group, her past experience provides an inductive basis for assessments. She will consider

---

6 Richardson, "Democratic Deliberation about Ends," unpublished draft.

what decisions and what lines of reasoning would be acceptable both to herself and to others. Where will she find common ground from which to start? Given that it is rational (not as a matter of self-interest) for each individual to look where agreement may be made or found, minority groups whose views are further from the center will be less active in such deliberations. That is, their influence will then be less, for they will not be partners in the sub-agreements or sub-intentions.

It is important not to confound the process of finding common values, ground, or principles with the strategy of forming alliances. There are numerous processes involved in finding principled accommodations or compromises, and I do not want to over-simplify. What I want to draw attention to is that, as rational, one does not merely listen to another person, and listen to oneself, and mysteriously plump for one's own or another's proposal. Reasoning involves looking for what will convince others, and oneself. But individuals learn from experience, and an individual may find that she has succeeded in the past with X and Y in arriving at principled compromises, never with A and B.

It will not help to appeal to the ideal of impartial reasoning. Suppose commitment to reaching consensus leads individuals to listen to everyone. Even where this is possible, it is nonetheless harder and requires more effort and time to come to an agreement with those whose views are more divergent from one's own. Merely equal effort and attention will not enable an individual to equally well understand the perspectives from which different individuals speak, or the very claims being made. The need for extra effort is especially apparent if one grants that the perspective of historically disadvantaged minorities will require recognition on the part of a majority member of her own unfair advantages. It is not, however, clear that unequal attention to those whose views are most divergent can be justified on simple procedural grounds or in the name of rationality. This will be elaborated in what follows.

It is important to see that theorists like Manin and Cohen have also left unquestioned the impartial and passive conception of reasoning. Their account of legitimacy seems to leave little theoretical room in which one might argue for legislative redress of the lack of success of minority groups. They argue that majority rule is legitimate, that there is nothing inherently unjust about the persistent lack of success of a minority group which is adequately represented in free deliberation.

Of course, it is only too easy to argue that deliberators in our world are never truly impartial, fail in many ways to listen in an open-minded way to considerations from all. Hence theorists can recognize the unfairness of lack of success in these cases. But that is not the whole story. Even where we believe agreement is possible (in the long run), disagreement can persist among the most idealistic of individuals. It is both unrealistic and potentially harmful to argue that in such a case disagreement must result solely from lack of empathy or impartiality. Seeing what is missing in the notion of reasoning which forms the backdrop here should help us recognize what is wrong with the persistence of a minority vote for a marginalized and relatively homogeneous group.

I have argued that the behaviour of rational deliberators committed to the public good can still fail to provide equal participation for the marginalized. If this is so, then the confrontation of views in free deliberation is not adequate to legitimize majority rule because the minority has not participated as an equal player in deliberation. This line of argument suggests some modification of the idea of unconstrained discussion.

I have not yet, however, confronted the strong criticism of Dworkin, that equalizing influence undermines our commitment to the truth. The problem seems to be that equal influence would require an individual to show epistemic deference for non-epistemic reasons. I will suggest that the reasons are not, however, unrelated to truth. I want to articulate the following factors: at least for an important subset, political truths are reached via deliberation. The pragmatist theory of truth has the advantage here over other theories of truth, in making sense of such a claim. Equalizing influence does not mean that an individual walks away from what she "sees" to be true or that, having gone through what she regards as the process adequate to truth, she reneges, or that she alters what must be admitted as the road to truth.

But still there is a changed view of impartial reasoning. I have argued that because of the process itself, more effort may be required to listen to and understand some views, to empathize with in the sense of considering the matter from another's perspective, especially when accusations of one's own injustice must be taken into account.

Now, it may be that one is not rationally in a position to require greater effort or further explorations of oneself without some kind of incoherence. For one has listened, discussed, and is convinced. This is, I believe, the force of Dworkin's criticism. He is persuasive because it does not seem coherent for a person to be committed to the truth (for all) and yet to urge on others or contribute to their accepting what she believes to be false. Just as one may find it pragmatically incoherent (incoherent given the point of assertions) to say "*p*, but I don't believe it," so, too, we are bewildered by someone who says "I have fully convincing reasons that all should accept for doing *x*, but I choose to let reasons for not doing *x* prevail." The incoherence is not less if we recognize our fallibility. For, as Mill noted, epistemic humility — accepting that I might be wrong — does not weaken the need to act on my views, nor to argue for them. It should lead me to open the doors to debate, not to retire to my room.

But does equalizing influence in a legislature undermine our commitment to the truth? First off, Dworkin is right to insist that one cannot simultaneously aim at the truth and impose constraints on seeing or letting others see it. But here it matters whether such imposition is direct or indirect, and whether political truths are attainable independently of political deliberation. Dworkin's criticism ignores the point at which the individual needs to invoke one's commitment to the truth, and so ignores a distinction between direct and indirect constraint. But general injunctions should be distinguished from those which are specific and occasioned at a given time. An individual may recognize, while reflecting, that she has often been wrong, even when she felt most certain, and take steps in advance that will force her to be more cautious in public utterance. That does not undermine a commitment to the truth. So, too, one can commit oneself in advance to more prolonged efforts than may seem warranted at a given time. An essay reads well to the author, but past experience prompts a policy of delay and later re-reading. An individual regulates his efforts to persuade others by endorsing these more strenuous rules, because mutual accommodation or agreement is more difficult the further apart are two initial positions.

What seems needed to equalize participation in decision-making for persistent minority groups, and what the individual can coherently support, are institutional changes which would force decision-makers to pay more attention to minority members.

Some of the proposed changes in decision-making rules which would force the majority to reason with the minority are not as easy to accommodate with democratic principles: to require a super-majority for some issues, for example, does not privilege any particular groups. But special group rights to a veto and cumulative voting look more difficult to justify. Iris Young would give a marginalized group a veto on those issues which are most important to it; Lani Guinier has proposed cumulative voting for those issues of particular interest to a minority. Each legislator would receive a number of votes which could be distributed in accordance with her highest priorities. But can one adapt such measures without undermining one's commitment to deliberation? Melissa Williams, for one, has argued that such measures prejudge substantive issues and discourage deliberation.[7]

Why should any group have a veto or more votes on a given issue? Deference to, or greater weight given to, a minority can be represented as a valid form of epistemic deference: it is a shift of burden of proof. It is easy to see why one must listen to all others. Given, let us say, the need to show that my end or principle is applicable in just this context, I need to take account of your characterization of our situation, for there may be considerations I have ignored. Why should I, however, given that I will listen to your view with an open mind, give it extra weight?

Some justification comes from the idea that another person knows best what is in her own interest or happiness. On those issues, the burden of proof is on the observer or outsider. So one can have a principled epistemic reason for trying harder to persuade the person who will be affected by a proposal. This is not acting in defiance of one's commitment to the truth. Arguments for fair group representation which privilege "voice" rest, in part, on this basis. The justification becomes more tenuous when what is contested is not the account of an individual's, or a group's, own needs, nor the best way in which they can be met, but rather a position regarding their relative priority, within a conception of what must be done for the public good.

At this point one may hope that a pragmatist view of inquiry and truth would offer a model of deliberation which could support special

---

7 Williams, *Voice, Trust and Memory: Marginalized Groups and the Failings of Liberal Representation* (Princeton University Press, forthcoming). I have greatly benefitted from reading Williams's defense of group representation.

efforts. On the pragmatist view, truth is the end of inquiry rather than an independent item; it is thus conceptually connected to the experiences and arguments of others. A seeker of truth must be committed to hearing out and understanding others.

There are, of course, many kinds of pragmatism. The most promising for our discussion is surely of the cognitivist-Peircian variety, although not in a form that can be attributed to Peirce himself. In the Cambridge Conference lectures, we find Peirce, who affirmed *in principle* a science of ethics, skeptical that jury deliberations are worth more than the flip of a coin, pessimistic in general about applying reason to "vital questions." But neither do we think one can rigidly adhere, as Dewey did, to applying the scientific method in ethics.[8] It is useful here to refer to the work of Cheryl Misak, a contemporary pragmatist indebted to Peirce, who eschews the two extremes. The relevance of her views to the issues under discussion is clear. On her view of the pragmatist program of inquiry, strict impartiality, according equal listening time for all participants, plays no part. The pragmatist reason for granting greater weight to an individual's representation, described above in terms of justifying a shift in the burden of proof, comes from the recognition that an individual is an expert regarding her own life. In terms of justifiable inquiry, the pragmatist can welcome the individual's expertise in her own life as a basis for special measures and demands placed on deliberation.

But arguments which would assign extra weight to an individual's opinion about her own good do not obviously extend to issues of prioritization for the community as a whole, or to claims made in the name of justice. Judith Shklar has claimed that we must privilege the voices of those who claim to have suffered injustice.[9] This may be seen as an attempt to shift the burden of proof in matters of justice, as one would in matters of personal good. But it does not seem easy to defend this in the name of expertise.

---

8 Cf. Comments of Hilary Putnam to Peirce's Cambridge Conference lectures, in *Reasoning and the Logic of Things* (Cambridge, MA: Harvard University Press, 1992): 555–57.

9 Shklar, *The Faces of Injustice*.

More radical norms for deliberation and legitimation of new procedures might be forthcoming, given that Misak acknowledges pluralism and divergence with respect to the truth-values of certain judgments. There is not only room for political deliberation to settle the matter, but a demand that it do so. But if there is pluralism, if there is under-determination of truth values for certain judgments, disagreement can persist despite the best deliberative procedure.[10] What justifies new institutional procedures?

A pragmatic program of inquiry, even coupled with recognition of under-determination and divergence of truth-values, cannot provide sufficient justification. They do not give a rationale for proposed changes in majority rule which would give voting or decision-making success to persistent minorities. Why not? Pragmatism is committed to open and public discussion, and, for some pragmatists, to those methods which will settle opinion in the long run. (A pragmatist like Misak may qualify such a commitment insofar as she is prepared for both under-determination and the possibility that some questions have no decent answer.) If a true belief commands convergence because it best accounts for all argument and experience, won't the pragmatist *require* us, in order that the debate-inquiry be justified, to take the measures needed to understand others? The difficulty is, unfortunately, in the details. What measures and what institutional changes should a pragmatist accept? Greater attention to those whose arguments have not previously been understood is called for, but we still have to figure out the standards and methods that apply to the deliberations under discussion. We cannot directly argue for any representation of long-suffering minorities in the outcomes, for there is no conceptual link between listening to others and the success of their arguments in particular political debates.

Peirce's views about scientific truths do not easily transfer; it is arguable that even if moral judgments are objective and can be true, they

---

10 The account of Misak's views comes from private discussions with Misak. Cf. her "Pragmatism, Empiricism and Morality," in *Essays for David Wiggins: Identity, Truth and Value*, ed. S. Lovibond and S. Williams (Oxford: Basil Blackwell, 1996) and *The True, the Just and the Good: A Pragmatist View* (London: Routledge, forthcoming).

are not independent of human thoughts and desires. Although scientific truths are for Peirce a product of human inquiry, his method of science recognized some external permanency upon which our thinking has no effect. The truth of moral judgments is essentially tied to human thought by way of volitions and desires. While arguing for the truth or objectivity of evaluations and directives, we cannot dispense with the need to carefully distinguish moral judgments from scientific claims.

Peirce's four methods of inquiry and his reasons for choosing the scientific method do not provide sufficient guidelines. Even if one accepts as the goals of moral inquiry either Peirce's stability of belief and convergence in the long run, or convergence over a given epoch, these goals will not settle the issues here. I will look at an argument from autonomy to provide a guide to equality of influence. Articulation of the value of autonomy, however, shows it to be independent of the pragmatist's concern for deliberation which will meet certain procedural criteria.

II

Autonomy is arguably the property of human beings which underlies democracy, for it is what makes us fit to govern ourselves, and is common enough to all humans that one can demand equality in its name. Kant thought of autonomy as the property of a will informed by reason, as a will which can act on principles. Political philosophers in the liberal tradition think of autonomy as the capacity to step back, critically, from one's ends before acting. In this tradition, whatever interpretation is given of reason informing the will, rational agency per se has been contrasted with successful agency, where success comes in degrees, both in determining the range (or some privileged range) of one's choices and in achieving their fulfillment.

There are many uses, however, of the terms "autonomy" and "autonomous." Frequently, someone is said to be (or her life is said to be) autonomous because her preferences and choices are sufficiently independent of group traditions or pressures, and she is equipped with those material resources to follow through on her choices. In this case it is rational agency as it is expressed with varying degrees of success, and in conditions which enable it to flourish, which is called autonomy.

Despite the shifting terminology, there are good reasons to maintain the contrast between, on the one hand, rational agency, as a threshold capacity common to all humans able to act, and on the other side, the numerous rational excellences as well as material conditions which permit people to live rich human lives. These excellences and material conditions are unevenly distributed among individual human beings. Because demands for political equality and popular control rest on the human capacity for agency, it is essential to distinguish the capacity of autonomy from what we see so unevenly manifested in individuals. Good enough. We can disregard as irrelevant to political equality the rational skills and personal talents which distinguish us. We can distinguish a capacity from the external resources which provide the means for it to flourish.

But the importance of this general human capacity has, I believe, led to the mistake of thinking of the will as a bare — that is, non-complex — capacity whose expression or exercise could be a single act of will or volition. It is not that people do not ever, at a given moment, decide, or form an intention to do something. It is rather that will and so autonomy of the will is more complex. The will is not to be located at a point in time, nor with one volition: many volitions are involved, for we must talk about perseverance, renewed and imaginative efforts in the face of obstacles. To will to do something is to be prepared to try again should one fail, to persevere, to look for ways around obstacles: it is not merely to will the means to one's end, but to *look* for them and look for other routes if the first fails.

The notion of autonomy as a simple capacity comes to us from Kant: granted his is meant to be a notion of rational agency as such, it is inadequate to think about will without thinking about the multiple capacities involved in perseverance, the power or strength of will. We need not fear that adding complexity will undermine the distinction between what humans have in common and their separate excellences. A complex as well as a simple notion of willing admits of the same distinction between what is common and what is differentially manifest in degrees of success.

I will argue that to acknowledge a more complex notion of willing and so a thicker idea of rational agency requires recognition of the role played by the acknowledged worth of the agent, and so her ends, expressed in social respect as well as self-respect. The respect necessary for activity and relations, for a willing which must persist over time, is respect for the particular individual one is. It is belief in oneself, necessarily tied to self-representations, which explains continued effort, perseverance, strength of will. Few would dispute the importance to willing of an individual's conviction that her ends are worth pursuing. What has been accepted is the fiction that this sense of self-worth can be adequately grounded in the pure and universal identity as a rational being. What I have called fiction is, nonetheless, deeply compelling. For there is a normative demand which I would not wish to dispute, that such rationality entitles an individual to respect. It is buttressed by a distinction between those conditions which enable a child to develop into an adult capable of acting on principles as well as pursuing her ends, and the seemingly analytical constituents of adult capacities.

One can acknowledge that the normative basis for respect is rationality without understanding our obligation as simply to respect the prized abilities within. We need to distinguish the person, what must be the focus of our action, and those characteristics which form the basis of the moral appeal. The individual's demand for esteem is for the person she is, with her own ends and principles as well as social identity. What should be universalized is esteem for other, equally specific people. This would at least clear the way for viewing the connections between self-respect and social respect as internal and necessary to the capacity for rational action.

The understanding of self-respect promoted in this paper has focused on an individual's evaluation of herself, as mediated by social recognition. What needs accommodation is an ever-growing awareness of the social world and its institutions as our making. To the extent that individuals see or feel this, they will see themselves as agents only if they are reflected in that world. Of course, to be an agent is not necessarily to be an active political participant, but there must be some social or political route by which the world is, and can be seen to be, partly of one's making, if one is to have a sense of oneself as agent.

Is this a genuine reconceptualization of autonomy or a characterization of what is needed in the real world to make the will effective? If it is only the latter, I will not have put in question the standard understanding of autonomy as a capacity, and with it, political equality. But the distinction between what is needed in the real world and the capacity for agency must be re-examined here.

We can, at least for some purposes and perhaps only temporarily, abstract from developmental conditions. The need to account for willing as persistent in time and in the face of obstacles will not, however, allow us so easily to dismiss the conditions we now see as needed for its continued practice.

Self-respect as thinking one's ends worth pursuing is not an external, or material condition but something internal and most intimately intertwined with agency. Self-respect is not simply connected contingently, or as a matter of psychology, to autonomy. It is equally a question of a rational connection. Esteem for the social, particular person requires social respect as well as effectiveness in the world.

These requirements for agency are reflected in political demands. Advocates of group representation have appealed to the value of what is called symbolic representation. This appeal has its basis in the connection between social respect and self-esteem. It is plausibly applied to groups when an individual's identity and sense of value is acknowledged to be mediated by one specific group to which she belongs. The argument is strong when it is used for those groups whose history manifests a lack of social as well as political recognition, where groups have been historically discriminated against or disadvantaged. Given that self-respect depends upon the respect others show one, a society may be judged as respecting full autonomy on the part of its members insofar as it fosters social respect for its individuals. If we grant that the sense of identity of members of disadvantaged and minority groups is strongly mediated by their group membership, it is particularly important for society manifestly to respect that group.

Although it is commonly accepted that self-respect depends upon the respect others show me, the connections are not transparent. One, however, seems to be the following. If my ends, expressed in my proposals within an assembly, are constantly losers in the assembly of citizens, my self-respect will be under attack. In the case of historically disadvantaged groups, where political agency is the last, ultimate hope, self-respect is most vulnerable. Political equality as the ideal of democracy is not exhausted by the idea that where multiple interests are at stake each person should have control over what affects her (and an equal vote given egalitarianism). Despite divergence of opinions, modern allegiance to democracy rests on the idea that where there is substantial inequality, political agency in a democracy is the forum for change.

Most proponents of reform in political representation see this as a precondition of social change. The demand that group action not be thought pointless is a general justificatory base for some reforms. Self-respect may be said to encompass all three items: that one's ends are worth pursuing, that pursuit is not pointless, and that the social world reflects one's agency in making it. To show equal regard to individuals whose sense of self is strongly mediated by group identity is to show equal regard to the groups to which they belong. Provided that representation preserves accountability, equal regard for autonomous individuals is politically expressed, in the first instance, by representation in political deliberation. I have tried to argue that autonomy is essentially connected to a conception of oneself as not only a participant in deliberation, but as maker of the social world via its institutions. This requires a notion of political influence which is not exhausted by mere presence in debate.

Two obstacles might be voiced to a search for justification of equal influence in autonomy and its component of social respect.[11] The first sees autonomy as an extraordinary human achievement — one which characterizes those moral heroes subjected to the most extreme trials who are yet able to abide by their principles. On this view, autonomy would provide too narrow a basis for the ideal of equal influence. The second, on the contrary, sees autonomy as it is here presented to be too general a basis. The moral obligation to respect particular individuals is seen as overly large. Respect would be due to neo-Nazis or to any minority group that does not succeed in political deliberations in order to acknowledge their autonomy.

The first objection carries its own response within it. For it acknowledges as extraordinary certain human achievements. The capacity to act on moral principles does not entail that an individual with such a capacity succeeds, no matter what the duress or special circumstances. It is to be hoped, but not reasonably expected, that we withstand all adversities.

---

11 Both objections have indeed been voiced in private discussion by Melissa Williams and Cheryl Misak.

Respecting autonomy has been tied to success in deliberations. Although every individual is an object of respect, the individual's own commitments and actions may alter the responses owed her. The position here is similar to that faced by anyone who grants the value of liberty and defends the liberty of each individual. Those who infringe the liberties of others by their actions are not free to perform them. Those who do not recognize the autonomy of others, who do not grant to other equal political participation in deliberations, should not enjoy success. One may also invoke as appropriate an answer given by Cheryl Misak, that groups like neo-Nazis are neither genuine inquirers nor deliberators.

Equal influence is a qualitative ideal. It is not *analyzed* in terms of numbers of votes or proportional satisfaction of interests or votes. Justified by our commitment to autonomy, it nonetheless insists that members of minorities have some substantial success in achieving their ends; it thus provides initial justification for certain reforms in legislative procedures.

Notes on Contributors

Judith Baker teaches philosophy at Glendon College, York University. She writes on Kant's moral philosophy, group rights, and forgiveness.

David Bakhurst teaches philosophy at Queen's University. He is author of *Consciousness and Revolution in Soviet Philosophy* (Cambridge, 1991) and co-editor, with Christine Sypnowich, of *The Social Self* (Sage, 1995). He is presently writing a book on culture and mind.

Joseph Heath is assistant professor of philosophy at Erindale College, University of Toronto. Recent publications include articles in *Mind*, *Law and Philosophy*, and the *Canadian Journal of Philosophy*. He is also author of a forthcoming book on practical rationality entitled *Communicative Action and Rational Choice*.

Christopher Hookway is professor of philosophy at the University of Sheffield. He is the author of *Peirce* (1985), *Quine: Language, Experience and Reality* (1988), and *Scepticism* (1990). A volume of his papers on Peirce and pragmatism will be published in 2000 under the title *Truth, Rationality and Pragmatism*.

Isaac Levi is John Dewey Professor of Philosophy at Columbia University. He is a member of the American Academy of Arts and Sciences and holds a Doctorate *honoris causa* from the University of Lund, Sweden. He is a former visiting Fellow at All Souls College Oxford, Corpus Christi, Cambridge, Darwin College, Cambridge, Wolfson College, Cambridge, the Australian National University, and the Institute for Advanced Studies at Jerusalem. He is the author of *Gambling with Truth, The Enterprise of Knowledge, Hard Choices, The Fixation of Belief and Its Undoing*, and *For the Sake of the Argument* as well as two collections of papers, *Decisions and Revisions* and *The Covenant of Reason*. He is an editor for *The Journal of Philosophy*.

Mark Migotti is an assistant professor of philosophy at the University of Calgary. He works chiefly on classical and contemporary pragmatism and on Nietzsche.

Cheryl Misak is professor of philosophy at the University of Toronto. She is the author of *Truth and the End of Inquiry: A Peircean Account of Truth* (Clarendon, 1991), *Verificationism: Its History and Prospects* (Routledge, 1995), and *Moral Deliberation: Truth, Conflict, Difference* (Routledge, 1999).

Henry S. Richardson is associate professor of philosophy at Georgetown University. He is the author of *Practical Reasoning about Final Ends* (Cambridge, 1994) and of "Beyond Good and Right: Toward a Constructive Ethical Pragmatism" (*Philosophy & Public Affairs*, 1995). He is currently at work on a book about democratic reasoning.

David Wiggins is Wykeham Professor of Logic in the University of Oxford. Previously he was Tutorial Fellow in Philosophy at University College, Oxford and Professor of Philosophy at Birkbeck College, London. He is author of *Sameness and Substance* (new edition forthcoming from Cambridge, 1999) and *Needs, Values, Truth* (third edition, Oxford, 1998). This is the first article he has written about C.S. Peirce.

Crispin Wright teaches philosophy at the University of St. Andrews. His most recent book is *Truth and Objectivity*.

Index